Why Americans Hate the Media and How It Matters

Why Americans Hate the Media and How It Matters

Jonathan M. Ladd

PRINCETON UNIVERSITY PRESS

PRINCETON AND OXFORD

Copyright © 2012 by Princeton University Press

Published by Princeton University Press, 41 William Street, Princeton, New Jersey 08540
In the United Kingdom: Princeton University Press, 6 Oxford Street, Woodstock,
Oxfordshire OX20 1TW
press.princeton.edu

Library of Congress Cataloging-in-Publication Data

Ladd, Jonathan M., 1978–
    Why Americans hate the media and how it matters / Jonathan M. Ladd.
        p. cm.
    Includes bibliographical references and index.
    ISBN 978-0-691-14785-7 (hardcover : alk. paper)   ISBN 978-0-691-14786-4
(pbk. : alk. paper) 1. Mass media—Political aspects—United States. 2. Mass media—
Objectivity—United States. 3. Mass media—United States—Public opinion. 4. Public
opinion—United States. I. Title.
    P95.82.U6L33 2011
    070.10973—dc23   2011017414

British Library Cataloging-in-Publication Data is available

This book has been composed in Sabon
Printed on acid-free paper. ∞
Printed in the United States of America
10 9 8 7 6 5 4 3 2 1

To my parents

Contents

Illustrations

TABLES

Acknowledgments

I ACQUIRED SO MANY DEBTS while pursuing this project that the thanks offered here are surely insufficient. First, I am deeply indebted to Larry Bartels. Larry has provided generous assistance and wise advice from the time we met to the present day. At Princeton, he seemingly always had time to discuss new ideas and read my work. Intellectually, Larry shaped how I look at all social science research. Most importantly, he taught me the importance of steering advanced social scientific tools toward addressing fundamental questions about democracy. At Princeton, I was lucky to be advised also by Doug Arnold, Tali Mendelberg, and Marty Gilens. They have been extremely generous with their time, reading drafts and providing insightful suggestions at all stages of the project.

I was also very fortunate to receive feedback from many other excellent scholars at Georgetown and Princeton and across the country. I thank Paul Abramson, Chris Achen, Mike Bailey, Adam Berinsky, Shana Gadarian, Amy Gershkoff, Bill Gormley, Doris Graber, Matt Hindman, Greg Huber, Karen Jusko, David Karol, Chris Karpowitz, Paul Kellstedt, Erika King, Dave Lewis, Skip Lupia, Nolan McCarty, Hans Noel, Diana Owen, Markus Prior, Kris Ramsay, John Sides, Steve R. Smith, Clyde Wilcox, John Zaller; seminar participants at George Washington University, Georgetown University, Princeton University, Temple University, and the University of Delaware; several anonymous reviewers; and especially Stu Jordan and Gabe Lenz. Of course, while the aforementioned should share credit for all positive aspects of this book, I am responsible for all deficiencies.

I received excellent research assistance at Georgetown from Holly Boux, Danielle Bush, Amy Cohen, Rebecca Delaney, Tyronda Gibson, Meghan Keneally, Sarah Levey, Amanda Spears, and Kristin Thorpe. I received financial support for various portions of this project from Georgetown's Graduate School of Arts and Sciences, Princeton's Fellowship of Woodrow Wilson Scholars, and Princeton's Mamdouha S. Bobst Center for Peace and Justice. Paul DiMaggio generously provided data from his reinterviews of 2000 General Social Survey respondents, which I use in chapter 6. James Chu of Princeton's Office of Information Technology provided assistance implementing the media trust and learning experiment, which also appears in chapter 6.

I never would have started this project if not for the education I received from Tufts's Political Science Department, especially Jeff Berry and

Jim Glaser. They introduced me to political science and its potential, inspired me to attend graduate school, and helped me get there. Additional special thanks go to Adam Berinsky, who taught my first graduate public opinion and research design classes, employed me as a research assistant, and has continued to provide advice, encouragement, and assistance.

My parents, Susan Cartmell and Larry Ladd, have always provided the greatest possible support to my academic endeavors. My debt to their passions for politics and intellectual pursuits is obvious. For that and many other reasons, this book is dedicated to them.

No person has experienced the day-to-day work of finishing this project as closely as my wife, Nancy. I am grateful for her seemingly endless patience and kindness. I am very lucky that she chose to journey through life as my love and best friend. Finally, special thanks go to my daughter, Ruth. While she did not directly aid in this book's creation, she did make the past two years extraordinary.

Why Americans Hate the Media
and How It Matters

1

Why Is Everyone Mad at the Mainstream Media?

IN THE MID-TWENTIETH CENTURY, the news media were one of America's most trusted institutions. The 1956 American National Election Study (ANES) found that 66% of Americans thought newspapers were fair, while only 27% said they were unfair. These views were bipartisan, with 78% of Republicans and 64% of Democrats viewing newspapers as fair. When the Roper Organization asked a similar question about network news in two 1964 polls, 71% and 61% of the public thought it was fair, while just 12% and 17% thought it was unfair. In 1973, when the General Social Survey (GSS) began regularly measuring confidence in various national institutions, only 15% of respondents had "hardly any" confidence in the press.

Prominent journalists were among the most respected figures in the country. A famous 1972 poll found that 72% of Americans trusted *CBS Evening News* anchor Walter Cronkite, a higher share than any other public figure received in the survey. In 1976, *Washington Post* reporters Bob Woodward and Carl Bernstein's investigations that uncovered the Watergate scandal were dramatized in a movie adaptation of their book *All the President's Men*. In the commercially successful film, the journalists were depicted heroically and played by Robert Redford and Dustin Hoffman, two of the era's most charismatic movie stars.[1] In popular culture, journalists were noble defenders of democracy and the public interest.

Today, the news media's place in society has changed. In the 2008 GSS, the portion of Americans expressing "hardly any" confidence in the press had risen to 45%. A 2004 *Chronicle of Higher Education* poll found that only 10% of Americans had "a great deal" of confidence in the "national news media," about the same as lawyers, in whom 9% of Americans had "a great deal" of confidence.

This decline in media trust was accompanied by a fragmentation of the news industry. Once, the media landscape largely consisted of a few national television news networks, local television news, and newspapers. The vast majority of these journalists were committed to a style of "objective" journalism that rose to prominence in the early twentieth century.

---

[1] See West (2001, 64). Details on the polling results reported in the first three paragraphs of this chapter are provided in chapters 3 and 4.

"So is Cameron Diaz really a babe, or is that another thing we've been led to believe by the biased media?"

Figure 1-1. Cartoon from the *New Yorker*. *Source*: The New Yorker Collection from cartoonbank.com. All Rights Reserved.

As a result, there was little diversity in coverage styles. Media choices have greatly proliferated in the past 40 years. New options include political talk radio, cable news channels, Internet news and opinion sites, as well as many entertainment-oriented media options. These choices offer a great variety of news styles, including more partisan and tabloid-oriented approaches.

As the media landscape has expanded, institutional (or mainstream) media outlets have come under increasing criticism from politicians, activists, and pundits. Sometimes these criticisms are transmitted by institutional news sources. Yet they also come through the newer, alternative media outlets. As a result, the trustworthiness of more professionalized forms of journalism is under steady assault.

Overall, those practicing conventional, objective journalism are in a much different position than they were a generation ago. They are dramatically less trusted by the public, face harsh and persistent political criticism, and must compete with less conventional news sources as well as many other entertainment options.

THE CONVENTIONAL WISDOM

It can be easy to see this shift as a fall from grace. Once, institutional journalists were powerful guardians of the republic, maintaining high standards of political discourse and routing out misbehavior by politicians and other public officials. Now, institutional journalists lack public trust and are swarmed by newer forms of reporting that flout the old standards, potentially leaving the public defenseless against political misbehavior. In this way of thinking, a powerful media establishment free of competition or political attacks is the natural and optimal state of the world, interrupted by strange, nefarious deviations in recent decades. These trends, therefore, should be reversed and journalism returned to its proper place in American politics and society.

In an article subtitled "Why Is Everyone Mad at the Mainstream Media?" Nicholas Lemann (2005), dean of the Columbia University Graduate School of Journalism, recalls some of his first memories of the media establishment from his childhood in the early 1960s:

> I remember being sent, as a child, from Louisiana on summer visits to my grandparents in New Jersey. My grandfather, who was a pediatrician in the town of Perth Amboy, would sit in his easy chair on Sundays reading the [New York] Times in a spirit not dissimilar to that of someone taking the sacrament. After finishing one article, he'd begin the next—who was he to decide what, of the material the Times' editors had chosen to publish, he had the right to skip? Quite often, the aural accompaniment to this exercise was the soothing music of WQXR, the Times' radio station, which between segments of classical music would occasionally air interviews with Times correspondents and critics—men, I inferred from their calm, distinguished voices, with neat Vandyke beards, their heads wreathed in contemplative clouds of pipe smoke. (170–72)

He goes on to recount the institutional media's glory days: "The civil rights movement, the Vietnam war (in particular, the Pentagon Papers), and Watergate all registered as examples of the big, prestigious journalistic organs asserting themselves, rather than merely passing along what government officials had said, and being rewarded with more power and influence and more admiration from the public" (172).

This is very similar to U.S. Supreme Court Justice Potter Stewart's historic interpretation.[2] In the *Hastings Law Review*, Stewart (1974–75, 634) summarizes his view: "The primary purpose of the constitutional

---

[2] For more on Stewart's views on the role of the press in American democracy and his inability to persuade a Supreme Court majority to accept them, see Cook (2005).

guarantee of a free press was . . . to create a fourth institution of Government as an additional check on the three official branches. . . . The relevant metaphor, I think, is the metaphor of the Fourth Estate." Consistent with this, MSNBC pundit and longtime *Newsweek* columnist Howard Fineman (2005) laments the changing place of the institutional media in American society by saying,

> A political party is dying before our eyes—and I don't mean the Democrats. I'm talking about the "mainstream media" . . . [which] is regarded with ever growing suspicion by American voters, viewers and readers, who increasingly turn for information and analysis only to non-[mainstream] outlets that tend to reinforce the sectarian views of discrete slices of the electorate. . . . Still, the notion of a neutral, nonpartisan mainstream press was, to me at least, worth holding onto. Now it's pretty much dead, at least as the public sees things. . . . It's hard to know now who, if anyone, in the "media" has any credibility.

Along similar lines, veteran journalist James Fallows (1996, 1) mournfully opens his book critiquing political journalism by stating, "Americans have never been truly fond of their press. Through the last decade, however, their disdain for the media establishment has reached new levels. Americans believe that the news media have become too arrogant, cynical, scandal-minded, and destructive." Ted Koppel (2010), longtime host of ABC's *Nightline*, expresses his own discontent with the demise of the mid-twentieth-century media regime, writing,

> To witness Keith Olbermann . . . suspended even briefly last week for making financial contributions to Democratic political candidates seemed like a whimsical, arcane holdover from a long-gone era of television journalism, when the networks considered the collection and dissemination of substantive and unbiased news to be a public trust. . . . While I can appreciate the financial logic of drowning television viewers in a flood of opinions designed to confirm their own biases, the trend is not good for the republic. It is, though, the natural outcome of a growing sense of national entitlement. . . . [A]mong the many benefits we have come to believe the founding fathers intended for us, the latest is news we can choose. . . . Much of the American public used to gather before the electronic hearth every evening, separate but together, while Walter Cronkite, Chet Huntley, David Brinkley, Frank Reynolds and Howard K. Smith offered relatively unbiased accounts of information that their respective news organizations believed the public needed to know. . . . It was an imperfect, untidy little Eden of journalism where reporters were motivated to gather facts about important issues.

While almost all commentators on the media at least briefly mention that there were previous exceptions to mainstream media hegemony, many still give the impression that this dominance is historically typical. It is the natural and superior state of the world. As quoted above, Fallows claims antipathy toward the media has "reached new levels." Similarly, former editor in chief of *The Hotline* and current *Congressional Quarterly* blogger Craig Crawford (2006, 25) writes, "Today's media is as bullied as ever."

Commentators depict the consequences of declining trust in the institutional media as severe. Crawford (2006) expresses concern that " . . . the vilification of the news media by politicians has diminished the power of an independent press" (11) and that "[p]ublic distrust of the news media is one of the most hazardous political challenges now facing Americans" (19). David S. Broder (2006), the longtime *Washington Post* columnist considered the dean of the Washington press corps, notes that "The hardest question any Washington reporter faces these days, whenever talking with voters outside the capital, is simply: Can I believe anything I'm told by those politicians in Washington—or by the press?" In lamenting the bipartisanship of attacks on media trustworthiness, then-editor of the *New Republic* Franklin Foer (2005) writes,

> Newspapers deserve an army of enemies that nag them to be less lazy, less timid, and less nice. But they don't deserve the savage treatment that they routinely receive in the blogosphere. . . . [T]he blogosphere nurses an ideological disdain for "Mainstream Media"—or MSM, as it has derisively (and somewhat adolescently) come to be known. Perusing the *Huffington Post*, a hub of liberal blogging, you'll find the MSM lambasted for its "usual sub-par, unsatisfactory, wholly misinformed, shitty job"; the MSM is, after all, filled with "lazy stenographer[s] . . . posing as journalist[s who] will gladly cut and paste this Republican propaganda." Or, to put it even more bluntly, the "Beltway media really makes no effort to do anything other than parrot totally out-of-touch conventional wisdom—no matter how inane, stupid and ridiculous it is." You would expect this kind of populism from the right, which long ago pioneered the trashing of the MSM . . . [but by] repeating conservative criticisms about the allegedly elitist, sycophantic, biased MSM, liberal bloggers have played straight into conservative hands. These bloggers have begun unwittingly doing conservatives' dirty work.

While no author puts things this plainly, I can roughly summarize this conventional wisdom with two assertions. First, a widely trusted, elite, professional media establishment is a natural part of national politics. Recent trends toward a more distrusted media establishment under fire from politicians and a more fragmented and heterogeneous media landscape, while not entirely unprecedented, are still perilous developments. Second, declining trust in the institutional media has large and potentially dire consequences, preventing journalists from checking political power and the public from learning essential information about public affairs.

An Alternative View

This book examines the role of the news media in the American political system. In doing so, it especially focuses on the causes and consequences of declining public trust in the institutional news media over the past 40 years. It finds that the type of conventional wisdom summarized above is only partially correct.

The conventional wisdom's first claim is false. The existence of an independent, powerful, widely respected news media establishment is an historical anomaly. Prior to the twentieth century, such an institution had never existed in American history. We should not misinterpret this circumstance, whatever its merits, as the historical norm.

There are structural factors working against the existence of a dominant institutional news media. Politicians who desire public support feel threatened by independent sources of information. Thus, they tend to use whatever means are available to prevent the media from becoming a trusted independent news source. Political leaders have used various methods for this task throughout history, including government suppression of independent media, founding and promoting government-controlled news outlets, and publicly attacking the credibility of outlets outside their control.

Another structural impediment is market demand for more partisan or entertaining styles of news. Even when journalists desire to produce informative, nonpartisan, nonsensational news, which can enhance the profession's respectability and trustworthiness, the market for this style of news is limited. It is difficult to find a large audience willing to regularly consume this type of news when other options are available. In this way, market pressure leads to more sensational and partisan forms of news. Both reduce trust in the institutional media, the former directly and the latter by transmitting partisan media criticism.

The mid-twentieth-century institutional news media briefly gained the public's trust for two reasons. First, low levels of economic competition enabled journalism to become highly professionalized. Journalists had the autonomy to enforce a professional norm of objectivity, greatly reducing salacious or explicitly partisan news coverage. Second, the lack of party polarization reduced political criticism of the institutional press. When these two things ended, trust in the media declined.

On the other hand, the conventional wisdom's second assertion, that media distrust has major negative consequences, is true to some extent. Media distrust is consequential. It changes the way people acquire information and form political preferences.

Overall, media distrust leads to substantial information loss among the mass public. Those who distrust the media both resist the information they receive from institutional news outlets and increasingly seek out partisan news sources that confirm their preexisting views. As a result, these individuals are less responsive to national policy outcomes, relying more on their political predispositions to form beliefs and preferences.

As the institutional media's mid-twentieth-century hegemony has ended in recent decades, journalists producing a professionalized style of news have not disappeared. Rather than returning to the media landscape that existed before journalism's professionalization, institutional journalists and news organizations now compete with newer news outlets employing different styles. As a result, institutional media trust has not become less important as the media has fragmented.

If anything, people now have stronger views about the institutional media, and those views are more consequential. Media trust's impact is large because people must regularly choose whether to believe messages coming from institutional or alternative sources as well as whether to simply rely on their partisanship to form their beliefs. In this way, declining media trust is a contributing factor to the polarization of the American political system (while also being a partial consequence of it). In the extreme, the partisanship and unresponsiveness to information that results from media distrust could prevent the public from holding politicians accountable for policy outcomes.

However, while largely agreeing that media distrust has potentially negative consequences, I add an important caveat. It is doubtful that returning to a depolarized party system with a highly respected and homogeneous news industry is either feasible or desirable. The mid-twentieth-century party system was a product of a unique historical circumstance, where civil rights constituted a salient national issue while remaining separate from the main partisan and ideological cleavages. Additionally, the lack of competitive pressure faced by news organizations was a product of a unique period in the media's technological development, which would be impossible to re-create.

In addition to being infeasible, restoring these circumstances is not necessarily even desirable. Party systems that fail to offer voters clear alternatives can also prevent them from holding elected leaders accountable, the same consequence we fear media distrust producing. Furthermore, there are other reasons to doubt whether the public should put all its faith in a homogeneous style of news practiced by a relatively small number of media organizations. What if the media establishment fails to live up to its professional ideal of providing accurate and objective information? In addition, is it not desirable for people to have the personal freedom to choose to consume more partisan or sensational news? Finally, would there be unintended consequences of policy interventions intrusive enough to completely reverse the tendency toward more a fragmented, less professionalized media landscape?

In light of these considerations, the United States should strive for a balance between a highly trusted, homogenous media establishment with little viable competition and an extremely fragmented media environment without any widely trusted information sources. In this middle path, individuals would continue to have a wide range of choices, including partisan, sensational, or conventionally objective news, as well as the option of avoiding news altogether. Yet the remaining institutional journalists and news outlets would continue to transmit important political information, with a significant portion of the public retaining enough confidence in the institutional press to use this information to hold government accountable.

Plan of the Book

This book marshals several types of evidence to make this argument. The next three chapters put the American news media's relationship with the mass public and place in the political system in historical context. Chapter 2 reviews relations between the press and political leaders from 15th-century Europe, following the invention of the printing press, through late-nineteenth-century America. It reveals that, through time, political leaders were consistently hostile to efforts by the press to become involved in politics as independent actors. While political figures often cultivated party- or government-controlled newspapers, they attacked newspapers that either strived for independent influence or affiliated with rival politicians.

Chapter 3 traces the evolution of the American news media from an eclectic mix of partisan, independent, or nonpolitical newspapers and journals into an influential political institution by the mid-twentieth century. The institutionalization of the American press coincided with less party polarization, a reduction in partisan media criticism, and a reduction in economic competition faced by media outlets. These trends peaked in the 1950s and 1960s.

Chapter 4 shows how all these patterns reversed from the 1970s through the 2000s. While reviewing this, I look carefully at attitudes toward the institutional news media in these decades. Using a variety of polling data, I examine what people mean when they express an opinion about the news media as an institution. I conclude that in recent decades Americans have had well-formed opinions about the institutional news media, which are stable over time and consistent across different question wordings.

Chapter 5 explores what factors cause people to distrust the institutional news media by analyzing data from national surveys and two original survey experiments. Despite many different claims in the literature, I find the strongest evidence supporting the role of two variables in reducing media trust: elite partisan media criticism and tabloid-style news coverage. While I find some effects of other variables, they tend to be either smaller in size, not statistically significant at comparable sample sizes and dosages, or more contingent on circumstances.

Chapter 6 explores the consequences of media distrust for the ways in which people learn politically relevant information, such as national conditions in major policy domains. Employing cross-sectional, panel, and original experimental data, I find that media distrust affects how people learn, particularly about national security and economic performance. Those who distrust the media are more resistant to new information about national conditions, instead relying more on their predispositions to form their beliefs.

Chapter 7 tests whether these effects on political learning have consequences for election preference formation. Using panel and pooled cross-sectional survey data, I find that distrust of the news media alters presidential and congressional voting through its effects on learning. Those who distrust the media base their votes more on partisan predispositions and less on current national conditions.

Chapter 8 returns to the overall argument outlined in this chapter. It reiterates that circumstances like those in mid-twentieth-century America, where the news media constituted a respected, powerful, independent force in politics, are rare. It further argues that the two major factors that reduce media trust—partisan criticism and tabloid-style news—are natural consequences of political and economic competition, respectively. The mid-twentieth century was unusual in that these competitive forces were both greatly curbed. I argue that extreme versions of either a centralized, homogenous, unchallenged, and trusted news media establishment or a fragmented, partisan, sensationalist media are both undesirable. I conclude by discussing several possible ways to achieve balance between these extremes.

2

Political Conflict with the Press in the Pre-Polling Era

TENSION IS INEVITABLE between those vying for political power and any independent sources of public information. Politicians' incentives lead them to favor information sources they can control and to try to reduce the influence of sources affiliated with rival political factions or with no faction. However, the tools available to political leaders have varied widely over time.

From at least the invention of the printing press, governments have used force to shut down independent or oppositional sources of news and have sponsored pro-regime periodicals and books. Repression of political printing was still prevalent in early American colonial history. Even as legal tools to control the press became more limited, colonial governments were still able to harass disliked printers enough to discourage most from serious engagement with politics.

The legal guarantees of press freedom placed in the U.S. Constitution did not end the incentives for politicians to limit independent news media influence. The Federalists pushed legal restrictions on newspapers to their constitutional limits. Most leading politicians in the young republic aggressively sponsored partisan newspapers and disparaged opposing ones. When newspapers outside party control acquired large circulations in the middle and late 1800s, they did so largely without gaining institutionalized power in the political process. Prior to the twentieth century, America had never experienced professionalized journalism wielding power as an independent political institution. A central reason is that politicians consistently used the tools at their disposal to prevent it.

THE RISE OF PRINTING PROVOKED POLITICAL CONTROL AND REPRESSION

In varying forms, conflict between political actors and the news media has been the norm throughout modern history. Since the introduction of the moveable-type printing press in Europe in the mid-1400s, media have offered their users the politically explosive power to transmit political information to the mass public.[1] At the same time, political leaders have

---

[1] Moveable type was used in Korea as early as 1241 (Emery, Emery, and Roberts 2000, 3).

consistently and aggressively attacked, persecuted, and attempted to co-opt political mass media. Largely as a result of this, American journalism was neither a professionalized field nor a respected, independent political institution prior to the twentieth century.[2]

The movable-type press dramatically increased all types of communication by lowering a book's production costs between 50% and 80% (Hirsch 1974, cited in Starr 2004, 26). Yet before 1600, government policies that severely restricted political communication, along with low literacy rates and the lack of societal expectations that ordinary people would follow politics (Starr 2004, 24), prevented the widespread use of print for political ends.[3] Still, the Protestant Reformation and Catholic Counter-Reformation in the 1500s illustrated the politically dangerous potential of printing. They showed, first, that printing could be a powerful weapon against one's political opponents (Eisenstein 1979). Second, they illustrated that printing's potency made competing political movements eager to increase their capacity (Starr 2004, 26–27) and political leaders eager to suppress any rival publishers.

By the 1500s, government leaders already realized the rapidly growing threat from inexpensive publishing. The goals of nongovernmental printers and their sponsors, which often included disseminating their political or religious views or selling more of their product to ensure a profit, inherently conflicted with the incentives of government authorities to get and hold political power. In response, most European governments initially tried to gain complete control over the press. For instance, the Catholic Church banned all books lacking church approval in 1543 and established an "Index of Forbidden Books" in 1559 (Febvre and Martin 1976 [1958], 310–11, cited in Starr 2004, 28). By 1551, the king of France banned all books except those approved by royal censors. Between 1529 and 1538, King Henry VIII of England set up a system that lasted until his death in 1547, under which the government maintained a banned books list, all printers needed royal permission to operate, and each book produced needed a royal license (Clegg 1997, 26–27; Emery, Emery, and Roberts 2000, 8–9; Starr 2004, 28; Copeland 2006, 28–29).

Despite their best efforts, European governments were unable to prevent the spread of the printing press. Political and religious censorship, while often successful in muffling domestic opposition, helped to spread printing technology and develop print distribution networks across the continent as presses relocated to avoid persecution (Starr 2004, 27). Also, capitalist development and trade generated roads and postal organization.

---

[2] This early history of the news media, prior to the American Revolutionary War, draws heavily on Paul Starr's *The Creation of the Media: Political Origins of Modern Communications* (2004).

[3] In 1530, literacy among males in England was approximately 25% (Grendler 2004).

This made printing more profitable, leading to its use by those primarily motivated by profit rather than just politics or religion (Febvre and Martin 1976 [1958], 249; Starr 2004, 25).[4]

While suppressing other printing, governments also used the press to consolidate their own power. Both England and France gave certain groups exclusive printing rights. In 1553, England's Queen Mary banned any printing without a royal license. In 1557, she gave the Company of Stationers, which in 1603 would evolve into a corporation called British Stock, the exclusive right to own and operate all printing presses, book publishing organizations, and book dealerships. It enforced official censorship through, among other means, search and seizure of any unauthorized presses, books, and so on (Clegg 1997, 14–25, 28; Emery, Emery, and Roberts 2000, 9; Starr 2004, 28–29).[5] The French crown similarly suppressed all printers and paper suppliers except a few in Paris affiliated with an organization called the Paris Book Guild, which was closely tied to the government (Starr 2004, 29).

Despite official hostility, some decentralized political communication networks developed when postal services began to grow. In the 1500s, pamphlets and books, delivered through the mail, were the predominant means of political communication. Private mail services were often used because government mail organizations, while more extensive, were consistently subject to censorship and monitoring by authorities (Starr 2004, 30–31).[6]

In this repressive environment, all recognizable forms of news media took time to develop. The first European newspapers published in native languages finally appeared in Germany in 1609 and then spread to cities all across the continent (Emery, Emery, and Roberts 2000, 7; Starr 2004, 32).[7] By devoting considerable space in each newspaper to restating news from other papers, these managed to serve as a decentralized communications network operating through the mail (Starr 2004, 32).

---

[4] On the connection between the rise of Protestantism, capitalism, and book commerce, see Wuthnow (1989, cited in Starr 2004, 27). On the connection between Protestantism and the rise of capitalism more generally, see Weber (2002 [1905]).

[5] Queen Elizabeth I (1558–1603) continued printing restrictions (through censorship and licensing) aimed at political and religious material, although they were somewhat less effective than under previous and subsequent monarchs (see Clegg 1997, 30–76).

[6] One early European postal service, privately owned and operated by the Thurn and Taxis family, began in the 1500s and at one time employed 20,000 people (Starr 2004, 30–31).

[7] Here I follow Emery, Emery, and Roberts' (2000, 8) definition of a newspaper: "it must be published regularly, on a daily or weekly basis; it must appeal to a general interest audience rather than a specialized one; and it must offer timely news." The first known European printed periodical devoted to news, titled *Mercurius Gallobelgicus*, began publishing in 1594 in Cologne. However, it appeared only semiannually, focused on military matters, and was in Latin (Starr 2004, 32).

As the political communication infrastructure grew, efforts by political figures to tame its power only intensified. Media historians Michael Emery, Edwin Emery, and Nancy L. Roberts (2000, 8) state, "It is significant that the newspaper first flourished in areas where central authority was weak, as in Germany, which at the time was divided into a patchwork of small principalities, or where rulers were more tolerant, as in the Low Countries. This explains why the development of the press lagged in England."[8] Across Europe, when governments had the ability, they censored or suppressed newspapers, especially any attempt to cover domestic politics. Sociologist Paul Starr (2004, 33) describes the attitude of the European aristocracy this way: "Newspapers could be especially dangerous to authority because of the immediacy and potential political sensitivity of news; they also seemed an affront and a vulgarity to some guardians of custom and social preroga-tive who upheld the traditional norms of privilege in political communica-tion." Leaders usually preempted independent newspapers by establishing official government-approved papers, whose coverage emphasized the cer-emony and majesty of the court (Starr 2004, 33).

The situation in England both illustrates these trends and provides context for the press's later development in the United States. In the early 1600s, foreign newspapers began mailing English-language news to sub-scribers in England, and domestic publishers began irregularly producing newsletters called corantos (Emery, Emery, and Roberts 2000, 10; Starr 2004, 32). In 1621, after issuing proclamations attacking "the great lib-erty of discourse concerning matters of state" in these publications, King James I banned all corantos except those with government licenses. Ob-taining a license required agreeing to cover only foreign news and to favor the Crown when doing so (Emery, Emery, and Roberts 2000, 10; Starr 2004, 32).[9] Later, Charles I completely banned newspapers from 1632 to 1637, while from 1637 to 1641 the Star Chamber (a secret court used to prosecute opponents of the Crown) implemented a strict licensing regime (Starr 2004, 33–34; Copeland 2006, 39–40; Clegg 2008, 186–207).

However, whenever serious divisions among English political elites erupted, the conflict spread into the newspapers. Yet even in these cases, the elite factions still labored to keep political communication firmly

[8] Throughout this book, I adopt a convention of identifying all academics other than political scientists by their discipline at the first mention of each name. One can assume that academics whose discipline is not named on first mention are political scientists. I do this to balance my desire to improve the accessibility of the book by providing some informa-tion about the researchers and my desire to avoid bogging down the text with numerous disciplinary identifications.

[9] In a 1663 proclamation, James I went further and imposed licensing requirements on books and pamphlets, complaining of "seditious, schismaticall, and other scandalous Bookes or Pamphlets" (Clegg 2008, 14–15).

under their control. For instance, during the term of the Long Parliament from 1640 to 1649, when opponents of the Crown dominated the legislature, refused to adjourn, then battled the king in the English Civil War, the Star Chamber and its licensing regime were abolished and both the Crown and Parliament produced competing authorized publications. Yet after Parliament executed Charles I for treason in 1649, both the republican governments of the Commonwealth period (1649–60) and the subsequently restored monarchy reclaimed governmental control through censorship and licensing (Starr 2004, 34–35; Copeland 2006, 42–49, 62–68).[10] After 1665 and for most of the rest of the 1600s, the official court newspaper, the *London Gazette*, was the only paper permitted in England (Starr 2004, 35).[11]

In 1694, Parliament allowed licensing laws to lapse. Control over the press shifted to a system of tight restrictions on access to political institutions, strict libel laws, and oppressive taxation (Emery, Emery, and Roberts 2000, 13). Reporting on parliamentary debates remained illegal through most of the 1700s (Starr 2004, 36). Courts interpreted common law prohibitions on seditious libel as outlawing any published criticism of the government (37).[12] On top of this, in 1712, Parliament passed legislation applying a stamp tax to news publications. It taxed printed materials based on their length, with a stamp affixed to the publication as proof of payment. This tax was so large that it initially increased the cost of a typical newspaper by 50% (38). The government also maintained a monopoly on postal delivery, keeping mail rates high to, among other things, increase the cost of distributing newspapers and pamphlets—except those produced by elected officials, which were mailed for free under their franking privileges (40).[13] By raising the price of a newspaper to approximately a day's pay for an ordinary worker, the stamp tax and postal fees effectively outlawed cheap mass-market newspapers (Emery, Emery, and Roberts 2000, 15; Starr 2004, 39). Newspapers that did operate at this time were

[10] On print during the Long Parliament, see Clegg (2008, 208–34) and Copeland (2006, 61–62).

[11] This is not to say that there were not breaches of restrictions on publishing. For instance, Oliver Williams published daily, "minute-by-minute" reports on parliamentary deliberations for four consecutive weeks in 1660 in his "small booklet," "Perfect Diurnal" (Emery, Emery, and Roberts 2000, 7). In his 1664 book *The Origin and Growth of Printing*, Richard Atkyns lamented that censorship had become overly lax, writing, "Printing is like a good Dish of Meat, which moderately eaten of, turns to the nourishment and health of the body; but immoderately, to Surfeits and Sickness." (Clegg 2008, 99).

[12] If the published account was true, this was considered an aggravating, not exculpatory, aspect of the crime (Starr 2004, 38).

[13] *Franking* refers to the ability of elected officials to send mail to their constituents for free through the government postal services.

pushed into a business model based on selling expensive papers to political and economic elites and receiving political patronage.

As a consequence, public access to political news became very limited. Estimates of the portion of the public able to access and read newspapers and pamphlets were difficult to make at the time and are little easier now. Edmund Burke estimated that 400,000 people in England acquired political information from newspapers in the 1790s, a figure that, if accurate, would have been only 5% of the population (Starr 2004, 41).

POLITICAL AUTHORITIES IN COLONIAL AMERICA AGGRESSIVELY REPRESSED THE PRESS

Most English printing regulations, such as the government-backed book-printing monopoly of the Company of Stationers, did not apply to the North American colonies. Colonial governments had autonomy to regulate the press (Starr 2004, 49–50). While different from that in England in some important ways, the relationship of colonial political leaders to the press in colonial America exhibited similar inherent tensions.

Government-press relations in the southern and Chesapeake colonies of English North America most resembled those in Europe. Printing was forcibly suppressed.[14] In 1641, the governor of Virginia wrote, "I thank God, there are no free-schools, nor printing . . . for learning has brought disobedience, and heresy, and sects into the world, and printing has divulged them, and libels against the government" (Starr 2004, 52–53). For instance, when one printer moved from Virginia to Maryland to avoid persecution and attempted to publish the proceedings of Maryland's colonial assembly, even Maryland's government quickly forced him to stop. There were no bookshops in the Chesapeake at this time, and book ownership was restricted to societal elites (52–53). As far north as Pennsylvania, the Quaker government suppressed any dissenting publications (54).

Literacy was more widespread in the New England colonies and the restrictions on printing less universal.[15] The first printing press in English North America was established in Massachusetts in 1639, three years after the founding of Harvard College (Starr 2004, 50; Copeland 2006, 107). In the next hundred years, an active book trade developed. It was customary for professionals, such as ministers, to own books. Even

---

[14] Literacy was also low in the southern and Chesapeake colonies. Approximately 60% of white men in the 1700s prior to the American Revolution were literate. Yet literacy rates were so low among women and slaves that, overall, only 25% of the populace could read (Starr 2004, 52–53).

[15] Literacy in New England is estimated at 70% for males and 30% to 40% for females in the early 1700s and 85% for males and 60% for females by the 1760s (Starr 2004, 52).

ordinary households tended to own "Bibles, almanacs, and [published] sermons" (Starr 2004, 52–53).

Yet even in New England, government did not leave publishing unmolested. Instead, there was an active and continuous struggle among publishers, the reading public, and political authorities to control information. For instance, Massachusetts passed its first law implementing "rigorous censorship" of published material in 1662, when there were only two active presses in the whole colony, both located at Harvard (Emery, Emery, and Roberts 2000, 21). Most scholars consider the first American newspaper to be *Publick Occurrences, Both Forreign and Domestick,* published in Boston in 1690 by Benjamin Harris. Harris had fled from London, where he had published a newspaper, was repeatedly arrested, and spent two years in prison for possessing seditious literature in his shop. Harris had intended to publish *Publick Occurrences* monthly. However, the first issue, which reported that the king of France took "immoral liberties" with his prince's wife and criticized the English government's military cooperation with the Iroquois Indians, antagonized colonial authorities. The Massachusetts governing council banned it after its first issue on the grounds that it lacked a license to publish. Another newspaper would not appear in the American colonies for 14 years (Sloan and Williams 1994, 1–23; Emery, Emery, and Roberts 2000, 22–23; Starr 2004, 55; Copeland 2006, 128–32).

Newspapers that later emerged adopted a different strategy. Rather than attempt independence, they wedded themselves to government authorities. For example, John Campbell, who was employed as a postmaster, began publishing the *Boston News-Letter* in 1704. Campbell "treated his role as that of a functionary, not a journalist, treating the newspaper as an extension of his work as postmaster" (Starr 2004, 55). He cleared every issue with the governor or the governor's secretary before publication and put "Published by Authority" on the front page, the same words printed on the front of the *London Gazette,* England's court newspaper (Cook 1998, 21–22; Emery, Emery, and Roberts 2000, 25; Starr 2004, 55). For the next 30 years, almost all colonial newspapers, such as the *American Weekly Mercury* in Philadelphia and the *New York Gazette,* followed this model. Almost all publishers were employed as either postmasters or government printers (which often enabled them to mail their papers for free under their franking privilege), followed some policy of government preclearance of content, and included the "Published by Authority" notice (Cook 1998, 22; Emery, Emery, and Roberts 2000, 23; Starr 2004, 56). In Starr's (2004, 55–56) words, "Like the court gazettes in Europe, these papers posed no challenge to authority; they primarily chronicled events across the Atlantic but provided little information about developments at home, much less any critical discussion of politics."

In 1721, James Franklin bucked convention by publishing a newspaper, the *New-England Courant*, with neither advance government approval nor the "Published by Authority" label. Yet by 1722, after Franklin criticized the colonial government's policy on smallpox inoculation and its poor defense against nearby pirates, he was jailed by the Governing Council for contempt. While he was eventually released, the council ruled that he "be strictly forbidden . . . to print or publish the *New-England Courant* or any pamphlet or paper of the like Nature, Except it be first Supervised by the Secretary of this Province" (Emery, Emery, and Roberts 2000, 25–28).

James Franklin's brother and apprentice, Benjamin, had better luck when he started his own paper in Philadelphia. Several years earlier, in 1719, the first American newspaper outside of Boston, the *American Weekly Mercury*, began publishing in Philadelphia. Like Boston papers of the time, it was run by a postmaster and received the colonial government's printing contract as a subsidy. In 1729, Ben Franklin became publisher of a recently founded rival, the *Pennsylvania Gazette*, and by 1730 he had won the government printing contract away from the *Mercury*. Ben Franklin attained tremendous commercial success, with both his newspaper and his *Poor Richards Almanack*, by producing entertaining copy with some opinions, while astutely avoiding offending the authorities. The *Gazette* would become the largest-circulation paper in America before Franklin retired from publishing in 1748 (Sloan and Williams 1994, 51–68; Emery, Emery, and Roberts 2000, 29–31).

While it was still very risky to directly attack colonial officials in print, the growth among some newspapers during this period was connected to the decline in the prevalence of convictions and severity of punishments. Prior to the Long Parliament and the English Revolution in the 1640s, punishment for sedition in the colonies often involved some type of "bodily correction," including possibly having one's limbs broken or one's tongue "bored through with an awl" (Starr 2004, 56). By the second half of the 1600s, these types of punishment were phased out. After a New York jury refused to convict John Peter Zenger of seditious libel in 1732, convictions for this offense almost entirely ceased in the American colonies (Cook 1998, 21; Emery, Emery, and Roberts 2000, 35–40; Starr 2004, 57–59; Copeland 2006, 153–63).[16] This is not to say that government authorities took a libertarian attitude toward the press. Harold Nelson reports that even after the Zenger case, "Printers were forever being called before the bars of legislative bodies to answer for 'affronts,' 'breach of privilege,' 'impudence,' 'indignities' upon authority, and 'libels'" (Nelson 1959, 163; see also Copeland 2006, 162). However, because acquittal

---

[16] On the Zenger trial, see Sloan and Williams (1994, 73–91).

was almost always the result if charges were brought, this was less persecution than petty political harassment.

Newspapers founded in this environment in the mid-1700s were usually owned and operated by individual middle-class artisans, who served
as printers, writers, and editors for their publications (Emery, Emery, and
Roberts 2000, 22–40; Starr 2004, 55–61). But they were certainly not independent checks on political power. Like Ben Franklin, most depended
on political subsidies from some combination of government printing
contracts and government advertising. Initially most of these publishers
also served as postmaster (at the pleasure of the colonial government),
but by the mid-1700s, this practice was fading away. During the period
just prior to the Revolution, most newspapers avoided controversy by
covering sensational crimes and accidents, disease outbreaks, and foreign
news—according to one calculation, Franklin's *Pennsylvania Gazette* devoted only 21% of its news coverage to British North America—and remaining "studiously neutral" on domestic political issues when they were
covered (Copeland 1997; Starr 2004, 60–61). By adopting this style of
neglect and neutrality toward continental politics, American newspapers
began to flourish.

Newspapers Were Tools of Political Movements in Revolutionary-Era America

The American Revolution changed the relationship between political elites and newspapers.[17] Yet as this happened, political leaders still
showed little tolerance for the press gaining independent agency. Instead,
where previously newspapers avoided domestic politics to dodge the various forms of repression print media were traditionally subjected to, now
they became effective tools of the independence movement.

Conflicts with Britain sparked in 1765, when it imposed a form of the
stamp tax, which had long been law in England, on the North American
colonies. Whatever the policy merits of the tax, it was a strategic mistake. It disadvantaged lawyers, printers, and other opinion leaders. Starr
(2004, 65) observes that it seemed practically "designed to inflame the

---

[17] While I use the term *American Revolution,* there is debate among historians about
whether this was a true social revolution (G. Wood 1993; Starr 2004, 62–63) or simply
a war of independence with social hierarchies left in place (Goldstone 1991). What seems
hard to dispute is that those writing at the time thought something important about the
bases of political power had changed. It was only at this time that the term *democracy*
acquired positive connotations and became widespread in America (Starr 2004, 62–63).
There is also significant evidence that popular sentiment shifted to believing that the people
were the source of government sovereignty (G. Wood 1993).

most articulate" (see also Davidson 1941, 226; Sloan and Williams 1994, 124–25; Emery, Emery, and Roberts 2000, 43; Copeland 2006, 202–6). Ben Franklin estimated that, by taxing newspapers for each page and each advertisement, it would reduce newspaper subscriptions and advertising by 50% (Starr 2004, 65).

Fueled at least partially by self-interest, many papers became crusading organs of the resistance movement. When a Boston mob burned a stamp tax collector in effigy on August 14, 1765, the act was covered favorably in many newspapers and consequently copied in other cities. The Sons of Liberty, founded in late 1765, used newspapers to publicize their message throughout the colonies (Starr 2004, 65).[18] In an example of how anti-British organizers used sympathetic printers, in 1768 and 1769, the Sons of Liberty produced the "Journal of Occurrences," a regularly printed collection of reports of atrocities (many of dubious veracity) committed by the British troops occupying Boston, which was published as part of the *New York Journal, Massachusetts Spy,* and *Boston Gazette* (Davidson 1941, 236–27; Sloan and Williams 1994, 148–50; Emery, Emery, and Roberts 2000, 51; Copeland 2006, 209). Many anti-British pamphlets, such as Thomas Paine's popular *Common Sense,* were similarly printed verbatim in revolutionary newspapers (Davidson 1941, 241; Emery, Emery, and Roberts 2000, 55).

By the start of the war, most newspapers had clear affiliations: overall, at least twice as many favored independence as sided with Britain (Davidson 1941, 226; Starr 2004, 68). Revolutionary newspapers were seen by both sides as such appendages of the cause that the *Massachusetts Spy* and *Boston Gazette* printing presses needed to be smuggled out of Boston when the British occupied the city after the battles of Lexington and Concord, to return only when the British evacuated the city in 1775 (Emery, Emery, and Roberts 2000, 54). Most people read the Declaration of Independence in pro-Revolution newspapers or learned about it when printed copies were read in public places (Starr 2004, 68).[19] After the war, newspapers would continue to serve the goals of these political elites. For instance, advocates for ratification of the federal Constitution employed the pro-Federalist *New York Independent Journal* to publish

---

[18] Printers who strongly allied themselves with the Sons of Liberty included Benjamin Edes and John Gill (producing the *Boston Gazette*), Isaiah Thomas (*Massachusetts Spy*), John Holt (*New York Journal*), Peter Timothy (*South Carolina Gazette*), William Goddard (*Pennsylvania Chronicle* and *Baltimore Journal*), and Solomon Southwick (*Newport Mercury*) (Emery, Emery, and Roberts 2000, 50–51). For a more complete list of pro-Revolution newspapers, see Davidson (1941, 227–45).

[19] The Constitution would later be publicized in a similar way. Hardly anyone at the time saw handwritten manuscripts like those shown in textbooks and displayed at the National Archives (Starr 2004, 71).

anonymous articles in favor of ratification written by James Madison, Alexander Hamilton, and John Jay, which later became known as the *Federalist Papers* (Madison, Hamilton, and Jay 1987 [1788]; Emery, Emery, and Roberts 2000, 63).

Newspapers' strong association with the independence movement greatly increased their standing in the eyes of revolutionary leaders, who would soon determine the U.S. Constitution's treatment of the press. In responding to British persecution of the *Boston Gazette*, the Massachusetts House of Representatives passed a resolution stating, "The Liberty of the Press is the great Bulwark of the Liberty of the People" (Starr 2004, 67). In 1774, the Continental Congress passed a resolution saying that a free press leads to political discourse "whereby oppressive officers are shamed or intimidated, into more honourable and just modes of conducting affairs" (76). By 1787, 9 of the 13 states had placed protections for freedom of the press in their state constitutions (Emery, Emery, and Roberts 2000, 62).

In 1787, when most of America's political leaders set out to replace the weak Articles of Confederation with the Constitution, the press's role in the revolutionary struggle was prominent in their minds. The framers found reinforcement for their ideas in contemporary political philosophy. For instance, John Locke's liberal, natural-rights-based republicanism supported a free press (Starr 2004, 62). As early as 1644, during the English Civil War, John Milton had criticized government restrictions on the press in *Aeropagitica*, an essay widely read in the Revolutionary era (Emery, Emery, and Roberts 2000, 12; Copeland 2006, 83–88, 143). American newspapers also extensively reprinted *Cato's Letters*, which were written by British radical Whigs John Trenchard and Thomas Gordon and originally published in the *London Journal* in the 1720s. In advocating republican principles, Trenchard and Gordon called the free press the "bulwark of liberty" (Emery, Emery, and Roberts 2000, 15; Starr 2004, 62; Copeland 2006, 97–100, 143).

The framers' recent experience of a free press serving their political self-interests, combined with the many arguments available in Enlightenment thinking that shaped their overall political outlook, created a powerful vogue for a free press. Given this, when it became clear that adopting an explicit bill of rights would be necessary to achieve ratification of the Constitution, there was little doubt that freedom of the press would be included.[20] The original draft of the First Amendment, which

---

[20] Interestingly, the original text of the First Amendment, as passed by the House of Representatives, was in the passive voice, implying that no entity could abridge these rights. It said, "The people shall not be deprived or abridged of their right to speak, to write, or to publish their sentiments; and the freedom of the press, as one of the great bulwarks of

Madison introduced in Congress in 1789, even called press freedom "one of the great bulwarks of liberty" (Starr 2004, 76).

Yet in guaranteeing freedom of the press, politicians at the time did not have in mind protections for a profession called journalism, because such a profession did not exist. In Timothy Cook's (1998, 23) words, "[t]he job of a reporter, as we know it today, was nonexistent." Nor did they have in mind an important political institution that would wield power independent of government and politicians. To the extent that those who produced newspapers and pamphlets were involved in politics at all, political elites (and likely the mass public as well) saw them as useful tools for politicians and political movements with little independent agency.

This interpretation of press freedom is made clearer in the preface to the state constitution Pennsylvania adopted in 1776, which explained, "the people have a right to freedom of speech, and of writing, and publishing their sentiments, therefore, the freedom of the press ought not to be restrained" (Starr 2004, 73). As Cook (1998, 22) puts it, to the founding generation "'Freedom of the press' . . . referred less to journalistic independence from government intervention than to the capacity of individuals to have free access to a printing press and thereby disseminate their views."[21] To the extent that press freedom was not associated with newspapers serving as propaganda arms of the Revolutionary movement, it brought to mind the early 1700s tradition of nonpartisan newspapers, which, when not ignoring domestic politics, accepted unsolicited opinion articles from those on all sides of a controversy.

In sum, we should understand the American founders' support for freedom of the press not as an indication that they felt unthreatened by a press corps exercising independent institutional political power. Rather, their support occurred in the context of not only Enlightenment political

---

liberty, shall be invaluable." In the Senate, however, the amendment was changed to the active voice, specifying that "Congress shall make no law . . ." No record remains of the reason for the Senate's change. James Madison actually proposed another amendment for the Bill of Rights that would explicitly protect speech and press freedoms from state governments, but it failed after passing the House and not the Senate (Starr 2004, 75). However, modern constitutional law has rendered this distinction largely moot because the due process clause of the Fourteenth Amendment is interpreted to imply that freedom of speech (*Gitlow v. New York* 1925) and freedom of the press (*Near v. Minnesota* 1931) apply to state governments under the incorporation doctrine.

[21] This is not to imply that this clause should not be used to guarantee broader rights for journalists. Such a view would be required only by a strictly originalist philosophy of constitutional law.

Clark (2005) agrees with the specifics of my description of the American press in the 1700s yet still concludes that by the 1790s it could be labeled an institution. Our disagreement seems to be only over semantics.

thought but also a recent history when newspapers either eschewed politics or were useful subordinate tools of the framers' own political movement.

NEWSPAPERS WERE ESSENTIAL ORGANS OF THE FIRST POLITICAL PARTIES

While most had modest readership, the number of American newspapers continued to grow in the new republic. Cities typically had many small newspapers, which tended to be expensive and cater to political and economic elites (West 2001, 16). Some scholars have suggested that this represented all newspapers in the early republic (19).[22] Others, such as Starr (2004, 70), find evidence that ordinary citizens also utilized small newspapers, which proliferated in rural areas, and other types of printing to express themselves.[23] Overall, while in 1775 circulation per capita in the American colonies was somewhere between 28% and 91% of English levels, by 1834 the new nation had 1,265 newspapers. In contrast, Great Britain had only 369 papers, despite having a larger population (68, 86).

At this time, American papers heavily emphasized both national and international politics (Starr 2004, 87). One estimate found that in 1831–32 political news and opinion constituted about 51% of the content of city papers and 73% of rural papers (Baldasty 1992, 123). Of course, as it would be a long time before journalistic professional norms would divide them, news and opinion mixed seamlessly in this coverage. Opinionated political newspapers quickly became part of the emerging first American party system. By 1810, 86% of newspapers would have some party connection (Thomas 1810; cited in West 2001, 16).

George Washington won the first presidential election in 1788 (and reelection in 1792) without notable opposition. Just before he assumed office in 1789, his supporters founded the *Gazette of the United States*, with its stated purpose "to be the organ of the government." Its editor, John Fenno, was kept on the Treasury Department's payroll as a way of subsidizing and keeping control of the paper (West 2001, 10).

---

[22] These scholars have estimated that newspaper readers were as few as 2% of the public at this time (West 2001, 19).

[23] This is consistent with de Tocqueville's observations that "the number of periodical or semiperiodical productions in the United States surpasses all belief" (2000 [1835–40], 184), there was an "astonishing circulation of letters and newspapers" in rural Kentucky and Tennessee (Starr 2004, 48), and a settler he met in Michigan had "plung[ed] into the wilderness of the New World with his Bible, ax, and newspapers" (de Tocqueville 2000 [1835–40], 303). In addition, in 1830, printer Isaiah Thomas observed that printers, usually producing some type of newspaper, operated "in all the principal inland towns and hamlets" (Thomas 1810, 18; cited in Starr 2004, 85).

Early in the Washington administration, a rift developed between Secretary of State Thomas Jefferson and Treasury Secretary Alexander Hamilton, which led to the establishment of the first American political parties. The Federalists, centered around Hamilton, advocated a strong national government and less-democratic institutions. The Democratic-Republicans, centered around Jefferson, favored a decentralized and participatory government as well as a more decentralized economy. The *Gazette of the United States* was controlled by Hamilton's faction. Jefferson described it as "a paper of pure Toryism, disseminating the doctrine of monarchy, aristocracy, and exclusion of the people" (West 2001, 11). He started his own paper, the *National Gazette*, to transmit his views, employing its editor, Philip Freneau, as a clerk for foreign languages in the State Department. The *National Gazette* accused Fenno and the *Gazette of the United States* of "preach[ing] in favor of monarchs and titles" (11). The *Gazette of the United States* called Freneau a "fauning parasite" and one of the "mad dogs" (11). Though President Washington had little interest or direct involvement in the *Gazette of the United States* (Pollard 1947, 6), he did not escape criticism because he was widely seen to have Federalist sympathies. For instance, the *National Gazette* accused Washington of "overdrawing his salary" and "unconstitutional" acts (West 2001, 11).

While the *National Gazette* folded and Freneau lost his job when Jefferson resigned as secretary of state in 1793, eventually Democratic-Republican newspapers proliferated to challenge the Federalists. Among the most influential Democratic-Republican papers was the *Philadelphia General Advertiser* (known as the *Aurora*), which was originally founded in 1790 with Jefferson's encouragement (Sheppard 2008, 25). Under editor Benjamin Franklin Bache (Ben Franklin's grandson), the *Aurora* called President Washington "treacherous" and "mischievous" and accused him of "pusillanimous neglect," "ingratitude," "insignificance," and "spurious fame" (Pollard 1947, 19). In 1796, the day after Washington published his farewell address, the *Aurora* proclaimed, "If ever a nation was debauched by a man, the American nation has been debauched by Washington. If ever a nation has suffered from the improper influence of a man, the American nation has suffered from the influence of Washington. If ever a nation was deceived by a man, the American nation has been deceived by Washington" (Mott 1950, 128).

Yet when Federalist John Adams defeated Jefferson in the election of 1796, in addition to the *Gazette of the United States*, he obtained support from about 80% of newspapers nationwide (West 2001, 13). The Democratic-Republicans' electoral strategy depended on changing this. Working together with supportive local printers, they increased the number of Democratic-Republican papers from 51 in 1798 to 85 in 1800 (Starr 2004, 80).

Federalists' worries about the Democratic-Republicans' use of newspapers were a prime motivation behind their passage of the Alien and Sedition Acts of 1798. The 10% of newspaper editors who were not American citizens, almost all of whom were Democratic-Republican sympathizers, were targeted under the Alien Act, which authorized the prosecution of many noncitizen immigrants. More political prosecutions came under the Sedition Act, which stated that the government could prosecute those who "write, print, publish or quote any false scandal or scurrilous writings against the government of the United States, the President, or either House of Congress" (Mott 1950, 148; West 2001, 13–14). Fifteen people were indicted and 10 were convicted under the Sedition Act. Benjamin Franklin Bache was jailed for seditious libel and died in prison awaiting trial (Starr 2004, 78–80).[24]

The partisan conflict between the Federalists and Democratic-Republicans, which peaked during the 1800 presidential campaign between Jefferson and Adams, was among the most vitriolic in American history. Most of the harshest rhetoric was expressed through party newspapers. During that campaign, a Federalist newspaper proclaimed that "should the Infidel Jefferson be elected to the Presidency, the seal of death is that moment set on our holy religion" (West 2001, 15). In the Democratic-Republican *Richmond Examiner,* Washington was called "a traitor, a robber and a perjurer." The *Examiner* called John Adams "a hoary-headed incendiary" (West 2001, 16). In 1802, as President Jefferson served his first term, the Federalist *New York Evening Post* attacked him for having several children with his slave Sally Hemings. The story originated with Virginia newspaper writer James T. Callender, whose articles labeled Hemings "Dusky Sally," "Black Sal," and "a slut as common as pavement" (West 2001, 15).

Most newspapers continued to be subordinate to politicians as the Federalists declined and the country moved toward the Era of Good Feelings (1815–24), when there was no strong opposition party. At this time, most papers, including most of those active in politics, supported themselves through advertising and subscriptions (Starr 2004, 93), but a significant and influential minority continued to receive direct political subsidies. For instance, when he took office in 1801, President Jefferson continued the practice of designating an "official" paper. The *National Intelligencer* served in this role from 1801 through 1828 (West 2001, 16). It was the official printer of the House of Representatives, allowing it to earn nearly a million dollars in government printing contracts during this period by producing publications like *Annals of Congress* and the *Register of*

---

[24] Benjamin Franklin Bache was actually arrested several months before the Sedition Act was even passed (Starr 2004, 78–79).

Debates, predecessors to the *Congressional Record* (West 2001, 16). In 1819, Congress adopted a practice that persisted until 1846 of allowing each chamber to elect a printer for each session (Baldasty 1992, 20; Starr 2004, 92). The *Intelligencer* consistently and enthusiastically advocated the government's positions, advertising that its pages were "always open for communications from politicians of the same political faith" (West 2001, 16). Its editors were given early access to government information and viewed it as their mission to be "the channel through which the federal administration carried its message to the people" (Ames 1972, 88; cited in West 2001, 17).

Newspapers that received congressional printing contracts consistently ran profits of 20% to 55% (Baldasty 1992, 20; Starr 2004, 92). Individual members of Congress also subsidized party papers through the franking privilege, which was interpreted very liberally in the 1820s and 1830s. Franked newspapers, sent under the authority of members of Congress, cost the federal government about $40,000 a year during this period (Baldasty 1992, 20). As for its subsidies, the executive branch spent an estimated $110,004 on printing in the 1831–83 congressional term, increasing to $174,244 during the 1839–41 term (Baldasty 1992, 20). Among these subsidies, the secretary of state had the discretion to choose a printer in each state to publish the laws enacted in the previous year (Starr 2004, 92), while other cabinet secretaries had similar arrangements.

When the Era of Good Feelings ended in 1824 with five candidates running for president, three (John Quincy Adams, John Calhoun, and William Crawford) were cabinet secretaries who used their departments to sponsor newspapers advocating on their behalf (Starr 2004, 92–93). Although Andrew Jackson won a plurality of the popular and electoral vote, Adams was elected president by the House of Representatives in 1824 because no candidate received a majority of electoral votes. Adams established the *National Journal* as his official newspaper and also continued to affiliate with the *Intelligencer*, which received the House printing contract (Baldasty 1992, 20; West 2001, 20). Both received patronage and wrote on Adams's behalf. Yet Jackson, who finally won the presidency in 1828, took political control and sponsorship of the press to unprecedented levels.

As part of Jackson and his campaign manager Martin Van Buren's creation of the first American political party with an ongoing mass-level organization, they sponsored newspapers extensively.[25] Opponents claimed that

---

[25] The Jacksonian era corresponded, of course, not just with a peak of partisan newspaper mobilization but also with an increase in mass-level political participation in general. The number of states directly electing their presidential electors increased from none in

Jackson's 1828 campaign had a $50,000 fund to bankroll party newspapers (Tebbel and Watts 1985, 77). Upon taking office, Jackson was unsatisfied with his first official newspaper, the *United States Telegraph*, and replaced it with the *Globe*. He conferenced with the *Globe*'s editor every night, when he "dictated ideas for future articles" and reviewed those in progress to ensure he approved (West 2001, 20). He appointed 56 newspaper editors and printers to government jobs and required all federal employees making over $1,000 a year to subscribe to the *Globe* (West 2001, 20–21).

Organizing newspapers was a core function of mass-based political parties in the Jacksonian era. For instance, when the Anti-Mason Party started to become a serious competitor to Jackson's Democratic Party in the late 1820s, its major institutional goal was to organize successful party newspapers (Baldasty 1992, 11, 15). The 1829 New York State Anti-Masonic Convention issued a report stating, "Free presses constitute the means upon which the country must rely to uproot and overthrow Free Masonry" (15). In 1832, the year Anti-Masons ran their first and only presidential candidate, they controlled 70 newspapers in New York, 32 in Pennsylvania, 5 in Massachusetts, and 1 each in Vermont, Virginia, and Washington, DC. Indeed, newspapers served as foundations of the party's rise to national prominence (17). Similar movements, like extreme states-rights activists in the South, also centered their organizing on creating and nurturing newspapers (17–18).

Newspapers were large and essential parts of party organizations (Pasley 2001, chap. 14). Party papers in state capitals and Washington, DC, served as "flagships" for the parties (Baldasty 1992, 15). Editors were replaced, or a rival paper created, if the editor abandoned his party loyalty (18). But this was seldom necessary because editors were often more activists than journalists. Communication historian Gerald Baldasty (1992, 29–30) explains, "Some editors were de facto county or state directors of their parties, while others were political lieutenants rather than party leaders. Whatever the position, a common pattern existed: editors did much more than edit newspapers. They were extensively involved in politics outside of newspaper offices. They served as central committee members, public speakers, and organizers of meetings and conventions." Yet after Jackson's presidency, direct control of newspapers by parties and the government began a steady but gradual decline. Still, as late as 1850, approximately 80% to 95% of U.S. newspapers had party affiliations (McGerr 1986; Baldasty 1992, 7). But the newspaper industry was transforming, as the number of party newspapers decreased and the number of papers following commercial business models grew.

1800 to every state except South Carolina in 1832. National voter turnout among adult white males increased from 9% in 1820 to 57% in 1828 (Baldasty 1992, 12).

The Partisan Press Was Attacked by Political Opponents and Generally Disrespected

With the subordination of professional standards to political objectives, newspaper writers of the partisan era suffered from a severe lack of prestige (West 2001, 9). Alexis de Tocqueville (2000 [1835–40], 185, 471) observed that "American journalists have a low social status, their education is only sketchy, and their thoughts often vulgarly expressed. . . . [T]he hallmark of the American journalist is a direct and coarse attack. . . . They certainly are not great writers, but they speak their country's language." This seems to reflect the prevailing view of journalists in the early 1800s.

While the founding generation preserved press freedom in the First Amendment and used newspapers to organize their parties, they tended to dislike newspapers that were not part of their own movement or coalition. For example, shortly after the revolutionary struggle, Thomas Jefferson wrote in a 1787 letter to Edward Carrington, "The basis of our governments being the opinion of the people, the very first object should be to keep that right [of a free press]; and were it left to me to decide whether we should have a government without newspapers, or newspapers without a government, I should not hesitate a moment to prefer the latter" (Mott 1950, 170; Kurland and Lerner 2000). However, running in three presidential elections and enduring constant criticism from Federalist Party–affiliated newspapers during these campaigns and in his two terms in office soured Jefferson on the press's role in the political process. In later letters, he wrote that "The newspapers of our country by their abandoned spirit of falsehood, have more effectively destroyed the utility of the press than all the shackles devised by Bonaparte" and that "[Federalists] fill their newspapers with falsehoods, calumnies, and audacities" (Emery, Emery, and Roberts 2000, 78). In an 1807 letter to John Norvell, he wrote,

> It is a melancholy truth, that a suppression of the press could not more completely deprive the nation of its benefits, than is done by its abandoned prostitution to falsehood. Nothing can now be believed which is seen in a newspaper. Truth itself becomes suspicious by being put into that polluted vehicle. . . . I really look with commiseration over the great body of my fellow citizens, who, reading newspapers, live and die in the belief, that they have known something of what has been passing in the world in their time. . . . I will add, that the man who never looks into a newspaper is better informed than he who reads them. (Whitman 1945, 232–33)

George Washington's relationship with the press took a very similar trajectory. Before returning to public life to preside over the Constitutional

Convention and serve as president, he expressed some concern about the accuracy of news reports. In a letter commenting on coverage of Shays' Rebellion, he said, "Newspaper paragraphs unsupported by other testimony, are often contradictory and bewildering" (Pollard 1947, 3). However, prior to any deep involvement in politics, his views were mostly dominated by a philosophical belief in the virtues of a free press. In June 1788 he wrote, "For myself, I entertain an high idea of the utility of periodic Publications. . . . I consider such easy vehicles of knowledge, more happily calculated than any other, to preserve liberty, stimulate the industry and meliorate the morals of an enlightened and free People" (5)."

But, like Jefferson, the more Washington participated in political conflict, the more hostile toward the news media he became. Like many politicians through the ages, Washington complained that the press did not pass on information unfiltered, writing in 1790, "It is to be lamented that the Editors of the different Gazettes in the Union, do not more generally, and more correctly (instead of stuffing their papers with scurrility and nonsensical declamation . . .) publish the debates of the Congress on all great national questions, and this with no uncommon pains, everyone of them might do" (Pollard 1947, 8). He wrote in 1796 that the *Aurora* and other Democratic-Republican papers were "void of truth and fairness" and "resort[ed] to misrepresentation and mutilated authorities." He complained, "it were to be wished that the enlightened public could have a clear and comprehensive view of the facts. But how to give it lies the difficulty, and I see no method at present" (18). Subsequent politicians would repeatedly echo Washington's themes: a wish that the press would simply relay politicians' messages unfiltered and hostility toward journalists' expressions of independent political power.

John Adams made no attacks on the press during his presidential term, despite receiving intense criticism. But he privately seethed. After leaving office, he wrote that he blamed his electoral defeat in 1800 on "the writings of Freneau, Markoe, Ned Church, Andrew Brown, Paine, Callender, Hamilton, Cobbet, and John Ward Fenno and many others. . . . Without a complete collection of these libels, no faithful history of the last twenty years can ever be written" (Pollard 1947, 46–47). In letters to Jefferson, Adams called newspaper criticism "the terrorism of a former day" and stated that "I have been disgraced and degraded and I have a right to complain. But, as I have always expected it, I have always submitted to it, perhaps with too much tameness" (47).

Not coincidentally, as the intense party conflict of the 1790s and 1800s gave way to the Era of Good Feelings, the relationship of political leaders with the press improved somewhat. President James Madison (1809–17), who faced little serious party opposition, even mustered some (very) modest praise for the press, writing, "In general, they give, though frequently erroneous and sometimes perverted, yet on the whole, fuller accounts of what is going forward than could be put into a letter" (Pollard 1947, 98). Similarly, President James Monroe (1817–25), while maintaining the *National Intelligencer* as the official government newspaper, paid little attention to it. Historian James Pollard (1947, 116) writes that Monroe had "little direct connection with the press of his time and only a casual appreciation of it." Similarly, journalism scholars John Tebbel and Sarah Miles Watts (1985, 57) state that Monroe was "less forceful about the press, either pro or con," than other presidents.

With the return of intense party conflict in the Jacksonian Era and Jackson's unprecedentedly large mobilization of partisan newspapers, the relationship between politicians and the press again became contentious. As noted above, Jackson took a very active role in directing his own partisan newspapers, largely to counter and surpass opposing papers. As long as the partisan press persisted, politicians continued to cultivate newspapers as part of their own political organizations and to attack most other papers, sometimes bitterly.

THE COMMERCIAL PRESS TURNED AWAY FROM POLITICS AND PURSUED DIVERSE NEWS STYLES

At the start of the nineteenth century, most newspapers were four-page weeklies or dailies, featuring advertising on the outer two pages and articles mixing news and opinion on the inner two pages. As the previous two sections describe, these often were part of a party apparatus or at least presented a clear political perspective (Schudson 1978, 14; Baldasty 1992, 3). By the end of the century, newspapers were "large-circulation, 8- or 12-page dailies that usually eschewed close political affiliation" and covered many more nonpolitical topics such as "business, crime, accidents, fires, divorce, suicide, labor, education, religion, sports, inventions, disease, weather, books, theater, music, fashion, recipes," and even "serialized fiction" (Baldasty 1992, 3). While in the partisan era newspapers' closest modern analog would probably be short political magazines like the *National Review* or *American Prospect*, by the late 1800s they most resembled modern urban tabloid newspapers like the *New York Post* or *Daily News*. Historian Michael E. McGerr (1986, 108) persuasively argues that three types of newspapers existed in the mid- to late-nineteenth-century United States: a decreasing number of partisan papers, "independent" papers, and "sensational" papers.

The last official presidential newspaper, the *Washington Constitution*, ceased serving that role when James Buchanan left office in 1861. The previous year, Congress had largely ended the federal government's direct subsidies to newspapers by establishing the Government Printing Office, eliminating the need for outside printing of most government documents (McGerr 1986, 109; West 2001, 28). As the partisan press continued to decline, its business model persisted predominantly among small, rural newspapers that relied on county-level government or party subsidies (McGerr 1986, 130).

Some newspapers, rather than maintaining strong party ties, adopted an independent style. While these papers engaged in political writing, they tended to adopt the various idiosyncratic styles and viewpoints of their editors rather than forming an institutionalized media establishment. High-profile editors like James Watson Webb of the *New York Courier and Enquirer*, James Gordon Bennett of the *New York Herald*, Horace Greeley of the *New York Tribune* and Henry James Raymond of the *New York Daily Times* each had their own styles and political prejudices. Each paper reflected the editor's philosophy of what journalism should be. This sometimes entailed focusing on specific issues, using a unique writing style, or feuding with other editors (West 2001, 29–31).

Bennett was one of the most colorful and successful. He founded the *Herald* in 1835 and operated it with virtually no other employees, focusing on scandals, crime, sex, and himself. To gain publicity, he sent a reporter to Africa from 1869 to 1872 to search for explorer David Livingstone and send back reports (McGerr 1986, 110). He wrote that other newspaper editors were "truly unfit by nature and want of capacity to come to a right conclusion upon any subject." He had particularly intense feuds with Webb and Greeley. The former feud resulted in Webb confronting Bennett on the street and beating him with a stick. When Bennett married, he announced his engagement with a large headline stating, "To the Readers of the Herald —Declaration of Love —Caught at Last —Going to Be Married —New Movement in Civilization" and an accompanying article providing more details. By 1860, the *Herald* had a circulation of 77,000, the largest of any daily newspaper in the world (West 2001, 29).

Independent editors eschewed blind partisanship, but not because they believed journalists could or would be impartial or objective. Editors freely expressed their own opinions and perspectives. They "deplored the notion of political neutrality: men must have principles after all" (McGerr 1986, 115). Some committed themselves and their newspapers to the campaign against slavery, such as Greeley's *Tribune*, Fredrick Douglass's *North Star* in Rochester, New York, or Joseph Medill's *Chicago Tribune* (West 2001, 33–34). Raymond's *New York Daily Times* had a much-publicized campaign against the Tweed Ring from 1870 to 1871 (McGerr 1986, 110).

The third type of paper that was prominent in the mid- and late nineteenth century was what McGerr calls "sensational." The success of sensational papers (and some independent papers) was closely related to the changing economics of the industry. Without political subsidies, papers were drawn away from political topics and toward those that increased readership or otherwise pleased advertisers. In Baldasty's (1992, 9) words, "Commercialization imposes the imperative that newspapers must entertain their readers. When entertainment is paramount, difficult issues or current events that are not inherently interesting or entertaining may well get short shrift."

Large technological changes also shaped the industry. The invention and proliferation of the telegraph, which led to wire services like the Associated Press (AP), allowed newspapers to share news-gathering costs (Emery, Emery, and Roberts 2000, 156, 114–15; West 2001, 26–27; Starr 2004, chaps. 5–6).[26] Costs were further reduced by easier transportation resulting from the proliferation of railroads (Emery, Emery, and Roberts 2000, 156; West 2001, 28).[27]

Printing presses increased in both capability and cost. In the 1830s and 1840s, it cost only approximately $5,000–$10,000 to start a newspaper in New York City. At least one paper (the *New York Herald*) started with an investment of only $500. After the Civil War, starting a New York paper cost an estimated $1 million (Baldasty 1992, 5). Newer printing presses, while expensive, had a much greater printing capacity. In the early 1800s, a fast press could produce 1,000 papers per hour (Emery, Emery, and Roberts 2000, 95). By the 1830s, a press could produce 4,000 per hour; by the 1850s, 12,000 per hour; and by the 1890s, 24,000 to 48,000 12-page papers per hour (Baldasty 1992, 85–86; Emery, Emery, and Roberts 2000, 95; Gentzkow, Glaeser, and Goldin 2006, 20). This meant that one printing press could supply newspapers for "a significant portion of a city's readers" (Hamilton 2004, 41). In addition, the cost of newsprint gradually declined through most of the early 1800s, rose during the Civil War, then fell dramatically from $25 per pound in 1870 to $10 per pound in 1910, further reducing the cost of printing each additional paper (Hamilton 2004, 41; Gentzkow, Glaeser, and Goldin

[26] The first telegraph message was sent in 1844, and by 1848 there were already over 5,000 miles of line in the United States (West 2001, 26). Telegraph lines continued to expand rapidly throughout the century, with Western Union quadrupling its telegraph network between 1880 and 1900 (Emery, Emery, and Roberts 2000, 156). The Associated Press was founded in 1949 by a group of New York newspaper editors, and it proceeded to sell telegraph news reports to newspapers across the country (114–15). By 1880, 52% of morning papers and 24% of evening papers in the United States used news obtained by telegraph (West 2001, 27).

[27] Railroads also grew rapidly. There were 9,021 miles of railroad track in the United States in 1850 (West 2001, 28), 93,000 miles in 1880, and 193,000 miles in 1900 (Emery, Emery, and Roberts 2000, 156).

2006, 19).[28] Combined, these higher fixed costs and lower marginal costs made large-circulation papers more profitable and smaller papers less so (Gentzkow, Glaeser, and Goldin 2006).

The forerunner of the sensational commercial press was the "penny press," which emerged in the 1830s. These papers, such as the *New York Sun*, surpassed their competitors in circulation by charging only a cent per paper or four dollars for a year's subscription (West 2001, 19–20). A business model based significantly on advertising revenue freed them from government subsidies. Their coverage was, "relatively speaking, indifferent to political events" (Schudson 1978, 21), instead emphasizing human interest and local crime stories on the front pages (West 2001, 20). For instance, the *Sun* began one short article on Congress by stating, "The proceedings of Congress thus far, would not interest our readers" (Schudson 1978, 21).

Large-circulation papers became widespread later in the nineteenth century partially because of urbanization. The portion of the U.S. population living in urban areas increased from 8.8% in 1830 to 34.5% in 1870 (Baldasty 1992, 49). In 1870, there were only two newspapers with a circulation over 100,000. By 1890, there were eight, with several New York papers maintaining a circulation of over 300,000. The average circulation of all daily U.S. newspapers rose from 2,200 in 1840 to 8,007 in 1904, reaching 16,684 by 1925 (McGerr 1986, 108). The portion of the population subscribing to a newspaper increased from about 3% in 1840 to about 4.7% in 1860 and about 20% by 1900 (West 2001, 27, 42). This facilitated an explosion in advertising revenue (Baldasty 1992, 52–80). Nationally, advertising revenue doubled between 1870 and 1880 and almost doubled again between 1880 and 1890 (McGerr 1986, 108). By 1900, newspapers relied on advertising for over two-thirds of their income (West 2001, 42).

New, large urban dailies, especially those owned by Joseph Pulitzer and William Randolph Hearst, employed "sensational and anti-political journalism" (McGerr 1986, 107). Starting with ownership of the *St. Louis Dispatch* and *San Francisco Examiner*, respectively, Pulitzer and Hearst had tremendous success increasing circulation and soon bought up many more papers. The flagships of both empires were their New York papers: Pulitzer's *World* and Hearst's *Journal*. Pulitzer increased the *World*'s circulation from 60,000 when he purchased it in 1883 to 250,000 by 1887 (West 2001, 43). By the 1890s, the *World* and *Journal* were the largest newspapers in New York City (Schudson 1978, 88). At the turn of the century, Hearst's media holdings were valued at $220 million and

---

[28] For more on the changing economics of the newspaper industry in the late 1800s, see Smythe (2003, chap. 7).

included 25 daily and 17 Sunday papers, 13 magazines, 4 syndicates, and a newsreel (West 2001, 46).

Hearst and Pulitzer emphasized "sensationalist coverage, big headlines and colorful graphics," a style known as yellow journalism (West 2001, 43). While the sensational press sometimes took on political crusades against misbehavior in government and industry, it generally eschewed party or ideological affiliations and placed a heavy emphasis on less political stories (West 2001, 44). In catering to prurient interests, "sensationalism . . . shifted public attention away from political events" (McGerr 1986, 122). Yellow newspapers "choked up the news channel . . . with a shrieking, gaudy, sensation-loving, devil-may-care kind of journalism," which "offered a palliative of sin, sex, and violence" (Emery, Emery, and Roberts 2000, 192). By emphasizing storytelling, entertainment, and gossip over political information, these papers successfully catered to the middle and working classes (Schudson 1978, 88–105; West 2001, 44).

Even the yellow press's coverage of the Spanish-American War fits this overall pattern. Before the war, Hearst and Pulitzer's papers portrayed Spain's Cuban occupation negatively. Yet prior to the USS *Maine*'s destruction in Havana harbor on February 15, 1898, the quantity of news about Cuba was inconsistent, with spurts of heavy coverage focusing on dramatic individual stories where political implications were secondary (Campbell 2001, 97–123). Communication scholar Michael Schudson (1978, 64) describes *New York Journal* reporter Richard Harding Davis's coverage of Cuba as "frequently a documentary fiction—the facts would be there, but their point was to entertain." In one example, Davis and illustrator Frederic Remington produced a heart-wrenching depiction of Spain's execution of a young Cuban rebel for the *Journal*'s February 3, 1897, front page (Campbell 2006, 135–43).[29] In another, in October 1897, *Journal* reporter Karl Decker and two others rescued Evangelina Cisneros, a 19-year-old Cuban imprisoned for plotting against the Spanish, and smuggled her from Cuba to New York City. The episode received widespread coverage nationwide, including dramatic front-page headlines in the *Journal* (Campbell 2006, 161–94).

While the *World* and *Journal* covered the *Maine*'s sinking breathlessly, including the *Journal* calling for war with Spain, other newspapers in New York and across the country were much more restrained (Campbell 2001, 116–19). Considering also that President William McKinley had

[29] Many historical accounts describe an episode where Hearst sent a message to Frederic Remington, saying, "You furnish the pictures and I will furnish the war." But this event is almost surely apocryphal (Tebbel and Watts 1985, 303; Campbell 2001, 71–86; 2006, 136–37).

Prior to the destruction of the *Maine*, Hearst's newspapers editorially supported Spanish withdrawal from Cuba in response to the Cuban resistance. But they did not emphasize the possibility of American military intervention (Campbell 2001, 86, 111–12).

run on a platform of Cuban independence (Tebbel and Watts 1985, 305), claims by some historians (e.g. Keller 1969) that yellow newspapers were politically influential enough to cause the Spanish-American War should be viewed with skepticism.[30]

Overall, the gradual decline of partisan newspapers and the rise of independent and sensational papers are reflected in the content of news across the 1800s. By one estimate, the percentage of newspaper coverage devoted to politics declined between 1831–32 and 1897 from 50.5% to 19.4% in urban papers and from 72.6% to between 42.7% and 22.9% in nonurban papers. Over the same period, the percentage of coverage devoted to "crime and courts, accidents, society and women, leisure activities" increased from 11.6% to 39.1% in urban papers and from 14.4% to between 27.1% and 34.3% in nonurban papers (Baldasty 1992, 123–24).

In sum, while the press became more independent of political parties in the commercial era, no independent, professionalized national media establishment developed. The styles of commercial newspapers varied widely, but a large portion deemphasized politics, especially policy and ideology. Coverage of sports, theater, crime, and scandal as well as colorful illustrations, comics, and sometimes fiction became prominent news features, especially among the yellow newspapers of Pulitzer and Hearst. In Baldasty's (1992, 107) words, "The measure of success in journalism was no longer political wisdom or advocacy but the ability to entertain, the acquisition of large circulations, and the generation of large revenues." In the relatively rare instances when commercial papers did cover politics, some adopted the styles and hobbyhorses of their editors, while others (like the yellow papers) subjugated their political views to the desire to increase circulation.

Commercial-Era Politicians and Activists Continued Criticizing the Press

Responses to the commercial press varied, but there is evidence that these newspapers continued to receive little respect and earned some hostility

---

[30] Tebbel and Watts (1985, 306) report that, once the *Maine* sunk, McKinley and his advisors thought that "nothing could prevent a declaration [of war]," even before they saw how it was covered in the newspapers. They go on to state, "McKinley could have resisted the clamor of the press if he had chosen to do so, but the pressures for war went far beyond the newspapers. Few advocates of moderation remained in Congress, and popular voices like those of Theodore Roosevelt . . . were whipping up passions everywhere in the country. There was real political danger in resisting. The Democrats would seize joyfully upon such an issue and win with it" (306–7).

from political leaders and other prominent societal figures. James Fenimore Cooper, the popular nineteenth-century American author of *The Last of the Mohicans*, responded to the rise of the penny press by writing in an 1838 essay:

> If newspapers are useful in overthrowing tyrants, it is only to establish a tyranny of their own. The press tyrannizes over publick men, letters, the arts, the stage, and even over private life. Under the pretence of protecting publick morals, it is corrupting them to the core, and under the semblance of maintaining liberty, it is gradually establishing a despotism as ruthless, as grasping, and one that is quite as vulgar as that of any christian state known. With loud professions of freedom of opinion, there is no tolerance; with a parade of patriotism, no sacrifice of interests; and with fulsome panegyrics on propriety, too frequently, no decency. (Cooper 1969 [1838], 183; cited in Schudson 1978, 13)

President Millard Fillmore (1850–53) wrote in 1850 that "In times like this, the telegraph in the hands of irresponsible and designing men is a tremendous engine for mischief aided as it is in many places by a mercenary and prostituted press. Agitation and excitement seem to pervade all the large cities, and this is greatly aggravated by unscrupulous partisans who desire to turn it to political account against the Administration" (Pollard 1947, 273).

While the press still had little popular respect or independent influence in policy making, as it became less involved in politics, political criticism appears to have become somewhat less frequent and intense. However, as James Fenimore Cooper's statement illustrates, this gap was often filled by criticism of the press from other sectors of popular culture. Characterizing the public standing of journalists in the commercial era, James Gordon Bennett's biographer described them as "little more than secretaries dependent upon cliques of politicians, merchants, brokers, and office-seekers for their position and bread" (Schudson 1978, 16).

In becoming more commercial and thus more associated with American big business, newspapers also became targets of criticism from political movements of the far right and left. In one early example of the former, an 1859 book by former newspaper editor Lambert A. Wilmer, titled *Our Press Gang; or, A Complete Exposition of the Corruptions and Crimes of the American Newspapers*, claimed the following:

> I assert that the American newspaper press is controlled and directed, in a great measure by MEN OF FOREIGN BIRTH; and that many of our most influential public journals are *Anti-American* in feeling and sentiment. I charge the newspaper press of America with practical hostility to our republican government and to all our free institutions. I charge

the newspaper press of America with a systematic and continuous effort to mislead the judgment of the public in relation to matters of
greatest national importance. I assert that the American newspaper
press is the zealous advocate and interested colleague of every form
of villainy and imposture; that it is the abettor and confederate of all
who defraud and plunder the public. (Wilmer 1859, 51; emphasis in
the original)

Activists of the Progressive Era depicted the commercial press as tools
of big business. In *The Brass Check: A Study of American Journalism*,
Upton Sinclair (1920, 222) wrote, "Journalism is one of the devices
whereby industrial autocracy keeps its control over political democracy;
it is the day-to-day, between-elections propaganda, whereby the minds of
the people are kept in a stance of acquiescence. . . . [W]e define Journalism in America as the business and practice of presenting the news of
the day in the interest of economic privilege." While the lack of modern
opinion polling prevents us from knowing with certainty how the commercial press was viewed by the public, contemporary figures like these
frequently belittled or attacked the press and believed the public shared
their views.

Newspapers that did involve themselves in politics fared no better, often
receiving harsh attacks from opposing politicians. The most extreme example of this came during the Civil War, when, in 1864, the *New York
World* and *New York Journal of Commerce* claimed, based on forged
documents, that President Abraham Lincoln planned to draft more New
Yorkers for the army.[31] Lincoln ordered the army to shut down the newspapers and jail their editors. The editors were released and the papers
resumed publishing when they agreed to publicly apologize and admit
the documents were fake (C. Crawford 2006, 62–63). Lincoln's written
military order stated,

Whereas there has been wickedly and traitorously printed and published this morning in the New York World and New York Journal of
Commerce . . . a false and spurious proclamation . . . you are therefore
hereby commanded forthwith to arrest and imprison in any fort or
military prison at your command, the editors, proprietors and publishers of the aforesaid newspapers, and all such persons as . . . print and
publish the same . . . and you will hold the persons so arrested, in close
custody, until they can be brought to trial before a military commission, for their offense. You will take possession by military force, of

[31] At this time the *World* was owned and edited by Marble Manton. Joseph Pulitzer
purchased it in 1883.

the printing establishments of the "New York *World*" and "New York *Journal of Commerce*," and hold the same until further order, to prevent further publication therefrom. (Richardson 1908, 237).

President Benjamin Harrison (1889–93) was often deeply angered by press coverage. One Washington reporter described a meeting Harrison held with several journalists at the end of his term this way: "Ralph [of the *New York Sun*], who was a cheery, friendly soul not easily abashed, started to tell the President of his innocent penchant for writing presidential valedictories, but was cut short by Mr. Harrison's abrupt condemnation of the newspaper press generally for what he described as their cruel, unfair, and discourteous references to himself and Mrs. Harrison since they had been living in the White House. He said the persecution had been persistent, and dwelt upon the subject at length" (Pollard 1947, 549).

Considering the dramatic events of his presidency and how they were covered by many newspapers, President McKinley was restrained in his comments about the press (Tebbel and Watts 1985, 295–317). He occasionally lavished praise on Republican partisan papers. In remarks to the Ohio Republican Editorial Association during the 1896 campaign, he said, "To be a real capable and worthy journalist, wise, honorable and efficient, is to attain the highest plane of human opportunity and usefulness. To love and proclaim the truth, for truth's sake, to disseminate knowledge and useful information, to correct misinformation . . . to mold and direct public opinion which is always the mission of journalism, is surely the noblest of professions" (Pollard 1947, 555). Yet McKinley had a more hard-nosed perspective on other journalism. According to some reports, during the Spanish-American War, McKinley and his cabinet grew so agitated by coverage in the *New York Evening Post* and the *Springfield Republican* that they debated indicting their editors for treason (Villard 1923, 53; Pollard 1947, 560–61).

The yellow newspapers of Pulitzer and Hearst received especially heavy criticism, though much of it came from other journalists. In the *Nation*, E. L. Godkin reacted to the *New York World*'s and *New York Journal*'s coverage of the destruction of the *Maine* by writing, "Nothing so disgraceful as the behavior of these two newspapers in the past week has ever been known in the history of journalism" (Pollard 1947, 561). As described in chapter 3, the *New York Times* marketed itself as more socially respectable than the yellow papers. In 1898, the *Times* published a letter stating that Pulitzer and Hearst's papers "are issued more for the amusement and excitement of a certain class of ignorant and uncultivated readers than for public enlightenment, and are the result of a morbid craving on the part of the lower order of mankind for sensational reading and illustrations" (Campbell 2001, 53). Similarly, one critic wrote in *Bookman* magazine in 1906 that "the banality and sensationalism of the bad papers are a shade above the banality and coarseness of the people who read them" (53). Another wrote in *Bookman* in 1907 that yellow newspapers were "Divorced completely from the world of truth and intelligence, they present nothing which an educated man would desire to read . . . they seem to address the half-blind eye and the wholly sluggish mind of the imbecile" (65). This provides a small representation of the widespread distain in which the yellow press was held by social and political elites.

The press has typically been viewed with hostility by elites—especially political leaders—from the time of its invention. Political leaders responded to printing in two basic ways: by attacking any press involvement in politics that they could not control and by cultivating press outlets they could control. The relationship between politicians and the press improved in several periods. It improved dramatically, but only temporarily, during and immediately after the American Revolution, when most newspapers were subordinate to American political movements. It also improved slightly when politicians were less threatened by party competition—as in the Era of Good Feelings—and when some commercial newspapers turned their focus away from politics. History to this point does not suggest that political elites were at all receptive to the news media becoming an independent, powerful, respected political institution. Chapter 3 takes up the story of how the media, for a brief period, came to play this role.

3

The Emergence of the Institutional News Media
in an Era of Decreasing Political Polarization

IN THE FIRST HALF OF THE twentieth century, the news media's place in
the American political system changed dramatically. Journalism developed widely held professional norms, greatly homogenizing the style of
news nationwide. Journalists and news organizations also became much
more autonomous and influential in the American political system. In
many ways, they became their own political institution, which enjoyed
high levels of public trust by midcentury.

They achieved this status in an unusual national environment. Competition in newspaper markets declined at the same time that legal and
technological limitations suppressed consumer choice in the television
and radio industry. As a result, news organizations faced abnormally little
market pressure, freeing them to follow their new professional norms
while avoiding behavior that, while drawing customers, might have reduced the public's esteem for journalists.

At the same time, America's party system was depolarizing. With ideological differences between the two major parties at historic lows, for a
brief period political leaders rarely used any of their traditional tools to
attempt to undermine an independent press. Politicians and party activists showed relatively little interest in attacking the institutional media's
credibility, sponsoring partisan news outlets, or practicing other types of
harassment. As a whole, this special environment allowed the media to
temporarily become a trusted, powerful, independent institution.

THE AMERICAN PARTY SYSTEM BECOMES LESS POLARIZED

The transformation of the American news industry took place alongside
a political system that was becoming dramatically less polarized. The
1930s through the 1970s was the nadir of partisan polarization in the
post–Civil War period. One way to measure American political polarization is to look at congressional voting. Political scientists conventionally
measure congressional voting patterns with DW-NOMINATE scores, which
are based on statistical analyses of all congressional roll call votes and
produce an estimate of the ideology of each House or Senate member

in each Congress.[1] The difference in DW-NOMINATE scores between the House Democratic and Republican parties was relatively large from the 1870s (when the current two-party system emerged) through the 1920s. This partisan divide narrowed dramatically in the 1930s and did not begin growing again until the late 1970s (McCarty, Poole, and Rosenthal 2006, 29). The pattern is very similar if one compares party median or mean scores, uses the Senate instead of the House, or excludes legislators from the former confederacy (McCarty, Poole, and Rosenthal 2006, 6, 29–30, 49).

Economic polarization in American society also reached its nadir in the middle of the twentieth century. In what economists Claudia Goldin and Robert Margo (1992) label "the great compression," the percentage of income going to the top 1% of Americans declined from over 19% in the 1910s to below 9% from the mid-1950s through the 1970s (Krugman 2002a; McCarty, Poole, and Rosenthal 2006, 8). Declining income inequality was accompanied by a reduction in the economic basis of partisan conflict. In the 1940s, Republican presidential candidates still did 15 to 20 points better among the top third of the income distribution than among the lower third. Yet from 1952 through 1960, with income levels increasingly compressed and the parties ideologically similar, there was almost no difference in the vote choices of the top and bottom third of the income distribution (Gelman et al. 2008, 45–46).

JOURNALISM PROFESSIONALIZES

From the dawn of printing into the 1800s, journalism was not professionalized. In a professionalized field, those who practice the craft follow uniform standards of practice, maintain barriers to entry and quality control, and often exercise independent power in society (Larson 1977; Zaller 1999b, 22–24, 31–33). Before approximately the turn of the century, styles of journalism varied widely, and news reporters most often served the interests of parties, powerful editors, or media moguls. While in the commercial era sensationalist newspapers often played an important role in policy making, their involvement tended to be unpredictable and haphazard, and the values they upheld were inconsistent. Because journalism was not professionalized, journalists were not an institutional part of the political process. As a result, they were not in a position to exert consistently an independent check on politicians and political outcomes.

---

[1] For more information, see Poole and Rosenthal (1991; 1997), McCarty, Poole, and Rosenthal (1997; 2006), and the website http://voteview.com.

In essentially all journalism up to this point, opinion fluidly mixed with fact and a newspaper often pushed a particular point of view (McGerr 1986; West 2001; Evensen 2002). However, by the late 1800s, prominent editors such as E. L. Godkin (who edited the *New York Evening Post* and the *Nation*) described journalists' main goal as "get[ting] accurate news" (Evensen 2002, 263), even though Godkin's own papers shamelessly crusaded "against American imperialism, government corruption and unsound money" (Alterman 1999, 26).

The *New York Times*'s emergence as a successful and influential newspaper was an important turning point in the evolution of American journalism. Adolph Ochs purchased the "failing and demoralized" *New York Times* in August 1896 (Schudson 1978, 110–11). That same month, he printed his editorial philosophy:

> It will be my earnest aim that the New York Times give the news, all the news, in a concise and attractive form, in language that is parliamentary in good society, and give it as early, if not earlier, than it can be learned through any other reliable medium; to give the news impartially, without fear or favor, regardless of any party sect or interest involved; to make the columns of the New York Times a forum for the consideration of all questions of public importance, and to that end invite intelligent discussion from all shades of opinion.

Yet, in the next paragraph, he did admit to a pro-business ideology, saying:

> There will be no radical changes in the personnel of the present efficient staff . . . nor will there be a departure from the general tone and character and policies pursued with relation to public questions that have distinguished the New York Times as a nonpartisan newspaper— unless it be, if possible to intensify its devotion to the cause of sound money and tariff reform, opposition to wastefulness and peculation in administering the public affairs and in its advocacy of the lowest tax consistent with good government, and no more government than is absolutely necessary to protect society, maintain individual vested rights and assure the free exercise of a sound conscience. (Schudson 1978, 111)

Ochs's *Times* catered to the tastes of wealthy readers by emphasizing business news. It covered real estate transactions and out-of-town buyers visiting the city and generally increased its financial coverage until it was known as the "Business Bible" (Schudson 1978, 108). Two months after taking ownership, Ochs put the paper's new motto, "All the News That's Fit to Print," on the front page (12). In selling itself, the *Times* emphasized its "decency" and social respectability as much as its accuracy (9).

For instance, on March 4, 1897, the *Times* proposed in an editorial that, if libraries decided to carry sensational newspapers, they should "make the reading of the new journals, except behind a screen, a social offense punishable with scorn and contempt" (114). To contrast itself with the yellow newspapers, the *Times* used the advertising slogan "It does not soil the breakfast cloth" (112). In another appeal for new subscribers, it claimed, "To be seen reading The *New York Times* is a stamp of respectability" (112). Elsewhere Ochs boasted that "no one needs to be ashamed to be seen reading" his newspaper (116). Having established it as a signifier of social standing, in 1898 Ochs lowered the *Times*'s price from six cents to one cent, producing dramatic increases in circulation, from 25,000 in 1898, to 82,000 in 1900, to 121,000 in 1905, and 343,000 by 1920 (114). Like many items associated with society's elite, the *Times* also had a very strong appeal to middle-class strivers once its price put it within reach (see Schudson 1978, 116–17).

Shortly after the *Times*'s rise to prominence, the Progressive movement reached its peak of influence. Progressivism of the 1890s through 1920s contained the belief that "partisan politics should be removed from the governmental process and that government administration should be professionalized" (West 2001, 54). The movement to professionalize spread not just to government but to several other classes of workers, where there were increased educational expectations, more standardized norms of conduct, and more autonomy. All these parts of the professionalizing trend took place in journalism.

In the 1800s, most reporters and editors did not attend college but worked their way up from "entry-level typesetting jobs" (West 2001, 50). In the 1860s, Horace Greeley considered a college education a "handicap" for journalists and avoided hiring college graduates at the *New York Tribune* (Schudson 1978, 68). However, by late in the century, college-educated journalists became much more common. The *Journalist*, a trade publication founded in 1883, reported in 1898 that every large New York newspaper had 10 college graduates on its staff (69) and stated in 1900 that "[t]oday the college bred men are the rule" (68). Prominent newspapers also increasingly made their writers salaried staff members, rather than relying on freelancers (69).

In the early twentieth century, Joseph Pulitzer became a strong advocate of more educated reporters and editors. Pulitzer not only publicly advocated for the cause, he left $2 million in his will to establish Columbia's School of Journalism, which opened in 1913, and the Pulitzer Prize (Schudson 1978, 152; West 2001, 50). Journalists began to found trade publications (such as the *Journalist*) and professional organizations. A National Capital Press Club was established in 1891 but folded a few years later. The National Press Club was launched in 1908 and survives to the present day (Schudson 1978, 70). A professional association of editors, the American Society of Newspaper Editors, was founded in 1922–23 (Schudson 2005, 29). Pulitzer himself argued that "We need a class feeling among journalists—one based not upon money, but upon morals, education, and character. . . . I wish to begin a movement that will raise journalism to the rank of a learned profession" (152).

Journalists were now expected to at least attend college, if not have a journalism degree. In terms of professional conduct, reporters were increasingly expected to follow what Schudson calls "the ideal of objectivity" (1978; 1990). Prior to the 1920s, journalists rarely used the term *objective*, preferring concepts such as *unbiased*, *uncolored*, and *realist*, which meant simply laying out facts and trusting that the truth would emerge (Streckfuss 1990, 973; Kovach and Rosenstiel 2001, 72–73). As noted above, the *New York Times*'s early reporting style was based on a strict emphasis on realism and presenting the facts, which reflected this earlier ideal. It appears that the term *objectivity* was imported from the emerging social sciences, which at this time were becoming heavily influenced by scientific naturalism, which maintained that there are no truths other than what can be "scientifically" (by which they meant empirically) demonstrated (Streckfuss 1990, 975). Epitomizing this new movement, the University of Chicago's social science building, dedicated in 1929, had inscribed above its entryway: "When you cannot measure your knowledge is meager and unsatisfactory" (975).[2] This scientific and apolitical notion of objectivity fit well with the Progressive movement's distrust of most forms of partisanship (McGerr 1986; Schudson 2005, 28).

However, the norm of objectivity that eventually took hold in journalism modified the Progressive Era's emphasis on simple empiricism (i.e., just presenting the "facts") with another major strand in Progressive thought: the importance of expertise. Major figures in journalism argued that, while journalists should be independent from party and ideological faction and avoid personal crusades, the facts did not speak for themselves. They needed interpretation. The professional journalist should play the role of a powerful, independent expert, sorting through the available information and telling the public what it all means (Schudson 1978, 134–60).[3]

---

[2] This is a paraphrased quotation from Lord Kelvin.

[3] The notion that facts do not speak for themselves is part of what Stensaas (2005, 46–48) calls "secularization," which he argues is the central cause of the rise of the norm of objectivity: "The secularization of culture and thought resulted in a shift to relativism—synthesis instead of antithesis. At its heart, this represents a change in the concept of truth. The implications for journalism and journalistic objectivity should be evident: If the journalist deals in truth and truth is relative, depending on the receiver, then the only course

The chief advocate for this type of professional journalism was Walter Lippmann. As a founder of the *New Republic*, Lippmann was a Progressive. But like many others who reported on World War I, he concluded after observing wartime propaganda that the public could not sift the truth out of news reports without the help of experts (Schudson 1978, 141–44; Lippmann 1997 [1922]). In his 1920 book *Liberty and the News*, he started the task of "turning newspaper enterprise from a haphazard trade into a disciplined profession" (1995 [1920], 71). He wrote that

> We need, first, to know what can be done with the existing news structure, in order to correct its grosser evils. How far is it useful to go in fixing personal responsibility for the truthfulness of news? Much further, I am inclined to think, than we have ever gone. . . . While it is not necessary, or even desirable that every article should be signed, each article should be documented, and false documentation should be illegal. An item of news should always state whether it is received from one of the great news-agencies, or from a reporter or from a press bureau. (65–66)

Later he commented,

> With this increase in prestige must go a professional training in journalism in which the ideal of objectivity is cardinal. The cynicism of the trade needs to be abandoned, for the true patterns of journalistic apprentice are not the slick persons who scoop the news, but the patient and fearless men of science who have labored to see the world as it really is. It does not matter that the news is not susceptible of mathematical statement. In fact, just because news is complex and slippery, good reporting requires the exercise of the highest scientific virtues. (74)

One of the first journalism textbooks was Nelson Antrim Crawford's *The Ethics of Journalism*. Published in 1924, it helped spread the term *objectivity* (supplanting the terms *unbiased*, *uncolored*, and *realist*) and devoted three chapters to "The Principle of Objectivity Applied."[4] In the text, Crawford drew heavily on Lippmann's writings and the scientific notion of objectivity (N. Crawford 1924, 178; cited in Streckfuss 1990; Stensaas 2005). Over the course of the 1920s, Lippmann served as editor of the *New York World* and continued to advocate for his views of the profession, frequently speaking to the annual meetings of the American

---

is to present 'value-free data' so that the recipient may fashion his own 'truth' from the 'facts'" (46).

[4] Ross's (1911; cited in Stensaas 2005) writing textbook is one earlier work that also favors an objective style of news writing.

Society of Newspaper Editors (Streckfuss 1990, 980–81). At its first convention, in 1922, the society adopted several "Canons of Journalism" to serve as a professional code of ethics. These included adherence to the principles of "sincerity," "truthfulness," "accuracy" and "impartiality," which, they stated, entailed that reporting "should be free from opinion or bias of any kind" (Schudson 2005, 29). With only slight revisions adopted in 1973, these guidelines still constitute the society's official code of ethics (Stensaas 2005, 37). By 1927, the dean of the School of Journalism at the University of Oregon commented, "If journalism means anything more than a mere trade and a technique, it must be based upon some depth of understanding. If it is, or is to become, a real profession—one of the learned professions—the thing the competent journalist must understand is the scientific bases of current life" (E. Allen 1927, 1–7; cited in Streckfuss 1990, 980).

The rise of news columnists illustrates the spread of the notion that expert reporters were required to objectively interpret the news. The job of syndicated news columnist was an invention of the 1920s. The first was Heywood Hale Broun of the *New York World*, whose column began in 1921. Lippmann's "Today and Tomorrow" column began in the *Herald Tribune* in 1931. By 1937, successful syndicated columnists included Lippmann (published in 155 papers), Arthur Brisbane (180 papers), David Lawrence (150 papers), and Frank Kent (125 papers) (Schudson 1978, 150). In 1933, the American Society of Newspaper Editors reflected the belief that interpretation of facts was part of good objective reporting by passing a resolution stating that "editors should devote a larger amount of attention and space to explanatory and interpretive news and to presenting a background of information which will enable the average reader more adequately to understand the movement and significance of events" (Schudson 1978, 148).

In addition, the spread of Lippmann's belief that journalists should be held accountable for their scientific analysis by having their name attached to their work was reflected in the spread of the use of bylines in regular news articles. For instance, in the *New York Times*, bylines were generally used only for foreign correspondents in the early 1920s. Yet by the 1930s, almost all articles were signed. The first byline in an AP article appeared in 1925, and in a few years the practice had become the norm (Schudson 1978, 145).

By the mid-1930s, a professional norm of objectivity relatively similar to that held by contemporary mainstream journalists had taken hold. While most papers continued to publish editorials, these were increasingly separated from the news pages (Stensaas 1986; West 2001, 53). The extent of this progress was evident from the change in Walter

Lippmann's assessment. In 1931 he wrote, in a satisfied tone, "The most impressive event of the last decade in the history of newspapers has been the demonstration that the objective, orderly, and comprehensive presentation of news is a far more successful type of journalism today than the dramatic, disorderly, episodic type" (Lippmann 1931, 439; cited in Streckfuss 1990).

A conventional definition of a profession involves the maintenance of codes of conduct and barriers to entry independent of employers (Larson 1977; Zaller 1999b, 22–24, 30–33). Among these standards of conduct that "identified journalists as a distinct occupational group with distinct patterns of behavior" was adherence to and support for norms of objectivity, which were uniform across the country rather than subject to the opinion and style of each editor or publisher. As Darrell West (2001, 53) writes, "journalists defined a new role for themselves that liberated them not only from outside parties and advertisers, but even from the owners and publishers within the communications industry." This professional notion of where journalists' loyalty should lie is still held up as an ideal today. Bill Kovach, chairman of the Committee of Concerned Journalists, and Tom Rosenstiel, director of the Project for Excellence in Journalism, provide a useful summary of the profession's standards at the turn of the millennium in *The Elements of Journalism: What Newspeople Should Know and the Public Should Expect* (Kovach and Rosenstiel 2001). They declare that "[j]ournalism's first obligation is to the truth" (37). In the chapter titled "Who Journalists Work For" they state that "[j]ournalism's first loyalty is to citizens" (51) rather than to media owners or their customers. In this way, reporters should "serve as an independent monitor of power" (112). Even as the ideologies of reporters and cultural trends have varied over time, these professional norms have continued to be a significant constraint on how reporting is done. Public editor of the *Chicago Tribune* Don Wycliff put it bluntly, saying, "[W]e may be liberals, but we have ideals of objectivity to which we aspire" (Lemann 2005, 174).

In *The Rise of Professionalism*, sociologist Magali Sarfatti Larson (1977) identifies several defining characteristics of professionalism that we can see adopted by journalists in the early 1900s. In professions, "apprenticeship is superseded, or at least necessarily proceeded, by formal training" (44). Also, "colleague sanction of individual talents becomes more legitimate" and based on standards prized within the profession rather than by the market or outside authorities (45). As a consequence, "professional identity is experienced as a shared expertise and therefore a sense of at least cognitive superiority with regard to the layman or irregular practitioner" (55). While journalism has never attained the same high degree of professionalization as fields like medicine or academia

(Larson 1977, chap. 3; Starr 1984; Zaller 1999b, chap. 4), it did increasingly adopt these characteristics.

Schudson argues that adoption of the norm of objectivity was not just an economic necessity or consequence of technology. While both of these, as discussed below, made the norm easier to maintain, he implies that the real cause of the persistence and uniformity of objectivity was the work of prominent journalists (such as Lippmann) and journalism organizations, which made objectivity "a norm with moral force" (Schudson 2005, 26). Only in the 1920s did journalism become autonomous enough to both socialize its members into its standards and sanction violations of those norms. Its most prominent norm, objectivity, "had no secure place until journalists as an occupational group developed loyalties more to their audiences and to themselves as an occupational community than to their publishers' favoured political parties" (Schudson 2005, 29). Fidelity to professional standards was now considered "the most legitimate grounds for attributing praise and blame" (Tuchman 1972; Janowitz 1975; Schudson 2005, 34).[5] For those in, or aspiring to join, the institutional news media, these group norms were now expected to be their primary loyalty. Tellingly, Hal Bruno, a longtime reporter and former *ABC News* political director who covered every presidential campaign from 1960 through 2000, commented, "Politics is what I cover, Journalism is my life" (Cook 1998, 89).

The News Media Become a Political Institution

At the same time that the style of coverage was becoming more uniform, the structure of the news business was also changing dramatically. With prices low, the number of newspaper readers continued to increase rapidly, even more quickly than the population. Total newspaper circulation in the United States increased from 3.1 million in 1880, to 15.1 million in 1900, 27.8 million in 1920, and 39.6 million by 1930 (Emery,

---

[5] Schudson (2005, 29) argues that group norms, such as objectivity in journalism, have four attributes. First, they are "encouraged by forms of ritual solidarity that call on a group or institution to celebrate itself, to honour its members, to recognize the introduction of new members of the group or the passing of old ones or the induction of fully adult or assimilated members to higher status in the group." Second, "cultural contact and conflict can provoke the articulation of norms inside the group." Third, "[w]herever people must be handled in batches and trained in the ways of the group, there will be a kind of pedagogical economy in saying out loud what the prescribed rules of behavior are. . . . The pedagogical imperative for the articulation of norms often leads to an overly rigid or absolute statement of norms and the overlearning of norms on the part of the students." Fourth, "[s]uperiors may wish to be free from normative constraints to act with their best discretion, but they would like their subordinates to be constrained by rules."

Emery, and Roberts 2000, 289). At the same time that readership and advertising revenues increased, the number of daily newspapers did not continue to grow, peaking at 2,200 in 1910 before declining to 1,942 by 1930. Newspapers continued to expand into more cities but faced less competition. While the overall number of newspapers declined, the number of cities with newspapers increased, causing the percentage of cities with at least two competing dailies to decline from 57.1% in 1910 to 20.6% by 1930 (Emery, Emery, and Roberts 2000, 289). This decline in local competition continued throughout the twentieth century. By 1992, only 2% of American cities had two or more newspapers (West 2001, 57). However, until late in the twentieth century, the decreasing number of newspapers did not correspond with a decline in the number of readers. In the 1930s, 1940s, and 1950s, most surveys found that 80% of adults reported regularly reading a daily newspaper (Prior 2007, 56). As a result, while at one time the newspaper business consisted of many small papers competing in a variety of news styles, it increasingly came to consist of larger papers with a more uniform news style and professionalized reporters.

This lack of competition made it much easier for professional journalistic norms to take hold. Larson (1977, 48) observes that professions are most autonomous when their supply is reduced, producing a "seller's market." Rather than being tempted to abandon professional norms in order to attract readers, journalists found that lack of competition reduced market pressures and allowed them to produce the type of news they thought (or had been socialized to think) was the highest quality (Zaller 1999a; 1999b, chap. 4). While news organizations surely could still have attracted readers and made money through partisanship or sensationalism, as they had successfully done in earlier eras (see Schudson 2005, 28), absent the necessity to do otherwise, journalists adhered to their professional norms.

Although newspaper editorials in the 1930s, 1940s, and 1950s endorsed Republicans at higher rates than Democrats (Ansolabehere, Lessem, and Snyder 2006; Stanley and Niemi 2010), news coverage had become much more insulated from these editorial positions.[6] A content analysis by journalist Harlan Stensaas (1986) illustrates how styles of news coverage became more homogenized and consistent with the emergence of professional standards. Looking at news articles in a variety of

---

[6] Nationwide, approximately 60% of newspapers endorsed the Republican presidential candidate in every presidential election from 1940 through 1960 (Stanley and Niemi 2010). This is consistent with endorsement patterns for other offices. Looking at all statewide and federal nonpresidential races, Ansolabehere, Lessem, and Snyder (2006, 400–402) find that newspapers had a two-to-one propensity to endorse Republican over Democratic candidates in the 1940s and 1950s.

U.S. newspapers from 1865 through 1954, he finds that the percentage of articles containing "observable or verifiable data," rather than opinions, increased from about 41% in 1865–74, to about 66% in 1905–14, to about 80% in the 1925–34 and 1945–54 time periods (12, 57). Other news-gathering routines associated with objective, professionalized journalism also diffused over this period. Reliance on authoritative sources (i.e., government officials), became a dominant practice of the mainstream political press corps (Tuchman 1972; W. Bennett 1990; Kuklinski and Sigelman 1992; Entman and Page 1994; Sparrow 1999, chap. 6; Zaller and Chiu 2000; W. Bennett and Livingston 2003; W. Bennett, Lawrence, and Livingston 2007, chap. 2), with the share of articles that used such sources increasing from about 28% in 1865–74, to about 43% in 1905–14, about 68% in 1925–34, and about 88% in 1945–54 (Stensaas 1986, 57). The use of the "inverted pyramid" style of news writing, consisting of a "summary lead followed by explanation of the lead, then further details," so that the "article could be cut from the bottom without destroying the story," increased from about 7% of newspaper articles in 1865–74, to about 82% in 1905–14, and about 93% to 95% in both the 1925–34 and 1945–54 time periods (Stensaas 1986, 15, 57; Mindich 1996, chap. 3; see also Pöttker 2005).

The rise of radio in the 1920s and 1930s further standardized news reporting. The percentage of American households with a radio grew from 46% in 1930 to 82% in 1940 (West 2001, 56). While precise estimates of the amount of news available on radio in its first several decades are difficult to find, the available evidence suggests it took up a very small percentage of airtime. Except for World War II coverage, then, as now, "radio was primarily an entertainment media and its newscasts short and easily avoided" (Prior 2007, 59). That said, with the introduction of radio networks, news was broadcast over large regions of the country and nationally for the first time (West 2001, 56). Many early radio stations were affiliated with major newspapers, which either owned the station or sponsored their newscasts (Emery, Emery, and Roberts 2000, 276), transmitting the values of professionalized journalism to radio news. The opportunity to reach so many people with (an admittedly small number of) reports "encouraged journalists to wring partisan and commercial excesses out of their programming" and adhere to the new professional norms (West 2001, 53).

During World War II, radio helped create national media celebrities like William Shirer, who reported from Berlin; Edward R. Murrow, who was lauded for his reports from the Battle of Britain (West 2001, 56); and George Hicks of ABC and Wright Bryan of NBC and CBS, who traveled with American troops to provide firsthand accounts of the D-day landing (Emery, Emery, and Roberts 2000, 345). While in the Civil

War journalists had served as tools of the competing sides and in the Spanish-American War the press had been sensationalist and jingoistic, in World War II journalists were seen as noble soldiers, sacrificing for the war effort like everyone else and embodying a mainstream patriotism. One of the most well-known war journalists was Ernest (Ernie) Taylor Pyle, known as the "columnist friend of the GI." He became famous and received the Pulitzer Prize for writing in detail about the daily lives of American soldiers while living with them in Ireland, North Africa, Sicily, Italy, France, and the Pacific (Emery, Emery, and Roberts 2000, 345). During the war, the U.S. military accredited 1,646 reporters, about 500 of whom were foreign correspondents. Among American casualties were 11 press association reporters, 10 newspaper correspondents, 9 magazine reporters, 4 news photographers, 2 syndicated reporters, and a radio correspondent (Emery, Emery, and Roberts 2000, 345).

Radio would soon be eclipsed by television as America's dominant news source, further increasing the nationalization of news and the celebrity of national reporters. The percentage of American households with television sets increased very rapidly, from about 2% in 1949, to 55% by 1955, to 87% by 1959 (Broadcasting Publications 1969; cited in Prior 2007). In merely a decade, television went from being a new, fringe technology to being ubiquitous and widely popular. The first network evening newscasts were CBS's *Douglas Edwards with the News*, which began in 1948, and NBC's *Camel News Caravan*, which began in 1949. ABC, the newest and smallest of the three networks, did not have an evening newscast it could convince its affiliates to carry until 1953, when it debuted *John Day with the News*. Typically, the news programs on the three existing networks all aired at the same time, so viewers could either watch news or turn off the set. *CBS Evening News* and NBC's *Huntley-Brinkley Report* expanded from 15 to 30 minutes in 1963, while the ABC evening news did the same in 1967 (Prior 2007, 62–63). Network news divisions grew as Sunday and morning news programs appeared, such as NBC's *Meet the Press* in 1947 and *Today Show* in 1952 and CBS's *Face the Nation* in 1954 and *Morning News*, which expanded in 1969 to a full hour to rival the *Today Show*'s two hours (Prior 2007, 63).

Like mid-twentieth-century newspapers, national television news faced relatively little competition. As Markus Prior (2007) has documented, these network news broadcasts not only faced few television news rivals but had few competitors of any sort. Before the mid-1950s, a large portion of media markets had only two stations that most televisions could clearly receive, usually a CBS and an NBC affiliate. While affiliates of these two networks usually broadcasted on VHF (very high frequency) channels, non-network stations and many ABC affiliates were on weaker UHF (ultra–high frequency) channels (Prior 2007, 61, 64). The portion of televisions in use that were even capable of receiving UHF channels was still 8% in 1960 and only 52% as late as 1970 (Bower 1973, 4).[7]

As noted above, the competition faced by network news divisions was further reduced because the two networks with the widest reach, CBS and NBC, aired their evening newscasts at the same time from 1957 on, first at 6:45 p.m., then at 6:30 p.m. (when they went to half-hour formats in 1963) (Prior 2007, 62–63). While local affiliates, at their discretion, sometimes put the news in a different time slot, in the 1971–72 season, for example, CBS and NBC stations aired their evening news programs at the same time in three-quarters of the 100 largest markets (Nielson Media Research 1972; cited in Prior 2007, 64). Furthermore, when stations ran a non-network news option in the 6:00–7:00 p.m. time block, it was usually local news (Prior 2007, 64). Restriction of competition, like that which technological limitations and station licensing policies achieved in the network television news business, is a quintessential characteristic of professionalized industries. As Larson (1977, 53) notes, almost always, "the professions' reliance on the state to control the access to their markets was and is justified in terms of protection of the consumer."

Patterns in editorial endorsements also reflect this trend away from partisanship and toward institutionalization. In each presidential election from 1940 through 1960, over 58% of American newspapers endorsed the Republican candidate. But subsequently, newspapers increasingly followed national tides. In each presidential election from 1960 through 1992, the majority of newspaper endorsements went to the winning candidate (Stanley and Niemi 2010).[8] For state and lower federal offices, newspapers moved from a significantly greater tendency to endorse Republicans in the 1940s and 1950s to an equal propensity to endorse either party in the 1970s and 1980s and a slightly greater propensity to endorse Democrats in the 1990s (Ansolabehere, Lessem, and Snyder 2006). Consistent with their institutionalization, newspapers also increasingly tended to endorse incumbents for these lower offices, regardless of party. While in the 1940s and 1950s newspapers made 1.3 incumbent endorsements for every challenger endorsement for state and lower federal offices, by 2000 they made four times as many incumbent as challenger endorsements (Ansolabehere, Lessem, and Snyder 2006, 398).

---

[7] Hamilton (2004, 160n) cites data from Media Dynamics (2001, 22) indicating that the average household received seven channels in 1960. This indicates that channel options may have been a bit more numerous in 1960 than Bower (1973, 4) indicates, but they were still quite narrow compared to later time periods.

[8] Subsequent to 1992, the Republican candidate received the most endorsements in the 1996 and 2000 presidential elections, while the Democratic candidate received more endorsements in 2004 and 2008 (Stanley and Niemi 2010).

Largely as a result of this professionalization and relative insulation from competition, in the mid-twentieth century the news media achieved a historically unique position as a respected, powerful, independent force. They had become their own political institution. Professional norms of objectivity and independence were thoroughly ingrained in the news culture, while reporters became "one of the best-educated groups in America" (Lichter, Rothman, and Lichter 1986, 21–22). A 1961 survey of Washington reporters found that 81% had college degrees (Rivers 1962, 6). By 1978, that number had climbed to 93% (Hess 1981, 165). Notably, the professionalized news media became an independent institution in the political system at a time when it faced relatively little resistance from politicians and relatively little competition in the media marketplace.

THE INSTITUTIONAL NEWS MEDIA ARE TEMPORARILY ACCEPTED INTO THE POLITICAL SYSTEM

By midcentury, for the first time in history, professional journalists and large news organizations acted as a respected, independent, influential, and institutionalized part of the American political process. Some newspaper reporters began regularly reporting from Washington as early as the mid-1800s (Emery, Emery, and Roberts 2000, 110).[9] The first president to ever sit for an interview with a reporter was Andrew Johnson in 1867 (Schudson 1995, 77; 2005, 25). However, President Theodore Roosevelt (1901–9) held the first presidential press conferences, provided White House correspondents with office space in the White House, released announcements of the president's daily activities, and staged events with reporters in mind (R. Rubin 1981, 86; Cook 1998, 48). President Woodrow Wilson was the first to allow reporters themselves to decide who would attend presidential press conferences (Cook 1998, 48). In 1909, Congress specifically authorized administrative agencies to use funds to work with the news media to publicize their agencies' activities, a behavior that only increased over time (Cook 1998, 50). Harry Truman (1945–53) and Dwight Eisenhower (1953–61) held formal news conferences that included hundreds of reporters. Eisenhower held 190 press conferences during his two terms and was the first to allow them to be recorded for television (Emery, Emery, and Roberts 2000, 364). President John F. Kennedy (1961–3) was the first to regularly hold news conferences live on

---

[9] Emery, Emery, and Roberts (2000, 110) describe Eliab Kingma, who reported from the capital for various publications from 1832 to 1861, as America's "first long-term Washington correspondent." In 1860, 23 correspondents reported on the House of Representatives, and 51 reported on the Senate (111).

network television (Liebovich 1998, 16). National wire services, such as the AP (reorganized into its modern form in 1900), the United Press Associations (UP, founded in 1907), the International News Service (INS, founded in 1909), and later United Press International (UPI, created in 1958 by the merger of UP and INS), were firmly entrenched in the media establishment. They represented the institutional media in Washington and disseminated their coverage of events to small newspapers across the country (Emery, Emery, and Roberts 2000, 110, 244).

For better or worse, political leaders accepted the media establishment as part of the national political process. Nicholas Lemann (2005, 170) observes that this institution, "encompass[ing] not only newspapers but national news magazines and network television and radio, occupied a dignified position" in American society. W. Lance Bennett, Regina G. Lawrence, and Steven Livingston (2007, 57–58) define the mainstream press as, "the New York *Times*, the Washington *Post*, the Wall Street *Journal*, and few leading organizations at the top, to the thousands of daily papers and local TV news operations that struggle to put together what they report from wire feeds, chain reporting, and video syndication services," which together constitute "the core information apparatus which has become so integral to government." Later, they proclaim, "[t]he press system in the United States is so uniformly organized across mainstream news organizations that it qualifies as an institution" (177).

Journalist Douglass Cater (1959) appears to be the first prominent author to call the press "the fourth branch of government." In Timothy Cook's (1998, 2) words, the news media became "a coherent intermediary institution without which the three branches established by the Constitution could not act and could not work." Quantitative analyses support this depiction of the media's power. Studies that track the issues the media, executive branch, and Congress devote attention to over time find that the media influence presidential and congressional attention at least as much as the reverse (Bartels 1996a; Edwards and Wood 1999).

Scholars of societal institutions define them as things that constrain behavior by providing formal or informal limits on choices and thus on behavior (see Sparrow 1999, 9). Bartholomew Sparrow argues that, given their prominence in almost all aspects of the political process, the major professionalized news organizations fit this definition of an institution. He says, "As an institution, the news media constrain the choice sets of these other political actors; that is, they structure . . . the actions of those working in the three formal branches of government, in public administration, and at various stages or parts of the political process" (Sparrow 1999, 10).[10]

---

[10] On the press as its own political institution, see also Hallin and Mancini (2004).

The behavior of the establishment press reflected its new, central role. Network newscasts of the 1960s had a greater focus on national political news (making up 60%–90% of stories aired) than newspapers had in earlier decades (R. Rubin 1981, 120, 152–53). What diversity there was among the different newspapers, radio stations, and television networks covering politics was minimized because they generally accepted the same professional culture and norms (Sparrow 1999, 10). Timothy Crouse criticized this phenomenon as "pack journalism" in his famous book, *The Boys on the Bus* (1973). He found that in addition to professional standards, a "herd" mentality "ensured that elite outlets would guide the coverage of other news organizations" (West 2001, 93). Independent studies analyzing the content of major network news coverage of the 1972, 1976, and 1992 presidential campaigns found quite similar content across networks (Hofstetter 1976; Patterson 1980; Just et al. 1996). As late as 1992, even coverage in newspapers and local television stations was similar across the country (Just et al. 1996).[11]

Many political leaders considered support from elite journalists for major policy undertakings to be critical to their success. For instance, when Walter Cronkite returned from a February 1968 Vietnam trip and announced on a half-hour CBS News special that the United States was losing the war, it influenced many political elites, including President Lyndon Johnson (1963–69). Journalist David Halberstam (1979, 514) argues that "Cronkite's reporting did change the balance, it was the first time in American history a war had been declared over by an anchorman. . . . [T]his affected Lyndon Johnson in two ways. First, he realized that he had lost the center, that Walter both was the center and reached the center, and thus his own consensus was in serious jeopardy. Second, he liked and admired Cronkite so much and thought him so fair a reporter, he found himself believing that if Walter Cronkite was reporting these things, he must know something." West (2001, 65) sums up the implications this way:

> The high source credibility and homogenous product of American journalists had major ramifications for the political process. . . . No other outside participants in the political system accumulated as much influence as journalists. . . . Without the press, political success was not possible. More than one successful politician groveled before the Washington press corps in order to win favorable coverage for a political cause. The 1960s and 1970s represented the pinnacle of power for American journalists. Not only had they carved out professional autonomy for themselves within media organizations, they had persuaded

[11] But see Dalton, Beck, and Huckfeldt (1998), who find diverse messages in local newspapers during the 1992 campaign.

the public that reporters were best-equipped to provide fair, balanced, and informative coverage.

However, it is easy to forget how late this transformation of the media occurred and how briefly its status went uncontested. As late as 1961, V. O. Key Jr. reflected the longstanding older consensus in his seminal book *Public Opinion in American Democracy*, writing that "radio and television have not become institutions of political influence in their own right. They have now and then a Murrow but they are more likely to have men of mellifluous voice who read the abbreviated news reports from the AP or the UPI" (Key 1961, 374). Yet only three years after those words were published, during the 1964 presidential campaign, politicians and activists would begin to try to knock the institutional news media off its new pedestal of popularity and elite respectability.

POLITICAL ATTACKS ON THE INSTITUTIONAL NEWS MEDIA WANE

While politicians had various reactions to the rise of the institutional political press, in general very few expressed support for the idea of a powerful independent news media establishment. For instance, President Theodore Roosevelt, whose administration helped institutionalize the White House press corps, had reasonably positive relations with the press. These good relations were not based on philosophical support for news media power, however, but on his consistent ability to attain positive coverage. He reasoned that his ability to get the press to convey his message rather than its own independent voice was a key to his success in the presidency. The press often covered Roosevelt like a charismatic celebrity. One reporter at the time commented on Roosevelt's public persona and the press's coverage of it, saying, "When Roosevelt was in the neighborhood [people could] no more look the other way than the small boy can turn his head away from a circus parade followed by a steam calliope" (Gould 2003, 140). Roosevelt's support from the Republican Party apparatus was often tenuous. As a result, he had little choice but to pursue a strategy based on cultivating his personal popularity and relying more heavily on the nonpartisan press to get his message out (R. Rubin 1981, 83–87). It was by necessity that he brought the press into the process of governing. Before leaving office, he famously described his power as coming largely because, "I have got such a bully pulpit" (Gould 2003, 140).[12]

---

[12] Roosevelt's resulting appreciation for the press is reflected in a 1910 speech were he said, "Almost, if not quite, the most important profession is that of the newspaper man," whom he called "as much public servants as are the men in the government service themselves" (Cook 1998, 48).

Politicians who could not rely on their personal charisma to command positive coverage were consistently more hostile to the newly institution-alized press. For instance, where Roosevelt brought reporters into the White House and intentionally gave them access, President William How-ard Taft (1909–13) "shut out" journalists during his presidency, including White House reporters (Gould 2003, 173). While President Woodrow Wilson (1913–19) resurrected many of the press-courting strategies em-ployed by Roosevelt, such as holding press conferences, other politicians were often more hostile.

Joseph Cannon, who from 1903 to 1911 served as one of the most powerful House Speakers in history, complained in the 1920s, "I believe we had better publicity when the party press was the rule and the so called independent press the exception, than we have now. . . . Then men repre-senting papers in sympathy with the party in power were alert to present the record their party was making so that the people would know their accomplishments, and those representing the opposition party were eager to expose any failures on the part of the administration." He claimed that, in the eyes of the new nonpartisan press, "The cut of a Congress-man's whiskers or his clothes is [considered] a better subject for a human interest story than what he says in debate" (Schudson 2005, 32).

President Franklin D. Roosevelt (1933–45) also had an often-contentious relationship with the press, viewing newspapers as biased against him and frequently denouncing them in speeches. Roosevelt's dis-satisfaction was not directed at the actual reporters who covered him. He cultivated good personal relationships with White House reporters and "service[d] their needs" whenever possible. But he viewed news-paper owners as thoroughly against him, blaming them for what he saw as an overall anti-Roosevelt bias in coverage (R. Rubin 1981, 127–28), frequently charging publicly that 85% of the press was biased against him (White 1979, 82–84). He often complained about "fool stories in fool press," "cuckoo stories in the press," "the opposition of the Hearst press," and "eastern managing editors" and contended that "freedom of the press is in jeopardy, not from the Government but from certain types of newspaper owners" (Winfield 1994, 41, 127).[13]

---

[13] Roosevelt's secretary of the interior, Harold L. Ickes, recounts one example of Roos-evelt's frequent frustration with his press coverage: "Where President Roosevelt is concerned, even some of the great news agencies cannot refrain from deliberate misrepresentations. On July 13, 1939, the United Press carried a dispatch—which at least one Washington correspon-dent headlined—to the effect that the President and the Secretary of State had differed on the vital question of neutrality. The President was so justly incensed at this bold fabrication that he took the grave step of issuing a public statement in which he accused a powerful press association of 'falsification of the actual facts'" (Ickes 1939, 47; cited in Stensaas 1986, 6).

In 1935 and 1936, Roosevelt's secretary of the interior, Harold Ickes, engaged in a two-year public debate with newspaper owners about the bias in their coverage. Shortly after Roosevelt's reelection in 1936, Ickes argued, "Last Tuesday we elected a President who was supported by less than 23 percent of our daily press. . . . [O]ur democracy needs more than ever before, a truly free press that represents no class or economic group and that will re-win the confidence of our citizens because it is worthy of re-winning their confidence" (Winfield 1994, 146). In his 1939 book, *America's House of Lords*, Ickes again criticized bias introduced by newspaper management. Referring to the American Society of Newspaper Editors' relatively new code of ethics, he said, "It is my personal conviction that if the publishers not only would tell their editors that they hoped they would live up to this fine code of ethics but expected them to do so, our newspapers would show wonderful effects overnight" (Ickes 1939, xii; cited in Stensaas 1986, 6).

Roosevelt's relationship with the press during his long presidency illustrates two classic symptoms of the inherent tension between political leaders and the press as a political institution. First, Roosevelt was frustrated whenever the press exhibited independent agency in how it reported information, preferring the press to simply convey his message unfiltered to the public. Richard Rubin (1981, 131) notes that "Roosevelt viewed the press's proper function as a channel through which information about government should flow to the people to keep them well informed. He saw the government itself as a major but not exclusive source of those 'facts,' and any 'opinion' added to those government 'facts' he perceived as a political distortion."

Second, Roosevelt intentionally employed the strategy of criticizing the press in order to induce the public to distrust critical coverage of his administration. He frequently criticized the AP and UP wire services by name for their alleged bias against him and their distorted coverage of national politics. In his campaign to undermine news credibility, he said, "There is a growing tendency on the part of the public not to believe what they read in a certain type of newspaper. . . . Lack of confidence in the press today is not because of the editorials but because of the colored news stories and the failure on the part of some papers to print the news" (Rubin 1981, 130).

Truman's administration did not engage in public campaigns of press criticism comparable to those conducted under Roosevelt. He initially had good personal relationships with Washington reporters as well. However, his relations with the press did deteriorate in his second term, when he became deeply unpopular nationwide (Pollard 1947, 847–49).

Overall, political rhetoric about the news media at midcentury was muted compared to previous and subsequent eras. President Eisenhower did not enjoy the media spotlight or courting reporters, but he expressed little hostility toward the press. He appears to have accepted the media establishment's role in the political process. Personally, he was simply not very interested in the press, heavily delegating media relations to his press secretary, James Hagerty (Emery, Emery, and Roberts 2000, 364). Unlike those in the Nixon, Roosevelt, and many other administrations throughout American history, members of the Eisenhower administration did not launch campaigns of media criticism. During this period of low political polarization, the administration preferred to stay above the fray in its media relations just as it did with much political conflict. At one press conference, Eisenhower said that, while he read newspaper coverage of world events carefully, beyond that, "the kinds of things you talk of, cartoons and unfriendly quips, I just can't be bothered with" (Emery, Emery, and Roberts 2000, 265). This attitude of disinterest is reminiscent of the sentiments expressed by James Madison during another period of low political polarization, the Era of Good Feelings.

Kennedy also accepted the press's dominant role in the political process and worked more actively to advantage himself within that system. Rather than attacking the press, he courted it. He granted frequent personal interviews and asked esteemed journalists such as Walter Lippmann for advice. His charm and rapport with Washington reporters was evident in his frequent live press conferences, where he affably and respectfully bantered with reporters (Liebovich 1998, 26; Emery, Emery, and Roberts 2000, 394). Kennedy and his press secretary, Pierre Salinger, rarely criticized the press and were well liked by White House reporters. One notable exception followed the failed invasion of Cuba at the Bay of Pigs, when Kennedy criticized reporters in a speech to the American Newspaper Publishers Association for not showing more restraint in reporting news during military conflict (Liebovich 1998, 18). But this was an exception, rather than the rule. Overall, Kennedy was usually complimentary. In another speech, this time before television broadcasters, Kennedy flatteringly stated, "The flow of ideas, the capacity to make informed choices, the ability to criticize, all of the assumptions on which political democracy rests, depend largely on communications. And you are the guardians of the most powerful and effective means of communications ever designed" (Gilens and Hertzman 2000, 371).

The Institutional Media Gain the Public's Trust

At the same time that the news media were becoming much more institutionalized, the development of polling technology was creating better measures of public opinion. Improved polling techniques began to be developed in the 1930s, although polling remained of low quality until the late 1940s (J. Converse 1987).[14] In addition, polls measuring public attitudes toward the news media from the middle of the century are sporadic and almost never use the same question wording repeatedly over time. This makes it very difficult to draw firm conclusions about changes in opinion over time (Mueller 1973, chap. 1). While acknowledging these limitations, it is worth briefly reviewing the polling evidence that does exist.

While results vary considerably, possibly resulting from poor and inconsistent sampling techniques, overall polls from the 1930s indicate only a moderate amount of trust in the media's fairness.[15] In 1937, Gallup found that 47% of respondents thought the newspapers they read were "fair in their treatment of political news," while 38% thought they were unfair. In the same year, a Roper poll asking simply "Is the press fair?" prompted 66% to answer yes. Yet in a 1939 Gallup poll only 29% of respondents thought "newspapers are fair in their treatment of political news," while 61% thought they were unfair. However, the 1937 Roper poll and the 1939 Gallup poll appear to be outliers. More mixed results like those in the 1937 Gallup poll were more typical. In 1946, when Gallup asked whether "you think the newspapers you read are fair or not fair in their reporting of the following news, excluding the editorials?" modestly more people thought news was fair than unfair in every category of news: news about Russia (44% to 31%), political news (45% to 35%), labor news (49% to 31%), news of Britain (50% to 26%), and news of international affairs (52% to 23%) (Erskine 1970–71, 635).

During this period, respondents were more likely to perceive anti-Roosevelt biases than the reverse. In a 1938 Gallup poll, among those who read a daily newspaper, 27% said their paper "usually support[ed]

---

[14] Commercial polling firms in the 1930s and 1940s used "quota control" and other sampling methods that modern survey researchers consider especially vulnerable to bias (Berinsky 2006).

[15] Some of the earliest poll questions about the media focused only on freedom from censorship. For instance, a 1936 Gallup poll found that 52% of the public thought "the press should have the right to say what it pleases about public officials" (Erskine 1970–71, 631). A 1939 Roper poll on behalf of *Fortune* magazine asked, "Do you feel that the press has abused its freedom in any way?" Only 21% of respondents said yes, while 64% said no (634). A 1941 Gallup poll found that 58% of Americans thought "newspapers should be allowed to take sides in their editorials during election campaigns," compared to 34% who opposed it (632). The National Opinion Research Center asked respondents in 1943 and 1946, "In peacetime, do you think newspapers should be allowed to criticize our form of government?" and found 66% and 64% support, respectively (632). Questions about press civil liberties have been a perennial topic of poll questions from the 1930s to the present day. While related, the main topic concern of this book is opinions on the trustworthiness of the news media, rather than legal rights.

President Roosevelt," while 42% said their paper opposed him. A year later, when Roper asked, "Is your newspaper for or against the New Deal?" 27% of respondents said their paper was in favor and 34% said it was opposed. In 1941, when Gallup asked if the newspaper that respondents read regularly "gave both Roosevelt and Wilkie [the 1940 Republican presidential nominee] an even break in its headlines and news accounts of the presidential election," only 36% answered no. Among those who thought their paper was biased, 76% thought it favored Wilkie, while only 19% thought Roosevelt (Erskine 1970–71, 639).

A complete dataset is available from a 1938 Roper Organization poll that probed the public's views on newspapers.[16] This is helpful because it allows us to see associations between opinions toward the news media and other attributes probed in the survey. As in most other polls from this decade, views on newspapers' trustworthiness were mixed. Forty percent of respondents believed that "newspapers furnish fair and unprincipled news about politics." Despite the Roosevelt administration's dissatisfaction with the press and editorial endorsement data showing most opposed him, FDR supporters were still more likely to think newspapers were fair. Forty-three percent of people who approved of FDR thought newspaper political coverage was fair, while only 36% of those who disapproved of FDR thought it was fair, a statistically significant difference ($p < .01$).

Like many early polls, this one does not ask party identification or any other question about partisan or ideological orientation, so presidential approval is the only available way to look at partisan differences. However, it does ask about respondents' occupations. Those with greater political awareness, often measured by education or objective political knowledge, tend to be more responsive to the positions and rhetoric of their party's political elites (Zaller 1992, 1994; Lupia et al. 2007). Figure 3-1 shows that political awareness does matter in 1938, but it has similar effects on supporters and opponents of FDR. Looking at respondents in high and low education occupations (no direct education question was

[16] This survey consists of a national quota-controlled sample, with face-to-face interviews. As with all commercial polling from the 1930s, we should interpret the results cautiously because of the poor sampling techniques used to generate the data. Berinsky (2006) lays out three weighting strategies for ameliorating some of the problems involved in analyzing quota-controlled samples. The only demographic variables available in this dataset for use in such methods are gender and a dichotomous age variable (20–40 or over 40). For both gender and age, the sample is almost exactly divided between the two categories, suggesting that these categories were likely used as quotas in the sampling design. When I employ regression-based reweighting (Berinsky 2006, 514–15) using these two variables, the results change very little. However, this is unsurprising given that these variables are set by construction to be already very similar to the population. Thus, despite this, we should still be reasonably skeptical whether the survey results presented in figure 3-1 are representative of the 1938 population.

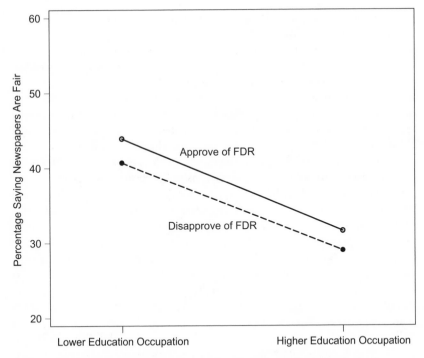

Figure 3-1. Belief in newspaper fairness was low among both parties in the 1930s. *Source*: August 1938 Roper Organization Poll, archived at the Roper Center for Public Opinion Research, University of Connecticut.

asked) suggests that political awareness has a similar effect regardless of one's political orientation. Moving from low education to high education decreases the percentage of respondents saying newspapers are "fair and unprejudiced" from 44% to 33% among FDR supporters and from 41% to 29% among FDR opponents.[17] On both sides of the American political

---

[17] The newspaper fairness question asks, "Do you believe that newspapers furnish fair and unprejudiced news about politics and politicians?" Education categories are constructed based on respondents' reported occupations because an education question was not asked in the survey. Those listed as "Professional," "Salaried-executive," or "Student" are coded as in higher education occupations. Those listed as "Proprietor-farm," "Proprietor-other," "Wages-factory," "Wages-farm," and "Wages-other" are coded as in lower education professions. Those listed as "Housekeeper," "Salaried-minor," "Retired," and "Unemployed" are excluded from this figure because their occupation leaves their education level too uncertain. The survey does not ask party identification or any other measure of partisan or ideological orientation besides presidential approval. The sample sizes for the four groups in this figure are as follows: low education occupation and approve of FDR (n = 1,871), high education occupation and approve of FDR (n = 433), low education occupation and disapprove of FDR (n = 910), and high education occupation and disapprove of FDR (n = 559).

spectrum, exposure to political rhetoric was associated with more negative views toward the news media.

Taken as a whole, poll results from the 1930s and 1940s show at best only modest levels of trust in the news media. Confidence in news messages seems to be modestly higher among FDR supporters and modestly lower among those more likely to be exposed to political discourse.

By the 1950s, most polling organizations had adopted better methods based on probability sampling. However, from the late 1940s through the early 1960s, when there was unusually little elite political media criticism, few thought even to ask survey questions about media trust. One exception was the 1956 ANES, which asked respondents, "Now talking just about newspapers. In reporting the news about the campaign and the candidates, do you feel the newspapers were equally fair to both sides or not?" In contrast to most polls from the 1930s and 1940s, in 1956, 66% of respondents thought newspapers were fair, while only 27% said they were unfair. Of those who said newspapers were unfair, as in earlier decades, most saw a Republican bias. Seventy-one percent of those saying newspapers were biased thought they favored Eisenhower and the Republicans, while only 10% said they favored Stevenson and the Democrats (see also Erskine 1970–71, 638–40).

Figure 3-2 shows the percentage of respondents who thought newspaper coverage was fair, broken down by party identification and political awareness.[18] Republican faith in the fairness of newspapers was high in 1956, with 78% of all Republicans saying they were fair. It was also remarkably consistent, ranging only from 68% to 81% across different levels of political awareness. Democratic beliefs about newspaper fairness were less consistent, showing a tendency to dip among the most politically aware individuals. While 64% of all Democrats thought

---

[18] Political awareness is measured with 12 objective political knowledge questions in the 1956 to 1960 ANES Panel Study. Following Zaller (1992, 340), I use whether working-class people vote for Democrats (v560142); which party is the congressional majority before the 1958 election (v580317); which is the majority after the 1958 election (v580318); naming the two house candidates in his or her district (v580394); naming which House candidate is the incumbent (v580395); Richard Nixon's home state (v600608), age in 1960 (v600609), and religion (v600611); John F. Kennedy's home state (v600612), age in 1960 (v600612), and religion (v600615); and which party is more conservative (v600798). Based on the number of correct answers to these questions, respondents are separated into six categories of political awareness with the following sample sizes: Democrats in first (lowest) awareness group (*n* = 22), in second awareness group (*n* = 47), in third awareness group (*n* = 28), in fourth awareness group (*n* = 29), in fifth awareness group (*n* = 38), in sixth (highest) awareness group (*n* = 56); Republicans in first (lowest) awareness group (*n* = 21), in second awareness group (*n* = 30), in third awareness group (*n* = 30), in fourth awareness group (*n* = 31), in fifth awareness group (*n* = 31), in sixth (highest) awareness group (*n* = 43).

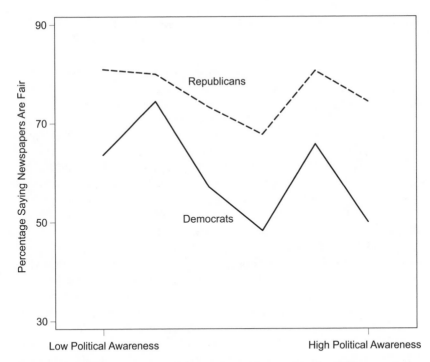

Figure 3-2. Belief in newspaper fairness was widespread in the 1950s, especially among Republicans. *Source*: 1956 ANES Time Series Survey.

newspapers were fair, among the most politically aware group, only 50% thought they were fair.[19]

In the early 1960s most people continued to view the institutional news media as fair. In two Roper polls in June and November of 1964, 71% and 61% of respondents, respectively, thought network news programs were fair and did not "generally favor one political party over another." Those believing them to be unfair constituted only 12% and 17% in these two surveys. These polls also found that only 19% and 18% of respondents thought "television programs dealing with candidates and issues in your area" were unfair (Erskine 1970–71, 636–37).

By the late 1960s, however, there was already some evidence that support for the institutional news media was softening. Prior to Vice President Spiro Agnew's attack on the press in 1969, the Nixon administration consulted one *Time*-Harris poll, which found that only about

[19] The lowest Democratic newspaper ratings were among the third most politically aware group, where only 49% thought they were fair.

one-fourth of the population trusted "national news." Based on this poll, they concluded that criticizing the media was unlikely to backfire (Perlstein 2008, 427).

The poll the administration consulted seems to be an outlier. At the time, most polls still found substantial trust in the news media, especially famous journalists. A large 1970 Roper poll asked respondents if "people who report the news on TV . . . let their opinions color the way they give the news." Only 30% of conservatives, 25% of moderates, and 26% of liberals said TV reporters colored the news (Bower 1973, 106).

This period may have been the peak of fame and respectability for network anchors like David Brinkley and Walter Cronkite. When the 1970 Roper survey asked people whether the TV anchor they watched most colored the news with bias, only 6% of respondents thought he did. Seventy-eight percent said their news anchor reported things "as it happened" (Bower 1973, 107). As noted above, President Johnson considered Cronkite's support essential to maintaining some public backing for the Vietnam War. Cronkite was often called "the most trusted man in America" after a 1972 poll found that 73% of the public trusted him. This was a higher share than any other figure in the survey earned, including the average senator (67%), the average governor (59%), President Nixon (57%), and Vice President Agnew (50%) (West 1999; 2001, 64). For this reason, the Nixon administration decided against attacking Cronkite personally. Nixon staffer Dwight L. Chapin wrote in a 1971 memo that "taking on Walter Cronkite cannot do us any good whatsoever. It is like taking on the Lord himself" (Oudes 1989, 218).

4

The Institutional News Media in an Era of Political Polarization and Media Fragmentation

IN THE LATER DECADES of the twentieth century, some of the unusual characteristics of midcentury America began to fade. As a result, the institutional media began to face some of the same obstacles that historically prevented a professional, influential, trusted media establishment from coming into existence. One change was the repolarization of the party system. As this happened, politicians and political activists began to aggressively attack the institutional media's trustworthiness. From the 1960s forward, this is the main way the historic tension between politicians and the independent news media has reasserted itself: through political attacks on the institutional media's accuracy and fairness.

Another change in the late twentieth century was the fragmentation of the overall media environment. Increasing numbers of alternative (noninstitutional) media outlets placed competitive pressure on the institutional media, pushing some institutional outlets to modify their style by reporting more "soft" news. Also, noninstitutional outlets with partisan perspectives amplified political criticism of the institutional media.

In the face of these changes, the public's confidence in the media as an institution declined dramatically between the early 1970s and the late 1990s. The decline was bipartisan. While Democrats had somewhat more confidence than Republicans at any given time, both parties showed major declines in confidence over the decades.

Yet while trust in the institutional media is diminished, people still have strongly held, clear views on the topic. Even though the media environment has fragmented and the institutional news media are only one part of a diverse media landscape, Americans know what survey researchers mean when they ask about "the media" or "the press." People think researchers are asking about journalists and outlets that adhere more to the professional norms that dominated in the mid-twentieth century. Despite the changing landscape, almost every American has a sense of what "the media" are and knows whether he or she trusts them or not.

THE AMERICAN PARTY SYSTEM REPOLARIZES

In the second half of the twentieth century, the United States became more politically and economically polarized. As mentioned earlier, voting patterns in the House, as illustrated by DW-NOMINATE scores, show that the parties remained relatively unpolarized until the late 1970s. From then on, voting patterns have increasingly diverged. By the mid-2000s, the parties' congressional votes were as polarized as at any point since the end of Reconstruction (McCarty, Poole, and Rosenthal 2006, 8, 29–30; 2009).[1]

At the same time, vote choice has become increasingly correlated with income. The 1956 and 1960 ANES surveys indicate that those in the highest income quintile were only slightly more likely to vote Republican than those in the lowest quintile. Yet by the 1990s, those in the highest quintile were twice as likely to vote Republican (McCarty, Poole, and Rosenthal 2006, 73–74).[2]

Concurrent with these trends, self-identified liberals and conservatives have increasingly sorted themselves into the Democratic and Republican parties, respectively. In 1972, when the ANES first asked for ideological self-placement, 27% of conservatives identified as Democrats and 41% as Republicans. By 1996, only 18% were Democrats, while 54% were Republicans (Green, Palmquist, and Schickler 2002, 31). In sum, from the mid-twentieth century to the present day, the two American political parties have increasingly represented divergent interests and ideologies.

THE MEDIA LANDSCAPE FRAGMENTS

While the party system was slowly but dramatically polarizing, the nature of the news industry was changing as well.[3] In the mid-twentieth century, V. O. Key Jr. (1961, 394) observed that what distinguished the American

---

[1] Again, these patterns are the same whether you compare party means or medians, look at House or Senate voting, or include or exclude the former confederacy (McCarty, Poole, and Rosenthal 2006, 8, 29–30, 49).

[2] Gelman et al. (2008, 45–46) find similar results using exit polls. This trend coincided with increasing overall income inequality. The portion of national income going to the top 1% of Americans increased from around 10% in the 1950s, 1960s, and 1970s to about 15% by the late 1990s and over 20% by the mid-2000s (McCarty, Poole, and Rosenthal 2006, 8; Bartels 2008b, 12).

[3] West's (2001) historical typology specifies an "interpretive media," which is separate from the "objective media" and the "fragmented media." In this book, however, I find it more useful to classify the interpretation done by establishment media figures like Walter Lippmann or David Broder, or "news analyses" done by otherwise "straight" reporters and appearing in the news section (West 2001, 71), as one way the institutional media exercises its power, by expressing its conventional wisdom in the political process. In contrast, I think

news media from their foreign counterparts was "the uniformity of their content" and "the relative ease of access to the public through the media for those who operate within the rules of the game." Different news outlets presented "a fairly uniform picture of the political world to all classes and kinds of people." In contrast to what Key observed, since the 1970s, the institutional news media has increasingly faced intense competition from various other news and entertainment options. These include cable entertainment and news channels, talk radio, and Internet news sources (R. Davis and Owen 1998).

Television options increased dramatically, mostly as a result of the shift from over-the-air to cable. Cable television was used by only about 2% of U.S. households in 1965 and about 8% by 1970. At this point, cable simply showed over-the-air channels to those who could not get clear signals in their homes. In the 1970s and 1980s, new channels started broadcasting only on cable, such as the Entertainment and Sports Programming Network (now officially just ESPN), the Cable News Network (CNN), Home Box Office (HBO), and the WTBS "Superstation" (West 2001, 84–87; Prior 2007, 94). By the 1990s and 2000s, cable or satellite subscribers had access to hundreds of channels. At the same time, the number of subscribers increased to one-third of households by 1983, more than half by 1989, 70% by 1997, and 85% by 2004 (Prior 2007, 94). By 2000, the average American household received approximately 63 channels (Media Dynamics 2001, 22; cited in Hamilton 2004, 160n). While most people regularly use fewer than 20 channels no matter how many are made available (Webster 2005; cited in Prior 2007), people vary considerably in which channels they settle on. As a result, news sources now compete not only with each other but also with a wide variety of television entertainment options (see Prior 2005, 2007).

The institutional media also faced competition from ideological talk radio programs. The rise of political talk radio can be traced to the abolition of the "fairness doctrine" by the Federal Communications Commission (FCC) in 1985. The doctrine had previously mandated that over-the-air television and radio provide balanced coverage of all political opinions (Jamieson and Cappella 2008, 45). Without this requirement, radio programming featuring political news and discussion proliferated (Hazlett and Sosa 1997). On AM stations, most of the increase in political content came from talk shows (95–96), where hosts often expressed strong partisan views. Most successful hosts were conservative. In 2004, *Talkers* magazine estimated that the two most successful conservative radio hosts, Rush Limbaugh and Sean Hannity, had audiences of 14.75

---

the punditry of clear partisans, who often do not have backgrounds as conventional news reporters, is best classified as part of the new alternative media.

and 13 million, respectively. A 2003 Annenberg survey found that 10% of Americans listened to Limbaugh's program every week, among whom 78% were Republicans and 85% were conservatives (Jamieson and Cappella 2008, 46, 92). Unsurprisingly, given talk radio's domination by conservative hosts, the total audience for all news and talk radio (including all news stations, public and commercial) also tilts Republican, with 36% of listeners identifying as Republicans and 27% as Democrats (Project for Excellence in Journalism 2007b).[4]

However, in radio there continues to be competition from the institutional style of journalism through NPR (formerly National Public Radio). Through its affiliate radio stations, podcasts, and website, NPR has substantially expanded its audience in recent decades, despite the increasing competition that has hurt most other highly professionalized news outlets. NPR's weekly radio audience was 22 million people in 2003, a 315% increase since 1985 (Project for Excellence in Journalism 2007b). This growth continued through the 2000s, increasing another 20% to 26.4 million by spring 2009 (Project for Excellence in Journalism 2010). Yet NPR continues to unapologetically follow a highly professionalized style of journalism directly descendent from that which dominated in the mid-twentieth century.[5]

The first national all-news cable channel was CNN. Founded in 1980 and quite successful by the 1990s, it broadcasts a mix of news and punditry (West 2001, 89–90). In the 1990s, CNN was joined by other news channels, including CNBC, MSNBC, and the Fox News Channel. By 2000, 60% of Americans reported regularly watching a cable news channel (West 2001, 86). Cable news's prime-time viewership has continued to increase in recent years, rising from an average of about 1.3 million a night in 1998 to 3.8 million in 2009 (Project for Excellence in Journalism 2009). Unlike CNN, which often adheres to the style of the institutional

---

[4] The well-documented tendency of people to consume information from sources that ideologically agree with them is called "selective exposure" in the political science literature (see Lazarsfeld, Berelson, and Gaudet 1948; Brock 1965; Sears and Freedman 1967; Sweeney and Gruber 1984; Iyengar, Hahn, and Prior 2001; Mullainathan and Shleifer 2005; Iyengar and Hahn 2007; Stroud 2008).

[5] NPR even restricts its employees' ability to attend political rallies or post political bumper stickers or yard signs. This is similar to restrictions on political contributions at some network news divisions and establishment newspapers. NPR Senior Vice President for News Ellen Weiss wrote in a 2010 memo to employees, "NPR journalists may not participate in marches and rallies involving causes or issues that NPR covers, nor should they sign petitions or otherwise lend their name to such causes, or contribute money to them. . . . [N]o matter where you work at NPR you should be very mindful that you represent the organization and its news coverage in the eyes of your friends, neighbors and others. So please think twice about the message you may be sending about our objectivity before you attend a rally or post a bumper sticker or yard sign" (Shea 2010).

media, Fox News, founded in 1996, adopted a more opinionated style similar to conservative talk radio. From its inception, Fox prominently featured conservative political talk shows, such as one featuring Bill O'Reilly and another with Sean Hannity and Alan Colmes.[6] By late 2004, 22% of Americans reported getting most of their news from Fox. Its ratings were greater than those for CNN, MSNBC, and CNBC combined (Jamieson and Cappella 2008, 47–48). Other cable networks increasingly copied Fox's style in order to improve their own ratings (51). MSNBC tried airing talk shows with both conservative (such as Alan Keyes and Joe Scarborough) and liberal (such as Phil Donohue, Keith Olbermann, Rachel Maddow, and Ed Schultz) hosts before eventually settling on a largely liberal evening lineup, which included hosts such as Olbermann, Maddow, Schultz, Chris Matthews, and Lawrence O'Donnell (see Kurtz 2009).

Opinionated cable hosts have attracted polarized audiences. In 2007, 38% of Fox News's overall viewership was Republican, while 31% was Democratic. In contrast, CNN and MSNBC viewership was only 22% and 19% Republican, respectively, and 45% and 48% Democratic (Project for Excellence in Journalism 2008). Turning to specific programs, in 2008, 66% of viewers of Bill O'Reilly's show identified as conservative, while 3% identified as liberal. Viewers of Fox's *Hannity and Colmes* show were 68% conservative and 7% liberal (Project for Excellence in Journalism 2009). One poll conducted the week before the 2010 congressional elections found that those planning to vote for Democratic candidates constituted 84% of MSNBC's viewers but only 5% of Fox's (Tesler 2010).

The Internet has provided another forum for the growth of alternatives to the institutional news media. Since the invention of the Internet browser in 1993, the World Wide Web has become an increasingly important part of life in developed societies (Hindman 2009, 1). It is now relatively easy for almost anyone to disseminate political news on the web. In his study of Internet usage, Matthew Hindman (2009, 60–64) found that most Internet traffic to news sites is focused on relatively few sites, many of which are the web incarnations of large, conventional news organizations, including CNN, MSNBC, the Weather Channel, Yahoo! News (which largely consists of wire service reports), Google News, *People* magazine, Yahoo! Weather, the *New York Times*, and so on.[7] Most traffic to political sites focused on opinion is also concentrated on the

---

[6] Colmes, the more liberal of the two, eventually left the program.

[7] Hindman (2009, 60–64) uses data that separates politically relevant websites into "news and media" sites and "political" sites. Of the 2.9% of all 2007 web traffic focused on "news or media" sites, the largest are almost all large news sites like those mentioned in the text.

relatively few most popular sites.[8] However, the popular opinion sites tend not to be run by large, traditional news organizations but to be sites like (in 2007) Freerepublic.com, HuffingtonPost.com, DailyKos.com, Townhall.com, Buzzflash.com, DemocraticUnderground.com, and so on (65–66). These sites often eschew the conventions of institutional journalism, seeing themselves instead as components of political movements of the right or left or simply as forums for political commentary.

Many of these political sites are either weblogs (known as blogs) or at least feature blogs prominently. Hindman (2009, 121) found that popular political bloggers were much more highly educated than ordinary journalists and slightly more educated than op-ed columnists for elite papers (126). A nontrivial portion (21%) of these bloggers consists of current or former professional journalists or columnists (122, 126). Yet whatever their background, most bloggers and other writers for prominent political opinion sites tend to mix opinion with information, in contradiction of the journalistic professional norms created in the early twentieth century. As with talk radio, criticism of the mainstream media is a major topic of commentary on these sites (Chait 2007, 24; Hindman 2009, 127–28).

While talk radio has been an especially hospitable medium for the development of conservative alternative information sources, the Internet has so far housed more successful liberal alternative sources.[9] This is possibly because liberal alternatives were less successful on other platforms, leaving an untapped market, and because web use for political purposes is more prevalent among liberals (Hindman 2009, 23). While still employing some magazines and liberal radio and cable talk shows, liberal alternative media discourse has been particularly focused on liberal Internet sites. Progressive alternative media outlets, centered on the web, have grown in numbers and popularity since 2000. Some of the most prominent members of the progressive alternative media label themselves a "movement," just as the Goldwater/conservative movement has labeled itself for decades, and have copied many other conservative tactics, including undermining the credibility of the institutional news media (Armstrong and Moulitsas 2006; Bai 2007; Chait 2007; Alterman 2008).[10] While conservatives have also used the Internet extensively, it, along with liberal cable talk shows and magazines, has enabled liberal alternative

[8] Among all web traffic in 2007, just 0.12% focused on "political" websites, which include only sites providing political opinions and advocacy (Hindman 2009, 60). Within this category, the top 50 "political" sites got 60% of all traffic (65–66).

[9] On the difficulties liberal talk radio has experienced, see O'Callaghan and Farrelly (2005).

[10] The progressive movement of the 2000s should not be confused with the original American progressive movement of the 1900s and 1910s. While both are movements of the political left, they are historically distinct phenomena.

media sources to now rival the size and emulate the message and coordination of conservative alternative media (Chait 2007).

As a whole, the Internet has become home to both large organizations that are part of the institutional news media and newer political news and opinion sites that serve as conservative or (more often) liberal alternatives to institutional journalism. As a result of noninstitutional outlets playing a relatively larger role online, studies find that, overall, Internet news consumers tend to be more ideologically extreme (Lawrence, Sides, and Farrell 2010) and more ideologically segregated across outlets (Gentzkow and Shapiro 2010a) than offline news consumers.

While the institutional media's journalistic style has remained much more consistent with mid-twentieth-century professional norms than the alternative media's style has, it did change in one important way over this period. Some prominent institutional outlets, especially network television, have come to provide more coverage of "soft" news, such as nonpolitical celebrities, the entertainment industry, and so on.[11] Economist James Hamilton (2004, 177–78) measured changes in evening network newscasts by counting how many of the "television stars, movie actors, sports figures, persons involved in famous crimes, and royalty" who were featured in *People* magazine's annual "25 Most Intriguing People" list were covered on the newscasts. He found that the percentage of soft news celebrities from *People* magazine covered on network news rose from 39.6% in 1974–78 to 51.9% in 1994–98. John Zaller (1999b, 48–49) illustrated this phenomenon by measuring changes in the content of CBS's newsmagazine *60 Minutes*, which has aired on Sunday nights since 1968. He coded reports on a scale of 1 to 5, with 1 indicating very soft news and 5 indicating very hard news. For example, coverage of President Nixon's Vietnam troop withdrawal plan was given a 5, while an interview with Elizabeth Taylor was given a 1. By this measure, *60 Minutes*'s news coverage had an average score of about 4.1 in 1968, which steadily declined to approximately 2.0 by 1998.

A central reason for this change appears to be more competitive pressure from alternative news sources and entertainment media (Zaller 1999b, chap. 3; Hamilton 2004, chap. 6). In a 2000 interview, *CBS Evening News* anchor Dan Rather said that his broadcast aimed for a "rich mix" of soft and hard news: "It's going to be entertainment and news all in a kind of bouillabaisse, and we do a lot of stuff that I think is pretty far over the line in the direction of entertainment" (Downie and Kaiser 2003, 135). Compared to when he started anchoring in 1981, he said, "What's

---

[11] Hamilton (2004, 165) defines the hard/soft news distinction as follows: hard news largely consists of "public affairs, government action, or international relations stories," while soft news mostly focuses on "celebrities, entertainment news, or tabloid crimes."

changed is there is a much—and I emphasize the word *much*—higher consideration given to competition. It is much larger and more ferocious than it was when I came to the broadcast. And I do want to emphasize the word *much*" (134). In a 1995 interview, *NBC Nightly News* anchor Tom Brokaw expressed similar sentiments, stating, "It's a relatively recent phenomenon of our business that people have so many choices at any given time. . . . [W]hen I started out in the 1960's, there were effectively two network news programs, and at 6:30pm people turned on either Huntley-Brinkley or Walter Cronkite and got their news for the day. I'd like to have that back again" (Mifflin 1995).

The more competitive media environment's effects on the newspaper industry are especially evident. In addition to facing competition for consumers from online, radio, and cable news formats, newspaper revenues have been depleted by free online classified services and more-targeted advertising options, such as those offered by Google (Fallows 2010). As a result, print newspapers are the portion of the institutional news media that have faced the most serious threat to their continued existence. Daily print circulation in the United States declined from 62 million to 49 million from the late 1980s to the late 2000s. Exacerbated by a recession, from 2006 to 2009, many newspapers experienced 25% declines in advertising revenue. Some, such as the *Chicago Tribune*, *Minneapolis Star Tribune*, and *Philadelphia Inquirer*, entered bankruptcy, while others, such as the *Seattle Post-Intelligencer* and *Ann Arbor News*, became online-only publications (West 2009, 2). The loss in newspaper audience has been much smaller than the loss in revenue, however, because many readers simply moved online. In 2008, Nielson estimated that approximately 75 million Americans read newspapers on the Internet (3).

As this section has shown, the American media environment has become more fragmented in recent decades with the introduction of cable television, political talk radio, and the Internet. However, while they have incorporated more soft news coverage, the institutional news media continue to be distinct from the rest of the media landscape and to serve as an important source of political information for many, thus retaining an important role in the American political system. Neilson ratings show that about 36% of Americans watched network evening news programs in 1970–71. Despite a steady decline, that number stood at 23% in 2000 and 15% by 2009 (Bartels and Rahn 2000, 3–4; Project for Excellence in Journalism 2010). In 2009, 22.3 million viewers a night watched the network evening newscasts, compared to cable news channels' combined prime-time viewership of around 3.9 million (Project for Excellence in Journalism 2010). Similarly, as Matthew Hindman has documented, websites from large news organizations that generally follow the conventions of professional journalism receive more web traffic than alternative media outlets on the Internet, despite the vitality of such alternative outlets (Hindman 2009, 60).

What has changed in the past 40 years is not that institutional news sources have gone away but that they now face intense competition. Among news options on the right, conservative talk radio, cable programs, and print media constitute what Kathleen Hall Jamieson and Joseph Cappella call an alternative "conservative media establishment" (Jamieson and Cappella 2008, ix). On the left, liberal websites, cable talk shows, and periodicals have more recently developed into an alternative liberal media establishment.[12] News consumers increasingly face a choice between institutional and alternative news media when deciding what to consume and whom to believe. As these sources often send very different messages, these choices can increasingly determine the facts a person receives about the political world.

In this way, from the 1970s to the 2000s, the ideological polarization of the major American political parties was accompanied by a greater availability of alternative news outlets more compatible with the increasingly divergent worldviews of liberal Democrats and conservative Republicans. Unsurprisingly, relations between political leaders and the institutional news media changed considerably when leaders were more polarized and knew competing news outlets were available to provide information more consistent with their divergent worldviews.

POLITICAL ATTACKS ON THE INSTITUTIONAL NEWS MEDIA INCREASE

After President Kennedy's assassination, in the mid-1960s the Johnson administration bristled at the elevated position reporters had come to

---

[12] There is a certain similarity between this and the development of the U.S. Congress. As Eric Schickler (2001) has shown, new congressional institutions do not sweep away and replace the old. Rather, in a process he calls "disjointed pluralism," new structures are created in addition to the old, so both exist in parallel, shaping congressional functioning. Similarly, new forms of media have risen up and been grafted on top of the existing institutional news media. While the institutional press have certainly not been unaffected by the expanded and fragment media environment, they still exist, with a structure and style distinct from their newer counterparts. Similarly, the role of the news media in the American political system is not clearly defined and is the result of a variety of similarly eclectic historical circumstances. Cook (1998, 39–40) describes the relationship of government to the media in historical perspective by saying, "One cannot say that there is a coherent and logical public policy toward the news media. Instead . . . such policies and practices emerged in incremental, particularistic, and inchoate manners, often by a process of explicit and implicit negotiation between political actors as a group and the news media as a group that ended up with mutual benefit far from philosophical questions of what kind of information is required for and in a democracy."

hold in Washington. Like FDR and so many other politicians throughout history, Johnson resisted reporters' attempts to be an independent source of information for the public. In Johnson's view, "Reporters were tools to be used to gain an end. . . . He believed that friendly reporters would write whatever he suggested they write, and unfriendly ones were not worth his time. But Washington was not Texas, and the press corps—White House reporters in particular—had come to expect the royal treatment" (Liebovich 1998, 43).

Indeed, as the relatively unpolarized style of national politics of the 1950s and early 1960s gave way to the polarized politics of subsequent decades, leading politicians became more hostile toward the news media establishment. This trend was evident not just in the Johnson administration but (even more so) in the emerging Goldwater movement. The solidly conservative faction of Republicans, after losing presidential nomination fights to "modern Republicans" such as Eisenhower (Dionne 1992, 170–86), finally succeeded in nominating Senator Barry Goldwater for president in 1964. The institutional and ideological descendent of the Goldwater movement—the new right or conservative movement—would come to dominate the party in subsequent decades. Criticism of the institutional news media was a defining characteristic of this political faction.

Several examples illustrate how antipathy toward the media was one of the basic characteristics of Goldwaterism. The night before the 1964 California primary, the Goldwater campaign held a televised rally that attracted 27,000 in person and a million more viewers at home. Historian Rick Perlstein (2001, 352) described the scene this way: "On the dais sat conservative leading lights like General A.C. Wedemeyer. . . . John Wayne looked down from the platform, locked eyes with [ABC news reporter] Howard K. Smith, and said in the throaty drawl he reserved only for the gnarliest of desperados, 'Ah-aystarn lab'ral prass!' . . . Then Ronald Reagan spoke. He was just as angry. But he made you want to stand right alongside him and shake your fist at the same things he was shaking *his* fist at. It was hard to remember exactly what they were. Clearly they were the enemy of all decent men" (emphasis in the original). Earlier, when Goldwater appeared on *The Steve Allen Show*, Allen tried to embarrass him by playing a recording of a "far-right hotline" sponsored by conservative activists thought to support his candidacy. The recording said, "Keep yourself well informed. Do not trust the newspapers, radio, TV, and newsmagazines for your information. These are the main weapons the enemy has to use against us" (Perlstein 2001, 350–51). Goldwater was equivocal, saying he didn't agree with everything on the recording but supporting the group's right to express itself.

Richard Nixon's long career illustrates many of the ways the relationship between the Republican Party and the institutional press changed over the course of the twentieth century. Nixon was affiliated, first, with the brand of extreme anticommunism of the late 1940s and early 1950s most closely associated with Senator Joseph McCarthy; second, with moderate, mid-twentieth-century "modern" Republicanism as Eisenhower's vice president; and third, with the emerging conservative movement during his 1968 comeback and presidency. Early in his career, he rarely criticized the press publicly. During his House and Senate races, he enjoyed strong support from the conservative *Los Angeles Times*. Investigating allegations of Soviet espionage against State Department employee Alger Hiss while a congressman, he worked cooperatively with Bert Andrews of the *New York Herald Tribune*. *Time* and *Life* magazines, owned by conservative Henry Luce, served as "practically Nixon megaphones" during his 1960 presidential campaign (Perlstein 2008, 58).

Yet later in his political career, Nixon became a frequent, public, and enthusiastic press detractor. The start of his serious public criticism of the institutional press occurred when he lost his race for California governor in 1962. He famously ended his concession press conference by saying,

> And as I leave the press, all I can say is this: for sixteen years, ever since the Hiss case, you've had a lot of fun—a lot of fun—that you've had an opportunity to attack me, and I think I've given as good as I've taken. . . . I leave you gentlemen now and you will write it. You will interpret it. That's your right. But as I leave you I want you to know—just think of how much you're going to be missing. You won't have Nixon to kick around anymore, because, gentlemen, this is my last press conference. And I hope what I have said today will at least make television, radio, the press, recognize that they have a right and responsibility if they're against a candidate to give him the shaft. But also recognize that if they give him the shaft to put one reporter on the campaign who will report what the candidate says now and then. Thank you, gentlemen, and good day." (Perlstein 2008, 59)

Nixon's substantive complaints resemble those of many other politicians before and since. They dislike the news media's propensity to serve as an independent information source for voters, wishing they would serve simply as amplifiers of the politicians' own messages (or in Nixon's words, "report what the candidate says now and then"). An autonomous, influential press is attacked. For instance, Nixon was most content with the press when they offered him partisan support, as the *Los Angeles Times* did early in his career, or when they transmitted his messages directly to the audience, as when *Reader's Digest* (the most widely read monthly in America at the time) gave him a regular column from 1965 to 1968 (Perlstein 2008, 85).

In addition to the emerging conservative movement in the Republican Party, other parts of the 1960s conservative backlash against liberal governance were also culturally hostile to the news media. In his segregationist campaigns for Alabama governor and president, George Wallace regularly attacked the press. In one example, at a rally during his 1966 gubernatorial campaign (technically his wife was running because he was constitutionally barred from seeking reelection), he attacked "these big northern newspapers having a fit because my wife is a candidate for governor." He pointed out Ray Jenkins, an *Alabama Journal* reporter in the crowd, and said, "I see we got the editor of the *Alabama Journal* here today. You know he's one of them Hahh-verd-educated intellectuals that sticks his little finger up in the air when he sips tea and looks down his long nose at us ordinary Alabamans. I had a goat one time, and I fed him a copy of the *Alabama Journal*. And the poor goat died" (Perlstein 2008, 79).

Police clashing with liberal 1960s protesters were frequently as hostile to the news media as to the protesters. At the famous protests during the 1968 Democratic National Convention in Chicago, many reporters were beaten by police and their cameras destroyed. On NBC's *Today* show, correspondent Jack Perkins reported, "In the darkness and confusion, policemen used their nightsticks with great zeal, clubbing and injuring about sixty people. Seventeen of them were newsmen—there trying to cover it—including a CBS cameraman . . . an NBC cameraman, and NBC news reporter John Evans. They beat cameramen to keep them from filming policemen beating other people, and newsmen not in spite of the fact they were newsmen but because of it" (Perlstein 2008, 312–14). Later, Mayor Richard Daly defended the behavior of the police in an interview on the *Today* show, saying, "The television industry is part of the violence and creating it all over the country." In an interview with Walter Cronkite, he said, "Many [reporters] are hippies themselves. They're part of this movement. Some of them are revolutionaries and they want these things to happen" (Perlstein 2008, 336–37).

After Nixon was elected president in 1968, he monitored the news with daily summaries prepared by advisor Patrick (Pat) Buchanan. Buchanan made a point of highlighting coverage that would offend Nixon's conservative sensibilities (Perlstein 2008, 407; Karpowitz 2009). While the Nixon administration's dislike of the institutional media was not new, the criticism intensified in 1969 when Vice President Agnew began regularly attacking the media in speeches. The attacks began with a November 13, 1969, speech written by Buchanan, edited by Nixon, and aired live on all three networks. In it, Agnew complained that a recently televised Nixon address was "subjected to instant analysis and querulous criticism" by a "small band of network commentators and self-appointed analysts." He called the elite news media this little group of men who not only enjoy a right of instant rebuttal to every presidential address, but more importantly, wield a free hand in selecting, presenting, and interpreting the great issues of our nation. . . . What do Americans know of the men who wield this power? . . . Little other than that they reflect an urbane and assured presence, seemingly well informed on every important matter. . . . To a man, these commentators and producers live and work in the geographic and intellectual confines of Washington, DC, or New York City. . . . They talk constantly to one another, thereby providing artificial reinforcement to their shared viewpoints. . . . Is it not fair or relevant to question [this power's] concentration in the hands of a tiny and closed fraternity of privileged men, elected by no one, and enjoying a monopoly sanctioned and licensed by government? The views of the fraternity do not represent the views of America. (Coyne 1972, 267–68; Agnew 1989, 67–69)

Agnew continued attacks along these lines for the next several years (Coyne 1972; Emery, Emery, and Roberts 2000, 436; West 2001, 65; Perlstein 2008, 439, 504–6, 525).[13] In response, conservatives sold Spiro Agnew wristwatches and bumper stickers saying "Spiro Is My Hero" and "Spiro of 76" (Perlstein 2008, 442, 446, 504). The main symptoms of journalism's transformation from a low-status trade to a high-status profession—greater education, more uniform and autonomous reporting standards and worldviews, and the resulting greater influence in politics—were precisely the things the administration found threatening and attacked.

By the time the Nixon administration reached its end, it was at war with the legitimacy of the institutional media on almost every level. At one point in 1971–72, it went almost a year without a primetime presidential press conference, holding only seven press conferences total in 1972. David Broder commented, "What we assumed, and it seems sort of dumb in retrospect, was that just because the presidential press conference had grown up from Wilson on and seven or eight presidents had adhered to it, it had somehow become institutionalized. It's not institutionalized at all. In fact, you could effectively say that Richard Nixon has abolished the presidential press conference as an institution" (Perlstein 2008, 568). The Office of Telecommunications Policy, under the direction of its general council, Antonin Scalia, designed plans to gain political control of the Public Broadcasting System's news programming,

---

[13] One of Agnew's most famous lines was delivered toward administration critics in general, presumably including the press. At a 1970 California Republican convention in San Diego, he said, "In the United States today, we have more than our share of nattering nabobs of negativism. They have formed their own 4-H club—the hopeless, hysterical hypochondriacs of history" (Perlstein 2008, 525–26).

wresting it away from, in Scalia's words, "the liberal establishment of the Northeast" (Perlstein 2008, 596). At a 1973 news conference, Nixon told reporters he "had never heard or seen such outrageous, vicious, distorted reporting in 27 years of public life" (Liebovich 1998, 61). When a new book, *The News Twisters* by Edith Efron (1971), claimed that television networks took "the elitist-liberal-left line in all controversies," biasing coverage against the "white middle class majority," the administration used $5,000 from a slush fund also used for Watergate-related activities to buy up enough copies to put it on best-seller lists. Boxes of *The News Twisters* piled up in the office of White House "plumber" Howard Hunt (Perlstein 2008, 596).

Nixon's White House went to political war with the institutional news media when the latter were close to the height of their prestige and influence. In the short run, the Nixon administration lost. Investigations begun by the *Washington Post*'s Bob Woodward and Carl Bernstein uncovered a pattern of illegal espionage conducted by the Nixon administration against its political opponents (collectively known as Watergate), eventually resulting in Nixon's resignation in 1974 (Bernstein and Woodward 1974; Emery, Emery, and Roberts 2000, 439–42). However, the attacks on the institutional media made by the Goldwater campaign and the Nixon White House became a fixture of the conservative movement and Republican political strategy. Over decades, they played an important role in eroding the news media's stature.

The increase in Republican media criticism slowed somewhat in the 1980s as the Reagan administration took a bit more conciliatory approach, trying to woo, not just bully, the media establishment. *CBS Evening News* executive producer Sanford Socolow recalled that the Reagan administration returned somewhat to the older strategy of "making the press part of your inner circle, or at least making them believe they were part of your inner circle" (Hertsgaard 1988, 43). Senior administration officials like Michael Deaver and David Gergen developed friendly personal relationships with elite Washington reporters (40–41). Advisor Lyn Nofziger believed that the press had attacked Nixon "because they could sense that hatred. Ronald Reagan likes everybody. He never had this feeling that the press as a group was out to get him" (42). In contrast to his criticisms of the institutional media while campaigning for Goldwater in 1964, when asked in an interview about press coverage of the 1982 recession, Reagan complained about the coverage but was philosophical about the reasons for it. He said bad economic conditions were being exaggerated because news organizations were "more concerned with entertainment than delivering the evening news. It's an entertainment medium, and they're looking for what's eye-catching and spectacular" (Cannon 1991, 227). It was only late in Reagan's second term, after the

Iran-Contra scandal broke in late 1986, that presidential rhetoric about the news media became harsher as Reagan became more disillusioned with his coverage and Pat Buchanan, now White House communications director, introduced stronger media criticism (Cannon 1991, 607–8).

By the 1990s, criticism of the institutional media had become a standard part of American conservative rhetoric. A popular bumper sticker in the 1992 presidential campaign read, "Annoy the Media, Re-elect Bush" (Dickerson 2007). During campaign speeches, 1996 Republican presidential nominee Bob Dole urged people to "rise up" against the media establishment. He said, "We've got to stop the liberal bias in this country. Don't read the stuff. Don't watch television. You make up your own mind. Don't let them make up your mind for you. We are not going to let the media steal this election. The country belongs to the people, not the *New York Times*" (West 2001, 104). Attacks similar to those from the "far right hotline" that had embarrassed Goldwater in 1964 were now actually coming from the Republican presidential nominee.

The conservative alternative media, with strong connections to the conservative movement and a commercial incentive to increase their audience, have always heavily criticized the institutional news media. One content analysis of the *Rush Limbaugh Show* found that the mainstream media was the second most frequent "issue" discussed (Barker and Knight 2000, 168; Barker 2002, 25–26), while another found that it was tied for the most frequent topic (Jamieson and Cappella 2008, 169). A 2007 content analysis of all talk radio programming found that the news media was the second most frequent topic, trailing only "election/politics" coverage (Project for Excellence in Journalism 2008).

Following in the footsteps of Efron's *The News Twisters*, conservative political activists from the late 1980s on have increasingly produced books attacking the institutional press. To get a sense of this trend, here is just a sample of some of the titles of these books: *Prodigal Press: The Anti-Christian Bias of the American News Media* (Olasky 1988), *Unreliable Sources: A Guide to Detecting Bias in News Media* (Lee and Solomon 1991), *Through the Media Looking Glass: Decoding Bias and Blather in the News* (J. Cohen and Sullivan 1995), *Bias: A CBS Insider Exposes How the Media Distort the News* (B. Goldberg 2002), *Journalistic Fraud: How the* New York Times *Distorts the News and Why It Can No Longer Be Trusted* (Kohn 2003), *Coloring the News: How Political Correctness Has Corrupted American Journalism* (McGowan 2003), *Weapons of Mass Distortion: The Coming Meltdown of the Liberal Media* (Bozell 2004), *South Park Conservatives: The Revolt against Liberal Media Bias* (Anderson 2005), and *A Slobbering Love Affair: The True (and Pathetic) Story of the Torrid Romance between Barack Obama and the Mainstream Media* (B. Goldberg 2009).

In the 2000s, George W. Bush's administration and other Republicans criticized and attempted to undermine the institutional news media in ways comparable to the Nixon administration's efforts. However, this behavior attracted much less commentary because it had become so commonplace. While the Nixon White House promoted *The News Twisters* covertly, President Bush openly endorsed Bernard Goldberg's *Bias: A CBS Insider Exposes How the Media Distort the News* (2002), prominently displaying a copy under his arm in front of photographers when leaving for a trip to Maine in 2002 (Streissguth 2006, 38). Bush held only 50 press conferences over the course of his two terms, compared to Clinton's 62 or Eisenhower's 190 (Emery, Emery, and Roberts 2000, 364; Bellantoni 2008; Loven 2009). In a 2005 interview with the *London Times*, he commented on his dislike of the institutional media and his preference to circumvent it, saying, "My job is to occasionally, you know, go out above the filter and speak directly to the people" (Watson and Baker 2005). When he did sit for interviews, he sometimes chose members of the conservative alternative media, such as talk radio and Fox News talk show hosts Bill O'Reilly (2004) and Sean Hannity (2009). During the third 2004 presidential campaign debate, when the moderator asked about health care and John Kerry cited analyses by "two leading national news networks" in favor of his position, it was not surprising when President Bush began his response by saying, "In all due respect, I'm not so sure it's credible to quote leading news organizations about—oh, never mind" (Commission on Presidential Debates 2004). This rhetorical pattern continued into the 2008 presidential campaign, in which Alaska governor and Republican Party vice presidential nominee Sarah Palin often attacked the national institutional news media. Shortly after the election, she argued, "This is for the sake of our democracy that there is fairness in this other branch of government, if you will, called the media. It is foreign to me the way some in the mainstream media are thinking" (Barr 2009).

At the same time, Democratic and liberal political activists developed a parallel genre. While modern liberal media criticism has never been as widespread or prominent, in content it resembles a mirror image of its conservative counterpart. Frequent themes are accusations that the media favor conservative policies and politicians. For comparison, a sample of these book titles includes: *Manufacturing Consent: The Political Economy of the Mass Media* (Herman and Chomsky 1988), *On Bended Knee: The Press and the Reagan Presidency* (Hertsgaard 1988), *Necessary Illusions: Thought Control in Democratic Societies* (Chomsky 1989), *What Liberal Media?: The Truth about Bias and the News* (Alterman 2003), *Big Lies: The Right-Wing Propaganda Machine and How It Distorts the Truth* (Conason 2003), *The Exception to the Rulers: Exposing Oily Politicians, War Profiteers, and the Media That Love Them* (Goodman 2004),

Figure 4-1. President George W. Bush displays
*Bias: A CBS Insider Exposes How the Media
Distort the News*, by Bernard Goldberg. *Source*:
Manny Ceneta / Getty Images.

*The Republican Noise Machine: Right Wing Media and How It Corrupts
Democracy* (D. Brock 2004), *War Made Easy: How Presidents and Pundits Keep Spinning Us to Death* (Solomon 2005), and *Lapdogs: How the
Press Rolled Over for Bush* (Boehlert 2006).

Liberal criticism of the institutional news media arose from its mid-
twentieth-century lull later than did conservative criticism. While left-
wing intellectuals such as Noam Chomsky were criticizing the media in
the 1970s and 1980s, prominent liberal pundits and Democratic politicians were less likely to attack the media than their conservative counterparts. As late as the 1988, 1992, and 1996 elections, between 92% and
96% of the media criticism during these presidential campaigns accused
the press of favoring the liberal or Democratic candidate (Domke et al.
1999). Its rise may have been helped along by the Clinton administration's contentious relationship with the Washington press corps. Like
Nixon, Clinton constantly fumed privately about news coverage (Emery,

Emery, and Roberts 2000, 477). Intensive coverage by major news organizations such as the *New York Times* and the *Wall Street Journal* of a series of Arkansas scandals collectively known as Whitewater and widespread coverage of Clinton's affair with Monica Lewinsky contributed to this hostility. After the Lewinsky scandal broke in 1998, David Broder revealed his feelings toward Clinton when he told *Washington Post* reporter Sally Quinn, "He came in here [Washington, DC] and he trashed the place, and it's not his place" (Quinn 1998). Clinton held news conferences only rarely, including just one in his first twenty months.

Only on a few occasions did he express his private hostility toward the institutional media. One such instance occurred when announcing his nomination of Ruth Bader Ginsburg to the Supreme Court, after Clinton teared up during Ginsberg's statement. ABC's Britt Hume posed what was intended to be the first question by asking about "a certain zigzag quality" to the nomination selection process. Journalist John F. Harris (2005, 62) describes Clinton's reaction to Hume: "Clinton glared, clenched his jaw, then spat back his answer: 'I have long since given up the thought that I could disabuse some of you [from] turning any substantive decision into anything but political process. How you could ask a question like that after the statement she just made is beyond me.' He quickly wheeled off the stage and returned to the Oval Office, bringing Ginsburg's announcement ceremony to an awkward close." Clinton's frustration also came out in several interviews. In one, he complained that his administration had many accomplishments but "the media didn't tell them" (Emery, Emery, and Roberts 2000, 477). In another, he said he "had not gotten one damn bit of credit from the knee-jerk liberal press, and I am sick and tired of it, and you can put that in the damn article" (Harris 2005, 146).

Media criticism by prominent Democratic politicians continued during George W. Bush's presidency. For instance, in a 2002 interview with the *New York Observer*, former vice president Al Gore argued, "The media is kind of weird these days on politics, and there are some major institutional voices that are, truthfully speaking, part and parcel of the Republican Party. Most of the media [has] been slow to recognize the pervasive impact of this fifth column in their ranks—that is, day after day, injecting the daily Republican talking points into the definition of what's objective as stated by the news media as a whole" (Kelly 2002a; Krugman 2002b).

As the previous section described, liberal alternative media that grew in prominence in the 2000s employed strategies similar to (and sometimes explicitly modeled on) movement conservatism and conservative alternative media, including attacking the institutional press. For instance, popular liberal blogs like DailyKos.com, run by Markos Moulitsas Zuniga, and Eschaton.com, written by Duncan Black, regularly criticized

Washington journalists as "Washington insiders" or as part of the "main-stream media," the "media elite," the "village" (meaning the District of Columbia), or the Washington "cocktail party" circuit (Bai 2007, 139, 232; Chait 2007, 22). Like conservatives, they criticized institutional journalism's claim to be loyal to professional, rather than ideological or partisan, standards. Duncan Black argued, "Lots of people imagine them-selves to be above the fray. The most obvious group which does this is journalists and their brethren. They fail to see themselves as actors on the political stage, instead of detached observers" (Chait 2007, 24). In addi-tion to stand-alone blogs, liberal alternative news sites like TalkingPoints-Memo.com frequently criticize press coverage, while MediaMatters.com follows the example of longstanding conservative organizations like the Media Research Center and Accuracy in Media in focusing solely on un-covering and publicizing news media bias (Chait 2007, 24).

Thus, while criticism of the institutional news media is not as common among Democratic politicians as among Republicans—there is nothing comparable to the prominent attacks on the media by their presidential and vice presidential nominees—among liberal activists at the base of the party and in the liberal alternative media, this criticism has become very common. As a result of all this, the institutional media is now regularly undermined by both sides of the political spectrum. Nicholas Lemann (2005, 174) reported, "I spoke to the heads of several large news orga-nizations, and all of them maintained that they get attacked from both political sides, and agreed that both the amplitude and the frequency of the attacks seem to be increasing."

Figure 4-2 provides one illustration of the changing nature of rheto-ric about the press among conservative and liberal activists. I coded all articles where the news media was an important theme in the *National Review*, a consistently conservative magazine, and the *Nation*, a consis-tently liberal magazine, from the mid-1970s to the mid-2000s.[14] I chose these two outlets because they have been journals of conservative and lib-eral activists over the entire period when partisan rhetoric about the press changed, allowing for a comparison over time. For each article, I coded whether it criticized the institutional media, praised the institutional media, or neither. The figure presents the net number of critical articles in each year. Media criticism was common earlier in the *National Review*, where there was a net of about 10 negative articles a year in the seven-ties and almost 20 per year in much of the 1980s and 1990s, punctuated by a temporary spike upward in the early 1990s. In the 2000s, criticism again increased significantly, up to a net of 40 critical articles per year. In

[14] Data from the *Nation* begin in 1971. Data from the *National Review* begin in 1975, as the magazine is not electronically searchable prior to that year.

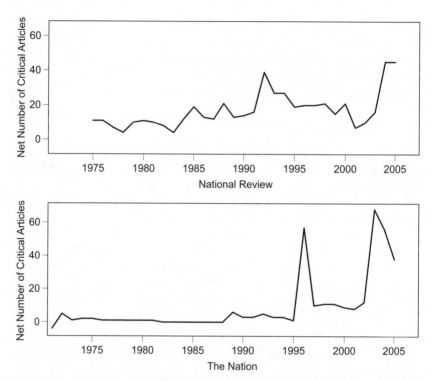

Figure 4-2. Criticism of the news media in ideological magazines, 1970s–2005. *Note:* Lines represent total number of articles in each year in which criticism of the news media is an important theme, minus the number in which praise for the news media is an important theme. *Source:* Coding performed by the author. Coding guidelines are available upon request.

contrast, there was almost no criticism of the institutional media in the *Nation* during the 1970s and 1980s, a temporary spike of about 50 net negative articles in 1996, followed by about 10 net negative articles per year through 2001, followed by a more sustained increase to over 40 net negative articles per year in the mid-2000s.[15]

---

[15] These trends do not appear to be driven by changes in the overall size of these magazines. To check for this, my research assistant, Amy Cohen, examined the size of these magazines for each year in the dataset. The size of the *National Review* showed no secular change over time. For instance, in 1975 it published 1,496 pages containing 547 articles, while in 2005 it published 1,356 pages containing 532 articles. The *Nation* showed a modest increase in size, from 1,534 pages containing 685 articles in 1971 to 2,026 pages containing 846 articles in 2005. Thus, if anything, accounting for magazine size slightly increases the difference in media criticism levels between these two magazines.

Another measure of elite political rhetoric toward the institutional press is the content of *Washington Post* op-ed columns. While the *Post* itself is a quintessential institutional newspaper, its opinion columns are a major forum for liberal and conservative (as well as centrist) opinion leaders to disseminate their ideas. My research assistant, Amanda Spears, coded all *Post* op-ed columns that commented on the news media from the late 1970s to the mid-2000s.[16] The top panel of figure 4-3 shows that both the number of *Post* op-eds at least mentioning the news media and the number in which the media was an important theme increased over this period. From almost no media commentary in the late 1970s and early 1980s, it became a regular topic of discussion from the mid-1980s through the 2000s. The bottom panel of figure 4-3 shows, as in figure 4-2, the net number of critical articles about the media. It indicates that the great majority of this media commentary that appeared regularly starting in the 1980s was negative.

A couple of examples illustrate this finding. The figure 4-3 data include a column by liberal pundit E. J. Dionne Jr. (2002) titled "The Rightward Press," in which he asserted, "It took conservatives a lot of hard and steady work to push the media rightward. . . . The media world now includes (1) talk radio, (2) cable television and (3) the traditional news sources (newspapers, newsmagazines and the old broadcast networks). Two of these three major institutions tilt well to the right, and the third is under constant pressure to avoid even the pale hint of liberalism. What it adds up to is a media heavily biased toward conservative politics and conservative politicians." The data also include a column where conservative pundit Michael Kelly (2002b) responds to Dionne, saying, "The question . . . —'Does a (still) largely liberal news media (still) exhibit a largely liberal bias?'—can be answered both as a matter of logic and as a matter of fact, and in both cases, the answer is: Sure." He attempts to undermine the institutional media's trustworthiness by denying journalism's professionalism and expertise: "[Journalists] don't have any professional training or discipline. Journalism is not a profession in the sense of medicine or law or science. Journalists do not go through years of brutal academic apprenticeship designed to inculcate adherence to an agreed-upon code of ethics (such as the Hippocratic oath) or an agreed-upon method of truth-determining (such as the method of scientific inquiry). We are not required to meet any standards of knowledge. We are not certified. We operate under no mandated professional set of rules. We need not even be decently educated, as consumers of news frequently notice."

---

[16] *Washington Post* articles are not available in full-text format on Lexis-Nexis prior to the late 1970s.

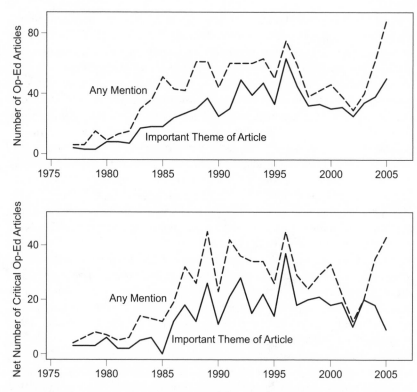

Figure 4-3. Commentary on the news media in *Washington Post* op-ed columns, 1976–2005. *Note*: The top section of the figure displays the total number of *Washington Post* op-ed columns containing commentary about the news media. The bottom section displays the total number of articles in which the commentary on the media is negative minus the number of articles where the commentary is positive. Articles in which the commentary is neutral or by the ombudsman are not used in this calculation. In both sections, the dashed lines indicate results when all articles with any mention of the news media are included and the solid lines represent results when only articles where the news media is an important topic or the entire focus of the article are included. *Source*: Search of *Washington Post* op-ed columns containing the words *media* or *press*, using Lexis-Nexis Academic. Coding performed by the author's research assistant, Amanda Spears, who did not know the purpose of the research project when the coding was done. Coding instructions are available upon request.

Figures 4-2 and 4-3 likely underestimate the increase in media criticism from ideological and partisan opinion leaders over this time period. This is because, in order to create time series that are comparable over time, I use outlets that existed in the 1970s. However, as I discuss in this and the previous section, many of the news media outlets that have come into existence in the past 40 years, such as talk radio shows and Internet sites, make media criticism a large part of their message. The growth in political attacks on the institutional news media comes from both greater criticism from existing opinion outlets and strong criticism from the new alternative media.

In 2009 and 2010, in their efforts to oppose newly elected president Barack Obama and Democratic congressional majorities, Republican politicians used media criticism as an important part of their strategy for returning to power. As just one minor example of the type of anti-media activism undertaken by conservative politicians and interest groups around the country, in June 2009, Congressman Lamar Smith of Texas founded what he called the Media Fairness Caucus with about a dozen other House Republicans. In 2009 and 2010, the caucus disseminated a weekly newsletter and coordinated attacks on the institutional media from House Republicans. Congressman Smith describes their strategy this way: "We'll come up with strategy, we'll coordinate the one-minute speeches, we'll coordinate news. There's strength in numbers, and getting more people involved, more members involved, will make us more effective in getting our message out there, about the dangers of media bias, as well as trying to get the media to be less biased" (Kessler 2009).

The Obama administration did not maintain warm relations with the press, either. Instead, the inherent tension between political leaders and the media continued to manifest itself. Unsurprisingly, the administration's strongest attacks fell on outlets it considered the most hostile. In an October 2009 interview, White House Interim Communications Director Anita Dunn accused Fox News Channel of being "the communications arm of the Republican Party" (Thompson 2009). A week after Dunn's remarks, Chief of Staff Rahm Emanuel and Senior Advisor David Axelrod reiterated this criticism on Sunday morning talk shows. On CNN's *State of the Union*, Emanuel described Fox as "not a news organization so much as it has a perspective." On ABC's *This Week*, Axelrod said Fox is "really not news—It's pushing a point of view" (M. Allen 2009).

While its harshest public attacks targeted Fox, the administration also tried to undermine the power of the institutional media. In April 2010, *Politico* reporters Josh Gerstein and Patrick Gavin interviewed a "cross-section of the television, newspaper and magazine journalists who cover the White House." The press corps perceived the administration as "thin-skinned, controlling, eager to go over their heads and even stingy with basic information." The *New Yorker*'s David Packer complained that the White House "seems to imagine that releasing information is like a tap that can be turned off at their whim." Reporters noted that hostility toward their independent institutional role "starts with the man at the top. Obama rarely let's a chance go by to make a critical or sarcastic comment about the press" (Gerstein and Gavin 2010).

The Obama administration's increasing hostility toward both alternative conservative outlets and the institutional press is further illustration of the inherent incentives for political leaders to undermine independent information sources. *Time*'s Michael Scherer (2009) described the evolution of Obama's media relations as follows: "[T]he White House decided it would become a player, issuing biting attacks on those pundits, politicians and outlets that make what the White House believes to be misleading or simply false claims . . . after eight months at the White House, the days of nonpartisan harmony are long gone—it's Us against Them."

Looked at from a historical perspective, elected leaders and other political elites appear to have had a contentious relationship with the news media throughout most of American history. Criticism has focused on news media whenever they attempt to express independent power or are affiliated with one's political opponents. The apparent exception to this was the 1950s and early 1960s, when the institutional news media achieved brief acceptance as an important political institution and was thus largely spared political criticism. However, in the past 40 years, political attacks on the institutional news media have greatly increased. They are now common among prominent politicians as well as alternative media outlets associated with the modern conservative and progressive movements.

Trust in the Institutional News Media Declines

From the 1970s to the 2000s, as elite discourse continued becoming more critical of the institutional press and alternative media outlets proliferated, trust in the institutional press greatly declined. One useful way to track changing opinions toward the media is with the General Social Survey (GSS), a large, national survey conducted every few years starting in 1972 by the National Opinion Research Center at the University of Chicago. Beginning in 1973, the GSS included a question about the press in a question battery probing confidence in various American institutions. As described in chapter 3, prior to 1973 it is difficult to track changes in opinions toward the institutional news media over time because questions were asked sporadically and with different question wordings. The GSS uses the same question wording and a similar survey procedure over time, making comparisons much easier. Figure 4-4 shows confidence in the press in the GSS from 1973 to 2008, as well as average confidence in all other institutions in the GSS battery. While average confidence in institutions has stayed reasonably steady, confidence in the press has notably declined. In 1973, 23% of those surveyed had "a great deal" of confidence

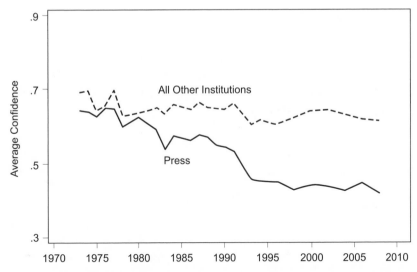

Figure 4-4. Confidence in the press compared to confidence in other institutions, 1973–2008. *Note*: Observations are weighted to account for the unequal probability of inclusion in the sample resulting from the GSS's procedures for subsampling of initial nonrespondents in the 2004–06 surveys and from variation in the number of adults in each household, using the "wtssall" weighting variable. For details, see appendix A of the GSS 1972–2008 codebook. Responses are coded so that 1 indicates "a great deal," .5 indicates "only some," and 0 indicates "hardly any" trust. *Source*: 1973–2008 GSS Cumulative File.

in the press, 62% had "only some," and 15% had "hardly any." By 2008, 9% had "a great deal," 46% had "only some," and 45% had "hardly any." The decline in press confidence occurs gradually, except between the 1991 and 1993 surveys, when it is somewhat steeper. Only a small portion of this early 1990s dip is mirrored in declining average confidence.[17]

Beyond the GSS, a variety of other surveys from the mid-1990s onward also reflect the institutional press's new unpopularity. For instance, a 1995 Times Mirror poll found that only 25% of respondents agreed that "[t]he news media helps society to solve its problems," while 71% instead agreed that "[t]he news media gets in the way of society solving its problems" (Sanford 1999). A 1997 survey sponsored by the Freedom

[17] Institutions included in the average calculation are all institutions, other than the press, where confidence was probed in every GSS from 1973 to 2008: major companies, organized religion, education, the executive branch, organized labor, medicine, television, the Supreme Court, the scientific community, Congress, and the military. Results are very similar if one uses the first principle component, rather than the mean, to summarize confidence in all other institutions.

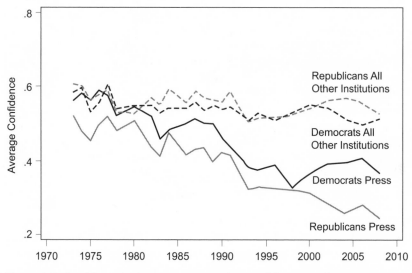

Figure 4-5. Confidence in the press compared to confidence in other institutions among Democrats and Republicans, 1973–2008. *Source and note*: See figure 4-4.

Forum's Newseum found that 62% of respondents thought the press was "too manipulated by special interests" and 63% thought news reporting was too influenced by "the profit motive" (Emery, Emery, and Roberts 2000, 481). A 2004 survey by the *Chronicle of Higher Education* found that only 10% of respondents had "a great deal" of confidence in the "national news media," while 49% had "some." These numbers are lower than those for most other groups in the *Chronicle*'s confidence battery but about the same as those for lawyers, in which 9% had "a great deal," and 49% had "some" confidence (2004). Finally, a 2007 survey by the Pew Research Center for the People and the Press found that only 39% of respondents thought "news organizations" "get the facts straight" and only 31% thought they were "careful to avoid bias" (Pew Research Center for the People and the Press 2007).

The decline in confidence in the institutional press has occurred in both parties and is only modestly larger among Republicans. Figure 4-5 shows confidence in the press compared to average confidence, as in figure 4-4, but now with each calculated separately for Democrats and Republicans. In both parties, confidence in the press has declined over time both in absolute terms and relative to other institutions. Democrats consistently have more confidence than Republicans, but the partisan gap varies over time. It is fairly modest from 1973 through the mid-1990s, drops to essentially nothing in 1998 when Democratic confidence falls following the

Monica Lewinsky scandal, then reaches its largest margin in the 2000s. Still, even though press confidence is higher among Democrats than Republicans in the 2000s, Democratic press confidence is still notably lower than for other institutions and lower than it was in the 1970s.

The ANES did not measure public opinion toward the news media between 1956 and the 1990s, when much of the decline in press confidence took place. In the 1993 ANES Pilot Study, a striking 83% of respondents agreed with the statement "Media coverage of politics often reflects the media's own biases more than facts." In 1996, 1998, 2000, and 2004, ANES surveys asked respondents, "How much of the time do you think you can trust the media to report the news fairly (just about always, most of the time, only some of the time, or almost never)?" Thirty-seven percent trusted the media "just about always" or "most of the time" in both 1996 and 1998. That portion increased to 48% in 2000 but dropped back to 35% in 2004. As in 1956, these ANES surveys are particularly useful because they contain objective political knowledge questions, which provide a good measure of awareness of political news and discourse. Figure 4-6 illustrates the relationship among media trust, partisanship, and political awareness in the 1993, 1996, 1998, 2000, and 2004 ANES surveys.[18] Here, we see that the partisan gap in news media trust, which we observed in the GSS data as well, is concentrated (at least in the past few decades) among the most politically aware. In each year, more politically aware Democrats have more trust than more politically aware Republicans, with the gap increasing with awareness. In contrast, on the lower end of the political awareness scale the relationship between partisanship and media trust shows no consistent pattern. In 1993, 1998, and 2004, Republicans have more media trust than Democrats among the less aware, but that relationship is reversed in 1996 and 2000.

PEOPLE STILL HAVE CLEAR OPINIONS ABOUT THE MEDIA AS AN INSTITUTION

What does it mean when someone expresses negative views toward the media in a poll? Given the fragmentation of the American media landscape in the past 40 years, one might wonder what now springs to mind when people are asked about "the media," "the news media," "the press" as an "institution," or something similar. Are people confused about which parts of the diverse media landscape survey researchers are asking

---

[18] While the 2008 ANES also included a question about media trust, results from that survey are not included in figure 4-6 because the ANES staff had not completed coding responses to the objective knowledge questions at the time this manuscript went to press.

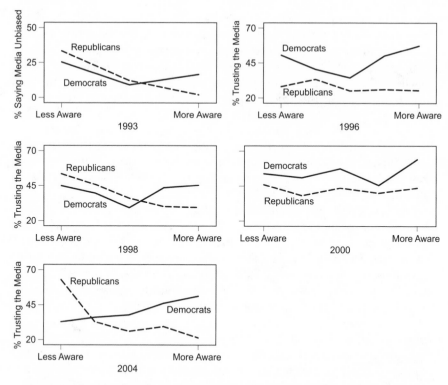

Figure 4-6. Levels of media trust across partisans diverge among the most politically aware. *Note*: In the top left panel, the vertical axis represents the percentage disagreeing with the following statement: "Media coverage of politics often reflects the media's own biases more than facts." In the other four panels, the vertical axis represents the percentage saying that they "trust the media to report the news fairly" "most of the time" or "just about always." In all panels, the horizontal axis represents political awareness, which is measured by a series of objective political knowledge questions. Because knowledge questions were not asked in 1993, I use questions from the 1992 ANES, which all 1993 respondents took part in. *Source*: 1996, 1998, 2000, and 2004 ANES Time Series Surveys; 1993 ANES Pilot Study.

them to evaluate? Do people no longer have views on the news media as an institution but only opinions about particular outlets? If either of these is true, the responses to questions about media trust could be particularly weakly held opinions or entirely constructed on the spot, what Phillip Converse (1964) labeled "nonattitudes."

Psychologists conventionally define an attitude as "a psychological tendency that is expressed by evaluating a particular entity with some degree of favor or disfavor" (Eagly and Chaiken 1993).[19] In this case, the attitude object is the news media as an institution, an abstract concept representing a series of major news organizations and journalists that aspire to the standards of professional journalism. This is what Starr (2004, XI) refers to as "a set of powerful institutions ('the media') that, much to the despair of grammarians, people generally speak of in the singular rather than the plural."

Despite these justifiable concerns, the evidence suggests that most Americans have relatively clear and firmly held attitudes toward the institutional news media. First, survey questions about the news media prompt an unusually low percentage of refusals or "don't know" responses. In the 2004 ANES, only 1 respondent out of the 1,066 asked refused to answer the media trust question and only 1 answered "don't know," producing refusal and "don't know" rates of 0.09% each. When asked the media trust question in the 2008 ANES, 6 of 2,322 respondents (or 0.26%) answered "don't know," and no one refused. As communication scholar Yariv Tsfati (2002, 67) has documented, rates of "don't know" and refusal for questions about the news media are consistently less than 1% and sometimes essentially zero in the ANES and a variety of other surveys.

Second, opinions about the news media are relatively consistent across different question wordings. As I have mentioned, poll responses are notoriously sensitive to small changes in question wording. To take just a few famous examples, respondents have given notably different responses when asked whether government should "forbid" versus "not allow" a communist to give a speech, whether money should be spent on "saving social security" or just on "social security," or whether it was a good idea to fight "the Korean War" or to send "troops to stop the communist invasion" of South Korea (Mueller 1973; Rasinski 1989; Schulman and Presser 1996 [1981]). Different survey organizations ask questions about the news media in quite different formats. Among the questions we have already looked at, the GSS asks about "the press" as part of a question battery probing "confidence" in "the people running these institutions," while the ANES asks in several years whether respondents "trust the media to report the news fairly" and employs several other wordings in various years. Are these questions and the others asked by other organization all tapping essentially the same predisposition?

Usefully, the 1998 ANES included three different questions where respondents evaluated the news media. In addition to the media trust

---

[19] Definitions by other authors are similar. For example, Crano and Prislin (2006, 347) define an attitude as "an evaluative integration of cognitions and affects experienced in relation to an object."

question, it asked respondents to place the "news media" on a "feeling thermometer" running from 0 to 100, and it asked if they "approve[d] or disapprove[d] of how the news media is handling these allegations (that President Clinton lied under oath about his affair with Monica Lewinsky)?"

As Figure 4-7 shows, responses to these three questions are substantially correlated. Those trusting the news media "just about always" have an average thermometer rating of 71, while those trusting the media "almost never" have an average rating of 29. Even though the Lewinsky question asks about coverage of a specific story for which one might expect coverage to be more aggravating to Democrats, who usually express more trust in the media than others, it is still positively correlated with the other two questions, although by a slightly smaller magnitude. Those who strongly approve of the Lewinsky coverage give the news media an average thermometer rating of 65, while those who strongly disapprove of the Lewinsky coverage give an average rating of 45.

In several instances, it is possible for us to go further and see whether responses are consistent when both different wordings are used and the questions are asked years apart. As part of the 1992–96 ANES Panel Study, about 450 respondents were asked both whether they agreed that "[m]edia coverage of politics often reflects the media's own biases more than facts" in 1993 and the media trust question in 1996. Figure 4-8 shows that, even though these questions are worded very differently and were asked three years apart, responses are still substantially correlated.

In another example, as part of the 2000–2004 ANES Panel Study, over 900 respondents who were asked the media trust question in 2000 were also asked the news media thermometer question in 2002, and over 700 were asked the thermometer question again in 2004. Figure 4-9 shows that responses to these three questions are also substantially correlated. Those trusting the media "just about always" in 2000 give the news media an average rating of 61 in 2002 and 62 in 2004. In contrast, those trusting the media "almost never" in 2000 give the media an average rating of 39 in 2002 and 27 in 2004.

Overall, attitudes toward the media do not seem to be overly sensitive to even major changes in question wording.[20] Furthermore, the stability of these responses over time suggests they are not transient reactions to recent events or news coverage. The 2000–2004 panel data are particularly illustrative of this. Between 2000 and 2004, the party holding the presidency changed, partisan control of the Senate changed twice, the terrorist attacks

---

[20] On the correlation of responses to different media evaluation questions, see also Kohring and Matthes (2007).

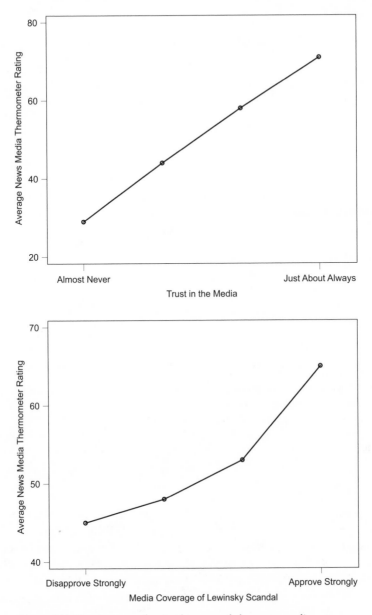

Figure 4-7. Consistency of attitudes toward the news media across question wordings. *Note*: The bivariate unstandardized regression coefficient of news media trust on thermometer is 0.0048 with a standard error of 0.0003. The Pearson's *r* correlation between these questions is .45. The bivariate unstandardized regression coefficient of opinion of scandal coverage on thermometer is 0.003 with a standard error of 0.0004. The Pearson's *r* correlation between these questions is .23. *Source*: 1998 ANES.

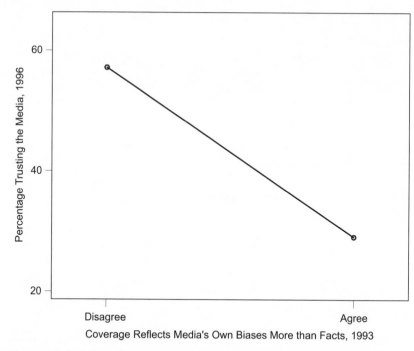

Figure 4-8. Stability of news media attitudes over time, 1993–96. *Note*: The bivariate unstandardized regression coefficient of 1996 media trust on 1993 perceptions of bias is -0.266, with a standard error of 0.037. The Pearson's *r* correlation between these questions is -.310. Respondents are coded as trusting the media if they said they trusted the media "just about always" or "most of the time" in 1996. *Source*: 1992–96 ANES Panel Study.

of September 11, 2001, transformed U.S. national security policy and altered everyday life in countless small ways, and the United States embarked on major wars in Afghanistan and Iraq. Yet those who distrusted the news media in 2000 still gave the media much lower ratings in 2002 and 2004, in response to a question with a different wording and format.

When Evaluating "The Media," Most People Think about the Accuracy and Bias of Institutional News Sources in General

While we have seen that people have relatively firm opinions about the news media, it is not yet clear what these opinions mean. The media as an institution is an abstract attitude object. It is not located in a designated place like Congress or the executive branch. It is reasonable to wonder

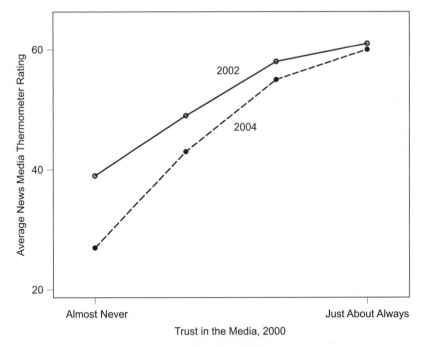

Figure 4-9. Stability of news media attitudes over time, 2000–2004. *Note*: The bivariate unstandardized regression coefficient of 2002 thermometer on 2000 media trust is 25.0, with a standard error of 2.5. The Pearson's *r* correlation between these questions is .31. The bivariate unstandardized regression coefficient of 2004 thermometer on 2000 media trust is 35.2 with a standard error of 2.9. The Pearson's *r* correlation between these questions is .40. *Source*: 2000–2004 ANES Panel Study.

what people are thinking about when they provide answers to closed-ended survey questions about the news media. To investigate this, I used a specially designed sequence of survey questions. In a survey conducted through Knowledge Networks, Inc., an academic and commercial survey firm, each respondent in a nationally representative sample of 1,018 was randomly assigned to be asked one of three different closed-ended questions about the news media.[21] These were the ANES media trust ques-

[21] The interviews were conducted March 8–10, 2005. The questions analyzed here were asked as part of a survey that included other questions unrelated to politics or the news media. Knowledge Networks draws its samples using random digit dialing. Those who agreed to participate were given a free television with Internet access in exchange for periodically answering commercial and academic surveys. Data from Knowledge Networks and other firms with similar methodologies have gained increasing prominence in political

tion, a media "feeling thermometer" question identical to the one I use in an experiment described in chapter 5 and similar to that used in the ANES, and the GSS's press confidence question.[22] For all respondents, the very next question asked, "Still thinking about the question you just answered, I'd like you to tell me what came to mind as you were answering that question. Exactly what things went through your mind?" After people finished answering this, they were asked, "Any others?" and given another opportunity to respond. Open-ended responses to the initial question and the follow-up were recorded for each respondent.

This format is very similar to the "retrospective" "memory dump" questions used by public opinion scholars John Zaller and Stanley Feldman (1992) to measure the "considerations" that come to mind when people answer survey questions (see also Zaller 1992). Zaller and Feldman argue that, on any subject, people "carry around in their heads a mix of only partially consistent ideas and considerations." When they are asked in a survey to evaluate an attitude object, they "call to mind a sample of these ideas . . . and use them to choose among the options offered" (Zaller and Feldman 1992, 580).

In exploring what considerations come to mind when respondents answer these three different questions about the news media, I address several concerns. First, I test whether people are confused about what to evaluate when asked about the news media in general or as an institution. Has the fragmentation of the media industry rendered these types of questions obsolete? Second, I test whether different question wordings, in addition to producing correlated responses as we saw in the last section, also bring to mind a similar mix of considerations? Only if they do can we say, by Zaller and Feldman's definition, that they measure essentially the same opinion.

The open-ended responses were coded by two of my research assistants, Danielle Bush and Amanda Spears.[23] For each respondent, the coders read their complete open-ended comments and recorded whether they mentioned any of 12 different media attributes. The coders were instructed not

---

science research (Hillygus and Jackman 2003; Clinton and Lapinski 2004; Hillygus 2005; Clinton 2006; Prior 2007). More details on Knowledge Networks's sampling techniques are available on its website, http://www.knowledgenetworks.com/ganp/index.html.

[22] As reassurance that the random assignment was executed correctly, the groups assigned to the three different questions were not substantially different in partisanship or education and were of similar size, with 339 given the media trust question, 331 given the thermometer question, and 344 given the press confidence question.

[23] This coding was blind, in that the research assistants were not told the purpose of the research project until all coding was completed. Written coding instructions are available from the author.

to treat the categories as mutually exclusive but rather to code as many attributes as were mentioned. Figure 4-10 presents the results.

This figure illustrates two important things about the considerations that make up people's attitudes toward the media. First, there is very little difference among the thoughts brought to mind by the different question wordings. This, along with the evidence in the previous section, indicates that opinions toward the news media are relatively firmly held. Second, the two types of thoughts mentioned by far most frequently both relate to the trustworthiness of the information the media provide. These were thoughts about news accuracy, which were mentioned by 41% of respondents, and thoughts about general bias or too much opinion overall, which were mentioned by 22% of respondents. Every other type of comment was made by less than 10% of the sample.

For example, here are the comments of an independent who gave the news media a thermometer rating of 40 and was coded as mentioning accuracy: "You cannot believe everything you read. Sometimes the media stretches the truth and clouds some stories that you don't know if it [is] true or not." Here is another independent, who gave the media a thermometer rating of 60 and also mentioned accuracy: "I think they try to report as close to facts as they can. Sometimes I think in some cases they give too much info." A Democratic-leaning independent, who had "only some" confidence in the press and was coded as mentioning accuracy, said, "The institution is manipulative, doesn't always give the full story, uses information to benefit itself instead of the cause of others." Another Democratic-leaning independent, who was coded as mentioning sensationalism, accuracy, and general bias even though he gave a thermometer rating of 70, said, "I think the news media tries to be fair and accurate, but those that control the purse strings are affected by what they perceive as what the public wants and what draws in an audience (what makes money)—sensationalism, hype and sound bytes." A weak Democrat who trusted the media "only some of the time" and was coded as mentioning both accuracy and general bias simply said, "I think that a lot of the media has their own biases that come through when they report the news—particularly in the area of politics." Another weak Democrat who had "hardly any" confidence in the press and was coded as mentioning accuracy and Republican bias said, "The press has not written the truth since Bush has been in office. [Any others?] That they are afraid to speak against this administration."

Turning to the other side of the political spectrum, a Republican-leaning independent who trusted the media "only some of the time" said this in a comment coded in the accuracy and general bias categories: "They seem to tell us whatever they think we want to hear and what will keep us watching them! [Any others?] They should not have a good

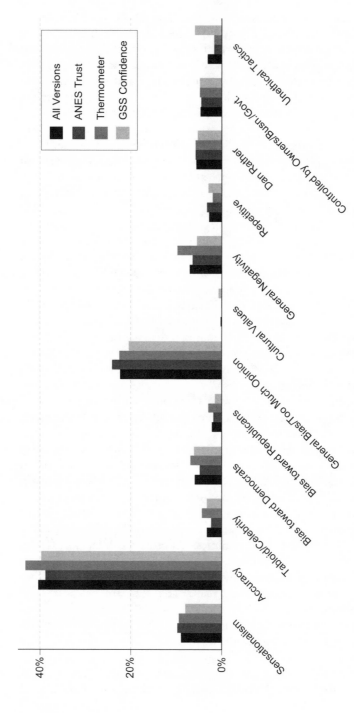

Figure 4-10. Different media evaluation questions prompt respondents to think about similar media attributes. *Note*: The vertical axis indicates the percentage of respondents mentioning the given media attribute in response to the open-ended "memory dump" question. The horizontal axis provides the categories of media attributes. The shaded bars indicate the media evaluation question respondents were asked before the "memory dump." *Source*: Survey conducted March 8–14, 2005, by Knowledge Networks, Inc. See the chapter 4 appendix for the questionnaire.

or bad opinion—just the news!" A strong Republican who had "only some" confidence in the press and was coded as mentioning accuracy said, "Sometimes the facts are distorted. They run to the press too fast before the facts are ironed out." A weak Republican who had "hardly any" confidence in the press and was coded as mentioning accuracy and Democratic bias said, "The press always lies. They'll always dig up dirt on the Republican and then try to cover up and things that will hurt the Democrat. This is starting to become a good against evil. The press is evil."

Of course, not everyone shared only negative thoughts about the news media. Some people rated the media more positively, and their thoughts in response to the open-ended probe reflected that. For instance, here are the comments of a strong Democrat who gave a thermometer rating of 60 and was coded as mentioning accuracy: "Very few times has word come out that a news story is false. Sometimes the story is presented in a way that that the reader may misunderstand." In another example, a weak Democrat who gave a thermometer rating of 85 said, "I feel that the media does a pretty good job with reporting what's going on in the world. I know that there are some things that go on behind the scenes, but they have done pretty good on reporting the war in Iraq. [Any others?] Yes, they are getting better in showing us things that happen here in America as they happen. They are staying on top of things a lot better."

Besides media attributes, my research assistants also coded the comments for any mention of specific media outlets or types of media outlets. Again, these categories are not mutually exclusive; each person's comments were coded in as many categories as applied to them. The results, presented in Figure 4-11, again show very small differences across question wordings.[24] However, the most striking finding in Figure 4-11 is how infrequent mentions of specific outlets or types of media were. The most frequently mentioned type of media was television in general, mentioned by only 7% of respondents. Eighty percent of respondents made no comments about any specific media outlet or type of media. In contrast, only 29% of respondents did not mention any media attribute. Comments about newer, alternative media outlets were particularly rare. Talk radio and the Internet were mentioned by 0.5% and 0.6% of respondents, respectively. The most frequently mentioned category that could be considered alternative media was Fox News/conservative cable talk shows,

---

[24] The biggest percentage-point difference across wordings is the difference between the thermometer question and the GSS confidence question in prompting comments about television in general. The thermometer question prompted 9% of the sample to comment about television in general, while the confidence question prompted 5% to comment about it.

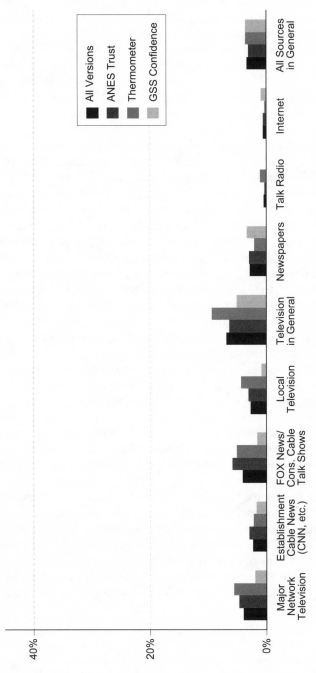

Figure 4-11. Media evaluation questions prompt respondents to think about few specific media outlets or types of media. *Note*: The vertical axis indicates the percentage of respondents mentioning the given type of media in response to the open-ended "memory dump" question. The horizontal axis indicates the different types of media. The shaded bars indicate the media evaluation questions respondents were asked before the "memory dump." *Source*: 2000–2004 ANES Panel Study.

which was mentioned by only 4% of the sample. However, even on the few occasions when alternative outlets such as Fox News were mentioned, it is almost always clear from the context of the responses that these outlets were not considered part of "the media."

Instead, people mentioned outlets like Fox News in order to draw a contrast between their feelings toward them and their feelings toward the institutional media, which they had just evaluated. For instance, a strong Democrat who gave the news media a thermometer rating of 75 said, "Some networks do a better job at being fair than others. For example, Fox News network claims to be 'fair and balanced,' but it is obvious that they are pro-Republican." This respondent's thermometer rating indicates that he or she trusts the institutional news media, which he or she sees as perfectly consistent with disliking Fox News. Similarly, a strong Republican gave the news media a thermometer rating of 30 and, when asked for his or her thoughts, said, "Dan Rather, Republican election exit polls. [Any others?] The news is very pro-liberal except Fox News." Another strong Republican who had "hardly any" confidence in the press said, "The last Presidential election coverage by the old mainstream media was so against President Bush it was terrible. Dan Rather was shameful! [Any others?] I am glad there is Fox cable news. I think Brit Hume is trustworthy."

Overall, very few people think about any specific media outlets when asked these media evaluation questions, and even fewer think about any alternative media. Those who do think about alternative media outlets consider them as a contrast to the institutional news outlets and professional journalism in general. They base their evaluations of "the press," "the news media," or just "the media" on their reactions to these latter objects.

Finally, we can also use these open-ended questions to see if Republicans, Democrats, and independents think about different considerations when they express opinions about the media. Figure 4-12 shows the prevalence of thoughts about different media attributes among Republicans, Democrats, and independents. It shows that the two most frequent types of comments, those about accuracy and those about general bias and too much opinion, were less common among independents than among partisans on both sides. Thus, in general, partisans are more likely to make comments concerning the trustworthiness of media information. The only other notable partisan differences were Republicans' greater propensities to mention bias toward Democrats, general negativity, Dan Rather, and sensationalism. Figure 4-13 reveals very little difference in the frequency of thoughts about specific types of media among Republicans, Democrats, and independents, although this is largely because very few people have these thoughts, whatever their party identification.

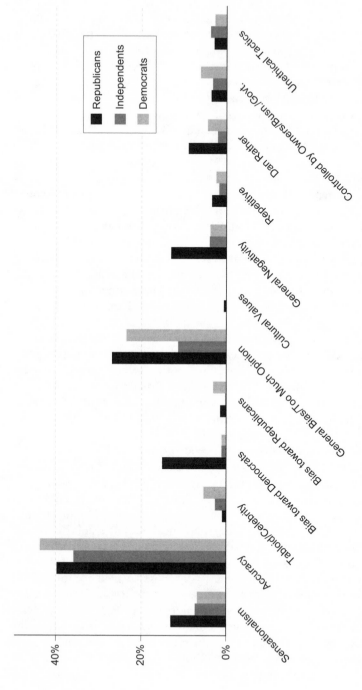

Figure 4-12. Few partisan differences in the media attributes people think about when answering media evaluation questions. *Note:* The vertical axis indicates the percentage of respondents mentioning the given media attribute in response to the open-ended "memory dump" question. The horizontal axis provides the categories of media attributes. *Source:* 2000–2004 ANES Panel Study.

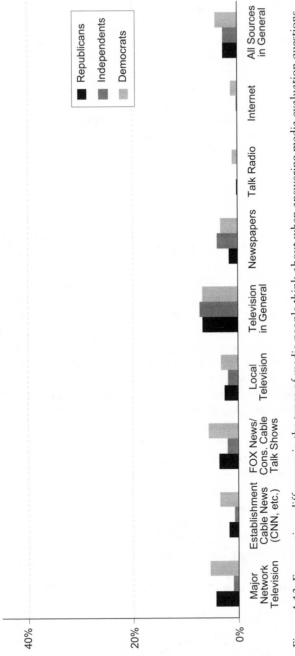

Figure 4-13. Few partisan differences in the types of media people think about when answering media evaluation questions. *Note:* The vertical axis indicates the percentage of respondents mentioning the given type of media in response to the open-ended "memory dump" question. The horizontal axis indicates the different types of media. *Source:* 2000–2004 ANES Panel Study.

Finally, one thing the coders did not find is also important. Only 2 of the 1,018 respondents (or 0.002%) said in their open-ended comments that the media evaluation questions were difficult to understand or too vague in a fragmented media world or complained about the questions in any other way. No one seemed to think, with all the different media options now available, that opinions about the media in general or (as in the GSS question) as an "institution" were no longer relevant. Instead, most people seemed to think they knew what the question meant and had something to say about it. Tsfati (2002, 67) found similar reactions when he asked 267 respondents to provide open-ended comments about "the press and journalists" and "the media." Only 1 of his interviewees (or 0.003%) asked for clarification of what the question meant.

The American people seem to have relatively firm opinions about the news media. They do not merely have views about specific news sources. Looking at the correlation between responses to media questions with very different wordings, the stability of these responses over time, the infrequency of people thinking of specific media outlets—especially alternative outlets—when answering these questions, and the fact that hardly anyone complained about (or refused to answer) these general questions, it is hard to disagree with Tsfati's (2002, 38; 2003, 68) claims that "people have some mental schema for what 'the media' are" and "media skepticism relates to the mainstream media as a whole rather than to a particular source." Furthermore, the open-ended survey responses indicate that when people do think of alternative outlets, they see them as the antithesis of the thing they are evaluating in these questions. Opinions on these questions are based on reactions to institutional, professional journalism, something that, in this age of fragmented media, people seem to feel as strongly about as ever.

In this chapter, we have seen that the news media, which became institutionalized through professionalization and homogenization in the early twentieth century, underwent more dramatic changes in the increasingly polarized political environment of the later 20th and early 21st centuries. Alternative media outlets increasingly challenged traditional journalism, both competing against it for consumers and disregarding its professional norms. At the same time, with the political system becoming more polarized, the traditional news media faced public criticism from politicians and activists on both sides of the political spectrum, much of it coming through alternative news outlets. As this happened, confidence in the media as an institution declined dramatically. In today's political environment, the merits of the institutional news media are a subject of intense public debate and strongly held opinions among the mass public. In the next chapter, I more carefully investigate what factors influence these opinions.

Appendix

Question 1

(There are three different versions of question 1. Each subject has a one in three probability of receiving each different version.)

Version A: "How much of the time do you think you can trust the media to report the news fairly, just about always, most of the time, only some of the time, or almost never?"

A. Just About Always
B. Most of the Time
C. Only Some of the Time
D. Almost Never

Version B: "We'd like you to rate on a scale from 0 to 100 whether you think the news media reports the news accurately and fairly. Zero means very unfavorable, and 100 means very favorable. Fifty means you do not feel favorable or unfavorable. You may use any number from 0 to 100. Where on this scale would you rate the accuracy and fairness of news media reporting?"

Rating: _____

Version C: "I am going to name an institution in this country. The institution is the press. As far as people running this institution are concerned, would you say you have a great deal of confidence, only some confidence, or hardly any confidence at all?"

A. A Great Deal of Confidence
B. Only Some Confidence
C. Hardly Any Confidence

Question 2

"Still thinking about the question you just answered, I'd like you to tell me what came to mind as you were answering that question. Exactly what things went through your mind?"

Question 3

"Any others?"

Sources of Antipathy toward the News Media

TODAY, A LARGE PORTION of the American public distrusts the news media as an institution. This has led to considerable debate about why media trust has declined nationwide since the mid-twentieth century and, relatedly, what causes individual people to distrust the media. This chapter considers several possibilities, including the hostile media phenomenon and exposure to news negativity, horserace coverage, tabloid coverage, and elite partisan media criticism. I investigate potential causes by considering the patterns found in chapter 4, results from two survey experiments, and the effects of exposure to alternative media outlets. The evidence indicates that elite partisan media criticism and tabloid coverage reduce media trust. These variables likely played large roles in the decline of media trust over recent decades.

THERE ARE SEVERAL POSSIBLE EXPLANATIONS FOR THE PUBLIC'S ANTIPATHY TOWARD THE NEWS MEDIA

With opinions toward the institutional news media becoming more negative over time, a variety of observers, including journalists, psychologists, political scientists, and communication scholars, have wondered what produces antipathy toward the media. They have proposed several possibilities. One is known as the "hostile media phenomenon" or the "hostile media effect." This is the tendency of people with divergent prior opinions on an issue, when consuming the exact same news report, all to view that report as biased against their views (Vallone, Ross, and Lepper 1985; Perloff 1989; Giner-Sorolla and Chaiken 1993; Christen, Kannaovakun, and Gunther 2002; Chia et al. 2007). Evidence of the phenomenon has been replicated by several researchers and for several topics.

However, there are reasons to doubt that the hostile media phenomenon can explain changes in press confidence over time. First, multiple studies find that it occurs only among those with strong views on, and deep involvement in, the topic of the news report. For instance, psychologists Robert P. Vallone, Lee Ross, and Mark R. Lepper (1985) observed the phenomenon when showing members of pro-Arab and pro-Israeli student groups a report on a massacre of civilians in a refugee camp in southern Lebanon. However, in studies where the viewers are not heavily involved in the issue covered, the hostile media phenomenon largely disappears (Vallone, Ross, and Lepper 1985; Perloff 1989; Giner-Sorolla and Chaiken 1993).

In addition, when the phenomenon does occur, a large portion of it results from respondents' preexisting beliefs about media bias (Giner-Sorolla and Chaiken 1993). Studies not specifically examining the hostile media phenomenon also find that prior beliefs about a source greatly influence perceptions of bias in its news reports, regardless of the content of those reports (Turner 2007; Anand and Tella 2008; Baum and Gussin 2008). Thus, while there is a small tendency for any news exposure to cause committed activists to trust the media less, the hostile media phenomenon mostly demonstrates that existing opinions about the media are firmly held and influential. It does not tell us where these existing opinions come from.

Another possibility is that negative attitudes toward the news media are caused by reactions to specific styles of news coverage. Journalist and media commentator Howard Kurtz expressed this commonly held belief when he lamented, "I think we bear 95 percent of the responsibility for the low repute in which we are held" (Shaw 1996; cited in Cappella and Jamieson 1997, 240). Similarly, former *New York Times* columnist Frank Rich (2005) claims, "What's missing from News is the news. On ABC, Peter Jennings devotes two hours of prime time to playing peek-a-boo with U.F.O. fanatics, a whorish stunt crafted to deliver ratings, not information. On NBC, Brian Williams is busy as all get-out, as every promo reminds us, 'Reporting America's Story.' That story just happens to be the relentless branding of Brian Williams as America's anchorman—a guy just too in love with Folks Like Us to waste his time looking closely at, say, anything happening in Washington." More specifically, at various times, commentators have claimed that several styles of news coverage produce media distrust. These styles fall into three categories.

First, some argue that consumption of negative and cynical political coverage creates antipathy toward the press (Sabato 1991; Jamieson 1992; Patterson 1993; Fallows 1996; Lichter and Noyes 1996; Cappella and Jamieson 1997; Sabato 2000). The press often plays the role of "critic of the established order" (Gronke and Cook 2002, 9), while reporters producing positive coverage are often derided by their peers as "shills" or "in the tank" (Cappella and Jamieson 1997, 31).[1] Furthermore, coverage of political candidates became increasingly negative

---

[1] Negativity may hurt the media's popularity because Americans tend to dislike disagreement and criticism in their political institutions (see, e.g., Hibbing and Theiss-Morse 1995, 2002).

over the same decades when confidence in the press declined (Patterson 1993, 20).[2]

A second and related school of thought claims that antipathy toward the media results from consuming news about the "game" of politics, such as politicians' strategies, poll results, and the campaign horserace generally, rather than policy. During these same recent decades, what Thomas Patterson (1993, 74) labels "policy schema" coverage has declined and what he calls "game schema" coverage has proliferated. Along similar lines, W. Lance Bennett, Regina G. Lawrence, and Steven Livingston (2007, 170) argue that "[t]he core preoccupation with power and partisan gamesmanship is largely what turns citizens off about their own government and the news messengers who seem implicated in the game."

A third possible source of media distrust is tabloid-style news. In this view, conventional news outlets' coverage of celebrities, sex scandals, and other topics once largely confined to the tabloids reduces trust in the media. This explanation is plausible because this trend in coverage has also grown over the same recent decades (Emery, Emery, and Roberts 2000, 479–85; West 2001, 104–6).[3]

The claims about the effects of all three styles of coverage are plausible. All three have increased over the same time period that confidence in the press has declined. Also, all three could help explain the widespread decline in positive media evaluations because each could plausibly affect all segments of the public. However, we should be cautious about drawing firm conclusions based on aggregate-level trends over time. It is worth investigating further by looking for individual-level causal connections between these styles of coverage and media distrust.

---

[2] Cappella and Jameson (1997, 139–59, 214–15) find that cynicism about politics is correlated with cynicism about the media. They also use an experiment to test the effect of cynical news coverage on an index of political cynicism. However, they did not experimentally test the effect of cynical coverage on attitudes toward the news media.

On the other hand, several recent experimental studies cast doubt on the notion that contentious, televised political debate affects attitudes toward the media. Arceneaux and Johnson (2007) fail to find a significant effect of viewing a contentious cable political talk show on general media trust, while Mutz and Reeves (2005) find that uncivil political debate has no detectable effect on evaluations of a television program's informativeness and actually increases assessments of how entertaining it is.

[3] Sensationalist coverage may be as good (or better) at informing the public (Baum 2002, 2003b; Zaller 2003; Baum and Jamison 2006), but consuming this type of news may still reduce consumers' respect for the news media. In her in-depth interviews with a small group of citizens over the course of a presidential campaign, Graber (1984) finds a tendency among her subjects to complain about the simplification and triviality of news while still choosing to consume that type of news rather than seeking more substantive media outlets. Tsfati and Cappella (2005) examine this tendency to watch news programs one reports disliking and find it to be concentrated among those high in "need for cognition."

Another possibility is that negative attitudes toward the media result from people viewing news that is biased against their predispositions. This claim is often implicitly or explicitly made in partisan books and articles attacking the institutional media, such as those mentioned in chapter 4. These critics claim that institutional news media coverage is biased in a liberal (if the commentator is conservative) or conservative (if the commentator is liberal) direction and that viewing this bias causes public distrust. While these claims are also plausible, we must again be cautious because we lack statistical evidence even of an association between exposure to biased news and antipathy toward the press, let alone evidence that such an association is causal. Still, looking for such evidence is certainly worthwhile.

These are the most common explanations for negative public attitudes toward the media. Yet, if we look beyond examinations of the media and toward scholarship on public opinion more generally, we find another possibility. Research on the formation of mass opinion is vast, but one of its most consistent findings is that elite rhetoric can influence opinions, especially among those who are politically aware and have the same political predispositions as the messenger.

To take just a few examples, the opinions of politically aware citizens tended to follow (over time) the rhetoric of political elites who shared their predispositions during World War II (Berinsky 2007, 2009), the Vietnam War (Zaller 1991; 1992, 102–3), and the first (Zaller 1994) and second (Jacobson 2007) Gulf Wars. When unsure of their opinion, many people seem to take cues from the positions of like-minded political elites (Brady and Sniderman 1985; Popkin 1991; Sniderman, Brody, and Tetlock 1991; Lupia 1994; Lupia et al. 2007). Panel surveys show that when citizens' opinions do not match the stances of the party they identify with, their opinions tend to move into conformity with their partisanship, while partisanship tends to resist change (W. Miller 1999; Lenz 2009). Experiments tend to find that people are much more receptive to political persuasion from those they perceive as knowledgeable and sharing their ideology (Lupia and McCubbins 1998). In one series of experiments, liberals and conservatives tended to support whatever welfare policy politicians from their own political party supported, even when that policy was contrary to their respective ideologies (G. Cohen 2003). Thus, in addition to the plausible sources of negative media evaluations put forward in books and articles about the news media, it is possible that these attitudes are shaped through elite opinion leadership.[4]

---

[4] Several studies find evidence consistent with elite opinion leadership on attitudes toward the media. Watts et al. (1999) find that perceptions of media bias in presidential campaigns are more strongly related to claims of bias by campaigners and opinion

In the remaining three sections of this chapter, I explore the sources of negative attitudes toward the news media. First, I use two survey experiments to test a variety of possible causal variables. Second, I examine one way that elite opinion leadership occurs: persuasive media criticism by alternative media outlets. In the final section, I draw conclusions based on the evidence in this chapter and the patterns presented in chapter 4.

In considering the effects of different variables, political predispositions will play a large role. In the public opinion literature, two types of predispositions tend to be most important in determining when opinion change occurs: partisanship and political awareness.[5] While the importance of partisanship is widely accepted, political awareness is often underappreciated outside of public opinion scholarship. Awareness is best measured with a series of objective political knowledge questions, such as naming which party holds the majority in Congress and identifying the vice president, Supreme Court chief justice, speaker of the House, and so on (Zaller 1985; 1992, appendix; Price and Zaller 1993), but education can often be used effectively as a proxy (e.g., Zaller 1994; Berinsky 2007, 2009). The politically aware are both more likely to be exposed to news and political discourse and more likely to respond to those messages based on their partisanship (see Zaller 1992). Upon receiving a message, the politically aware are more likely than the unaware to be persuaded when the message comes from their party, but they are less likely than the unaware to be persuaded when the message comes from the opposite party. Beyond that, the aware tend to have more consistent ideologies across issues (P. Converse 1964) and more overall interest in politics (Zaller 1992).

Consequently, when looking for elite opinion leadership, we should expect to find elite criticism's largest effects among politically aware partisans of the same party as the media critic. Also, when looking for effects

---

commentators than to the tone of news coverage of the candidates. Gunther (1992) finds that political engagement, which can expose citizens to elite messages (Zaller 1992, 1996), is strongly related to perceptions of newspaper bias. Also, perceptions of news bias tend to correlate with discussion with ideologically similar individuals, where elite messages can be spread, but not with political discussion in general (Eveland and Shah 2003).

Dalton, Beck, and Huckfeldt (1998) find that, during a presidential campaign, Republicans and Democrats both perceive local newspaper coverage as biased against them, regardless of the actual slant of that coverage. This could be consistent with either the hostile media phenomenon or elite opinion leadership.

[5] The seminal works making this point are by Converse (1962, 1964) and Zaller (1992). Following Zaller (1992), here I use the term *awareness* interchangeably with similar terms like *sophistication* and *engagement*. Though, in theory, these terms could denote different attributes, in the literature they are usually treated synonymously because they are so highly correlated among the mass public.

of consuming biased political coverage, we might expect politically aware partisans to be the most responsive to the direction of bias. Finally, it is also worth checking whether the effects of different styles of coverage depend on political awareness and partisanship, even though we have less clear expectations of what the relationship may be.

PARTISAN RHETORIC AND TABLOID NEWS REDUCE MEDIA TRUST: EVIDENCE FROM TWO SURVEY EXPERIMENTS

One way to test possible sources of negative attitudes toward the media is with an experiment. Experiments, where treatments are randomly manipulated by the researcher, are generally considered the best research design for drawing causal conclusions (D. Rubin 1974; Holland 1986; Green and Gerber 2002; McDermott 2002; Shadish, Cook, and Campbell 2002).[6] Here, I employ two survey experiments. This involves randomly assigning survey respondents different versions of survey probes and then measuring the effects on subsequent responses. An advantage of survey experiments, which has made them increasingly popular in political science and psychology, is that it is easier to conduct them with nationally representative samples, allowing one to generalize to the entire population more confidently. In contrast, it is very difficult to conduct a conventional laboratory experiment with a nationally representative sample of subjects (Piazza, Sniderman, and Tetlock 1989; Sniderman and Grob 1996).[7]

These experiments are based on defining an attitude as the sum of the considerations at the "top of the head" when responding to a survey question, as explained in chapter 4. People's opinions change when they

[6] The chief advantages of experiments are in largely avoiding reverse causation, omitted variable bias, and measurement error in the independent variables.

[7] Besides experiments (or an instrumental variables model as in the next section), there are several additional possible approaches for assessing what variables affect attitudes toward the media. One could allow survey respondents to state for themselves why they dislike the media, using closed-ended survey questions as in Dautrich and Hartley (1999) or open-ended questions as in the retrospective memory dump questions used in chapter 4 and in Tsfati (2002). The main problem with this approach is that psychologists have long documented that people are notoriously poor at introspecting about their own psychological processes. Simply put, when people report what they think has caused their opinion to change, they often get it wrong (see Nisbett and Wilson 1977). Another approach would be to examine which variables are correlated with negative media attitudes in cross-sectional observational survey data (S. Bennett, Rhine, and Flickinger 2001; Kiousis 2001; Jones 2004). Unfortunately, it is very difficult with this type of data to rule out reverse causation or spurious omitted variables. A third approach is to look at change over time. However, even when observing changes in media evaluations over the course of several years (Barker 1999), during a campaign (Dautrich and Hartley 1999) or over several decades (Patterson 1993), it is still difficult to rule out omitted variable bias.

bring different considerations to bear. This can happen either because the individual absorbs new, salient considerations or because existing, non-salient considerations have now come to the top of the head.[8] Either way, one way to investigate why attitudes toward an object change is to look at the effect of different considerations on survey responses. These survey experiments do that. The treatments bring different considerations to the top of respondents' minds to see how they influence attitudes toward the institutional news media.[9]

The experiments were conducted by Knowledge Networks, Inc., under my direction.[10] Interviews for the first experiment took place between March 15 and 22, 2007, with 1,014 respondents completing the relevant questions. Respondents were told about a recent news report and asked if they had heard about it. I am not primarily concerned with their answers to this question; rather, I use it to bring various types of news stories to the top of respondents' minds.[11] The question's preface was identical for everyone: "We are interested in how well the news media gets information out to the public. There are so many news stories these days that most people have trouble following them all. We want to ask about some stories the news media has reported to see if you happened to hear about them." The story they were subsequently told about varied randomly among six different versions (see the appendix to this chapter).

Two versions of the question were designed to test how elite messages affect media attitudes. One mentioned Democratic elite criticism, stating, "Recently, Democratic politicians have criticized the media for being too friendly with President Bush," while the other mentioned analogous Republican criticism, stating, "Recently, Republican politicians have criticized the media for being overly critical of President Bush." To test

[8] See Zaller and Feldman (1992) and Zaller (1992), as well as Tourangeau (1987), Tourangeau and Rasinski (1988), and Tourangeau, Rips, and Rasinski, (2000). The phrase "top of the head" comes from Taylor and Fiske (1978).

[9] How should we describe this approach? In this area, the academic jargon often confuses more than it clarifies. Specifically, the terms *framing* and *priming* are frequently used in the persuasion literature but with often-inconsistent definitions (for reviews, see Althaus and Kim 2006; Chong and Druckman 2007b). Chong and Druckman (2007b) propose clarifying these concepts by defining framing broadly, to encompass any process by which an expressed opinion changes because of changes in the relative salience of considerations related to the attitude object (105). Within this framework, they classify priming as a type of framing where the consideration made salient is a "separate issue dimension or image used to evaluate" the object (115). While other scholars may classify things differently, using this typology, this study's research approach qualifies as a type of framing, where I make salient a series of different considerations representing variables hypothesized to reduce evaluations of the news media.

[10] For more details on Knowledge Networks, see chapter 4, note 21.

[11] This design is based on one employed by Gilens (2001). It is also similar to Kuklinski and Hurley's (1994) design.

whether coverage critical of all politicians induces people to dislike the media, in another version respondents were told, "Recently, the media has reported stories that criticize both President Bush and the Democrats in Congress." To test the expectation that people are turned off by the media's focus on horserace coverage, another version told respondents, "Recently, the media has reported on President Bush's standing in opinion polls, especially when his popularity has increased and decreased." To test the effect of tabloid coverage, another version told respondents, "Recently, the media has reported on the death of Anna Nicole Smith." This example was chosen out of a desire to use a contemporary and well-known tabloid story. There had recently been a "feeding frenzy" of coverage of the death of Smith, a former *Playboy* Playmate of the Year and reality television star (Project for Excellence in Journalism 2007a; Shafer 2007).[12] The sixth and final version of the questionnaire served as the "control." Those assigned to this condition received the same question preface but were not reminded of any particular news story or style of coverage. They were simply asked, "Have you been following stories in the news media recently?" As the dependent variable, later in the question battery all respondents were asked a media feeling thermometer question identical to the one sometimes used by the ANES.

I calculate treatment effects by comparing thermometer ratings of those who received each treatment with those in the control group.[13] Figure 5-1 presents the average effect of each treatment across all respondents (for details, see table 5-1 in the appendix). Among all respondents, only two variables significantly reduce media ratings. Thinking about tabloid coverage reduces ratings by about 7 degrees, while thinking about Democratic elite criticism reduces ratings by about 5 degrees. For every other

---

[12] The story was covered extensively on cable news channels and network newscasts. According to the Project for Excellence in Journalism (2007a), between her death on February 10 and her burial on March 2, 2007, Anna Nicole Smith's death was the third most covered story in the American news media as a whole, making up 8% of all coverage, behind only "a crucial House vote against the President's surge policy" (2) and the 2008 presidential race, which each took up 9% of coverage. On cable news channels, 32% of Fox News Channel's programming, 20% of MSNBC's programming, and 14% of CNN's programming focused on the Smith story, making it "far and away the biggest cable news story in that period." On major network morning news shows, it took up 20% of the first half hour of airtime on CBS, 17% on NBC, and 10% on ABC.

[13] A simple and concise way to present the results is in the form of a multiple regression. In this setup, each experimental condition is a "dummy'" explanatory variable coded 1 if the respondent received the treatment and 0 otherwise. The control condition is the excluded category. Here, the coefficient for each variable becomes simply the difference in means between the treatment and control groups, with its statistical significance equivalent to a difference-of-means test. I analyze the results with regression models presented in the chapter appendix, tables 5-1, 5-2, and 5-3. Figures 5-1 and 5-2 in the text graphically present the treatment effects from table 5-1.

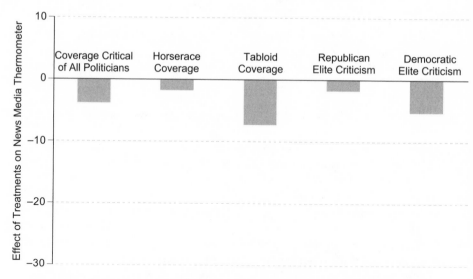

Figure 5-1. Effects on news media thermometer ratings in survey experiment. *Note:* Bars represent the difference in the average thermometer ratings between the control group and those receiving the given treatment. For more details, including significance tests, see table 5-1. *Source:* Survey experiment conducted by Knowledge Networks, Inc., March 15–22, 2007.

treatment, the effects are not statistically distinguishable from zero. However, I expect some of these variables' effects to depend on predispositions. Figure 5-2 presents the treatment effects separately for all Democrats and all Republicans and also for only well-educated liberal Democrats and well-educated conservative Republicans (for details, see table 5-1).

Unsurprisingly, the effect of Democratic elite criticism is stronger among Democrats than Republicans. Among all Democrats, Democratic criticism reduces ratings by about 8 degrees, while among liberal Democrats with education through at least some college, it reduces ratings by 17 degrees. Even among Republicans, thinking about Democratic elite criticism is associated with lower media ratings, but these differences—3 degrees lower among all Republicans and 9 degrees lower among educated conservative Republicans—are not statistically distinguishable from zero. The effects of Republican elite criticism show an analogous pattern, the main difference being that they are less widespread. Republican criticism has no distinguishable effect on any group except educated conservative Republicans. Among them, however, its effect is large, reducing media evaluations by about 24 degrees. Yet in contrast to Democratic elite criticism, here the responsive group is too small to produce much of an average effect among the whole sample. If we combine the effects of both Democratic and Republican elite criticism on the entire

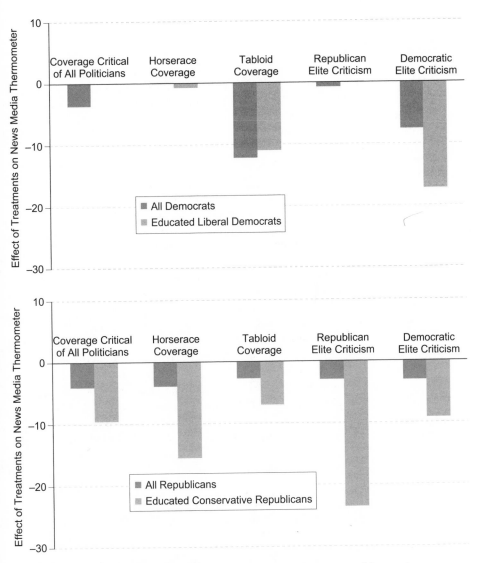

Figure 5-2. Effects on news media thermometer ratings separated by partisanship. *Source and note:* See figure 5-1.

sample's media ratings, however, overall they reduce media evaluations by about 7 degrees.[14]

[14] However, due to the imprecision of the estimate of Republican criticism in the entire sample, this combined effect is also imprecisely estimated. Its standard error is 5.1 and its *p*-value is .18.

Educated conservative Republicans' media evaluations seem particularly sensitive. They are the only group significantly affected by thinking about horserace coverage or coverage critical of all politicians, with these treatments reducing their evaluations by about 16 and 10 degrees, respectively. Among Democrats, and even among all Republicans grouped together, these treatments have no significant effect. On the other hand, the effect of thinking about tabloid coverage is significantly larger among Democrats, although there is some evidence of a substantial effect among educated conservative Republicans here as well.[15]

Overall, this experiment confirms the power of elite messages to reduce evaluations of the news media. Criticism from Democratic elites has the potential for more widespread influence. Yet Republican elite criticism is very influential among those predisposed to be most receptive to it: politically aware conservative Republicans. Of the other variables, only tabloid coverage has the effect often attributed to it: an overall reduction in media evaluations. In contrast, critical coverage and horserace coverage only reduce politically aware conservative Republicans' media evaluations, but the effects are not large or widespread enough to create much change in the population's overall evaluations.[16]

One possible source of negative news media evaluations that this first experiment does not explore is reactions to biased news. Given that partisan media critics sometimes argue that confidence has declined because of biased coverage, I conducted another survey experiment to explore this possibility.[17] To make the results comparable to the first experiment, I stayed as close as possible to the its format. This time, 1,000 respondents completed the relevant questions between March 4 and 11, 2008. The first question began with the same preface as in the first experiment: "We

[15] The difference in the effect of tabloid coverage between the parties is statistically significant at $p < .02$. Among educated conservative Republicans, the effect of tabloid coverage is about negative 7 degrees but not statistically significant at conventional levels ($p < .18$).

[16] Here, I estimate heterogeneities in the effects across predispositions by dividing the sample. In Ladd (2010a), I find similar results by pooling all respondents and estimating a model with interaction terms. However, the results here show some differences with those in Ladd (2010a), caused by a difference in how I classify liberal and conservative respondents. Here, liberals include those who place themselves at 1, 2, or 3 on the 7-point ideology scale while conservatives include those at 5, 6, and 7. However, in Ladd (2010a), liberals include only those at 1 and 2 on the scale and conservatives only those at 6 and 7. Because this led to very small sample sizes in the different conditions, such as only 50 educated liberal Democrats divided among six conditions, I decided to use a broader definition of liberal and conservative here. This coding change substantially alters only the effect of horserace coverage among educated liberal Democrats (where the effect estimate becomes smaller) and coverage critical of all politicians among educated conservative Republicans (where the effect estimate becomes larger).

[17] This study was also conducted through Knowledge Networks, Inc.

are interested in how well the news media gets information out to the public. There are so many news stories these days that most people have trouble following them all. We want to ask about some stories the news media has reported to see if you happened to hear about them."

This time, the remainder of this question randomly varied among three different versions. To test the effect of thinking about coverage favoring Democrats, in one version, respondents were told that "Recently, the news media has reported stories critical of President Bush and supportive of the Democratic majority in Congress." In the second version, to make respondents think about coverage favoring Republicans, respondents were told, "Recently, the news media has reported stories supportive of President Bush and critical of the Democratic majority in Congress." The third version, serving as the control, simply said, "Recently, the news media has reported stories about President Bush and the Democratic majority in Congress."[18]

As elite criticism often contains accusations of bias, I designed the experiment to check also whether effects of bias depend on the nature of elite rhetoric. After the first question, respondents had a one-third chance of being told about Democratic media criticism, a one-third chance of being told about Republican media criticism, and a one-third chance of not receiving any follow-up question at all. The elite criticism treatments had the exact same wordings as in the first experiment. Again, I look at the effects of those treatments on media feeling thermometer ratings given later in the survey.

The experiment finds very little evidence that the bias of news directly alters media evaluations. As table 5-2 in the appendix shows in detail, neither coverage favoring Democrats nor that favoring Republicans has a significant effect among all respondents together or among all Democrats or all Republicans. Even in the presence of elite criticism, bias has no detectable direct effect among these groups.

Looking only at educated liberal Democrats and educated conservative Republicans, direct effects of coverage bias are still very limited. As table 5-3 in the appendix shows, there is no detectable effect among educated conservative Republicans, regardless of elite rhetoric. Educated liberal Democrats are affected by bias only when they also hear Democratic criticism. When they do, coverage favorable to Democrats increases their media ratings by about 10 degrees, while coverage favorable to Republicans still

[18] The key assumption in this experiment is that partisans differ in their perceptions of reality. In what political psychologists call "motivated reasoning," partisans tend to perceive reality in ways that confirm their preexisting views. As a result, I expect conservative Republicans to see coverage critical of President Bush as biased and liberal Democrats to see coverage favorable to President Bush as biased, whatever the reality.

has no detectable effect. Still, educated liberal Democrats who hear Republican criticism or no elite rhetoric are not affected by any coverage bias.

Together, these two survey experiments suggest several conclusions about the origins of news media distrust. First, elite opinion leadership can play an important role in reducing media evaluations. Second, tabloid coverage can also significantly reduce media evaluations among the public overall. Third, educated conservative Republicans are particularly responsive to negativity and horserace coverage. Yet the effect of these two types of coverage on the public's media attitudes overall is small because no other group responds to them.

In the absence of elite criticism, I found no instances of bias significantly affecting evaluations. Even in the presence of elite criticism, the only circumstance where coverage bias had its own significant effect was when educated liberal Democrats received Democratic criticism, where coverage favoring Democrats improved their evaluations. However, all failures to detect effects in these experiments should be treated with caution. Relationships can fall below the threshold of statistical significance for several reasons, including insufficient sample size or insufficient dosage of the treatment.

It is still possible that biased coverage has some effect among partisans who also hear consistent elite rhetoric. Among Democrats, favorable coverage increased their media ratings by 4 degrees if they also heard Republicans criticizing that coverage, while unfavorable coverage reduced their ratings by 5 degrees if they also heard Democratic criticism. Similarly, among Republicans, favorable coverage increased their media ratings by 3 degrees if they heard Democratic criticism, while unfavorable coverage reduced their ratings by 6.5 degrees if they heard Republican criticism. It also is possible that Democratic criticism reduces media ratings among educated conservative Republicans, where the treated group's ratings were 9 degrees below the control group's. However, all these relationships are not statistically significant, meaning that we cannot be certain whether they reflect real effects or just random variation.

It is fair to say the following about these variables. The two survey experiments had similar sample sizes. By design and intention, each type of consideration was primed in a very similar way. Thus, I am unable to clearly detect effects of variables like biased coverage when I use a similar sample size and a similar dosage of treatment to that which detects other effects. Yet it is still possible that some effects that these experiments could not detect would be detected with a stronger treatment dosage or larger sample size, especially in the case of biased coverage accompanied by consistent elite rhetoric.[19]

---

[19] In the case of dosage, while it is possible that variables with no detectable effect here might have some effect if the dosage was increased, an increase in dosage would also likely

Alternative Outlets Convey Elite Media Criticism: Cross-Sectional Survey Evidence

One way elite criticism of the institutional news media may reach the public is through alternative media outlets. Of course, the media criticism of politicians, political activists, opinion columnists, and others is covered in the institutional media. However, new types of outlets that have grown in prominence in the past 30 years have also been an important venue for these attacks. Chapter 4 reviewed how media criticism is a staple of discussion on political talk radio as well as on blogs and other alternative news websites. Thus, if elite criticism is an important source of negative attitudes toward the institutional media, one place we should see that influence is in the effects of consuming news from alternative media outlets.

In 2008, for the first time, the ANES asked respondents whether they "read, watched, or listened to information on the Internet about the campaign for President." This allows me to examine the relationship between political website exposure and distrust of the media. Among all respondents, there is no significant relationship between political Internet use and media trust. However, most political Internet use centers on institutional outlets' websites. It is less widely viewed sites, with partisan perspectives, that criticize the institutional media. Given this, we might expect politically aware partisans to be both more likely to use partisan websites and more accepting of the rhetoric they find there.[20] In addition, because the intensity of media criticism tends to be greater among Republican elites, effects might be strongest among politically aware Republicans.

To test this, I look at the relationship between political Internet use and media trust among five different groups: politically aware conservative Republicans, politically unaware conservative Republicans, independents, politically aware liberal Democrats, and politically unaware liberal Democrats. In doing so, I control for other attributes that may be correlated with Internet use, including education, income, age, and (among independents) ideology.[21] Internet usage is not discernibly associated with media trust among either group of Democrats nor among politically unaware conservative Republicans. Yet among politically aware

---

cause variables with detectable effects to have even greater effects. Thus, while it may be the case that, in instances where variables lack significant effects here, they do in fact have some small effect, the effects of variables that are influential here are likely to be larger at comparable dosage levels.

[20] Zaller (1992) argues persuasively that politically aware partisans are most receptive to elite messages from their side of the political spectrum when they do receive them. This is because, in Zaller's receive-accept-sample model of opinion change, they understand the political implications of the message yet "partisan resistance" does not prevent acceptance.

[21] Of course, party identification and ideology are largely held constant in the other groups as well, because the groups are selected based on these attributes.

conservative Republicans, as well as independents, those who use the Internet to learn about politics trust the media less. Among politically aware conservative Republicans, using the Internet for campaign information "a good many times" decreases one's probability of trusting the media "most of the time" or "just about always" by .21.[22] Among independents, the relationship is similar but substantially smaller. Using the Internet "a good many times" decreases one's probability of trusting the media "most of the time" or "just about always" by .10 (for details, see table 5-4 in the appendix).

A second popular alternative news medium is political talk radio. Similar to blogs and partisan news websites, talk radio features opinionated hosts who regularly criticize the institutional press. One difference is that liberal talk radio programs have been less successful than liberal Internet sites in attracting audiences comparable to their conservative counterparts. Thus, for talk radio, we have even greater reason to suspect effects to be strongest among politically aware Republicans. Using questions measuring talk radio usage in the 1996 and 2000 ANES surveys, I find a negative relationship between media trust and talk radio exposure when all respondents are grouped together. On average, listening to talk radio "every day" corresponds with a .11 lower probability of trusting the media "most of the time" or "just about always."[23] This relationship persists even when controlling for education, income, age, and ideology.

However, this overall relationship appears to be driven largely by Republicans. I again look at the relationship separately among politically aware Republicans, politically unaware Republicans, independents, politically aware Democrats, and politically unaware Democrats, in each case controlling again for education, income, age, and ideology. Among politically aware Republicans, those who listen to talk radio "every day" have a .24 lower probability of trusting the media "most of the time" or "just about always." Even among less politically aware Republicans, listening "every day" corresponds to a .19 lower probability of trusting the media "most of the time" or "just about always." Among independents and politically aware Democrats, there is no statistically significant relationship between talk radio exposure and media trust. Among politically unaware Democrats, there is even a positive relationship. In this group, listening to talk radio "every day" is associated with a .17 greater probability of trusting the media "most of the time" or "just about always" (for details, see table 5-5 in the appendix).

---

[22] Effects of using the Internet for political information "a good many times" are in comparison to not using the Internet for political information at all.

[23] Here and throughout the analysis of talk radio, the effects of listening "every day" are in comparison to not listening at all.

Even with control variables, there are still reasons to doubt whether these relationships between media trust and alternative media use result from persuasion. First, there could be other attributes I have not controlled for that lead people to both use alternative media sources and trust the media less. Second, I suspect (and demonstrate with evidence in chapter 6) that distrusting the media leads one to seek out more partisan media outlets. Because of this, it is difficult to know how much these associations result from alternative media persuading individuals to trust the media less and how much they result from omitted variable bias and reverse causation.

One way to tease out the persuasive effect is to find something else that increases exposure to alternative media outlets without directly influencing one's views on the media.[24] The number of miles a person drives each day may fit these criteria. The 1996 and 2000 ANES surveys ask, "And finally, about how many miles do you drive in a typical day?" Respondents provided an exact number of miles. As figure 5-3 shows, driving more often appears to lead to greater consumption of talk radio. If the additional talk radio listening exposure from driving more causes people to trust the media less, we can be more confident that talk radio has a persuasive effect whenever people listen to it.[25] In this analysis, I include additional control variables that might be correlated with driving more. In addition to education, income, age, and ideology, I control for whether individuals are employed, what type of area they live in (urban, suburban, or rural), and their type of profession (professional/managerial, clerical/sales, service, nonfarm laborer, farmer, or homemaker).

With this method, estimates of the effect of talk radio on politically unaware Democrats and Republicans become much less precise. We can no longer say with confidence that there is any persuasion among these

[24] In econometrics, this is called an instrumental variables model. Stated more formally, to identify a causal effect with this type of model, the exogenous variable(s) must satisfy two assumptions. The first is that the covariance between the instrument and the explanatory variable must not be zero. The second is that any effect of the instrument on the dependent variable must be through the explanatory variable (Hanushek and Jackson 1977, 243; Kennedy 2003, 159; Wooldridge 2003, 484). Figure 5-1 illustrates that the first assumption holds in this case. The second assumption, that the miles driven each day affects trust in the media only through talk radio exposure, is not empirically testable (Angrist, Imbens, and Rubin 1996; Wooldridge 2003).

[25] Barker (2002) also uses an instrumental variables model to estimate the persuasive effect of talk radio on media trust and employs miles driven as one of his instruments. The two differences between his analysis and mine are that, first, he uses several other variables as instruments as well, and second, he does not estimate the models separately for different groups as in table 5-3. In addition, Barker and Knight (2000), Jamieson and Cappella (2008), and Jones (2004) document an association between talk radio exposure and media distrust. Jones (2004) finds that this association is concentrated among conservatives.

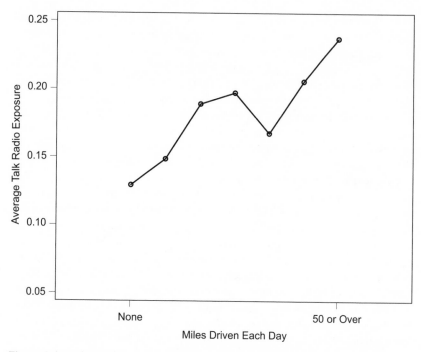

Figure 5-3. Miles driven and talk radio exposure. *Note:* Talk radio exposure is coded as in tables 5-5 and 5-6. Dots are averages for each category of miles driven. Categories are for presentation only. The actual number of miles driven is used in the analysis. *Source:* 1996, 2000 ANES.

groups. The effect estimate among independents also becomes much less precise, remaining indistinguishable from zero. Among politically aware Democrats, the effect is relatively precisely estimated yet so small it is also indistinguishable from zero. The group in which we can detect persuasion is politically aware Republicans. Among them, listening to talk radio "every day" leads people to move about one response category (out of four) lower in media trust (for details, see table 5-6 in the appendix).

Thus, we cannot rule out the possibility that the negative relationship between media trust and talk radio exposure among politically unaware Republicans and the positive relationship among unaware Democrats result from omitted variables or reverse causation. Persuasion may take place among these groups, but our estimates based on miles driven are too imprecise to be certain. However, the evidence strongly suggests that talk radio exposure persuades politically aware Republicans to distrust the media. Thus, at least for Republicans, alternative news outlets are an avenue through which elite rhetoric reduces trust in the institutional news media.

Any effects of Democratic elite media criticism appear not to flow through these alternative outlets in a large enough magnitude to be detected here.

WHY DID CONFIDENCE IN THE PRESS DECLINE?

As I noted at the start of this chapter, many commentators provide different, sometimes conflicting, explanations for Americans' increasingly negative attitudes toward the institutional news media. Based on the evidence in this chapter and the last, we can make some progress assessing these claims. Any explanation for the public's declining confidence in the press over the past 40 years should be consistent with both the results in this chapter and the relationships among attitudes toward the press, time, partisanship, and political awareness illustrated in figures 4-4, 4-5, and 4-6.

First, consider the hostile media phenomenon. As I noted earlier, the main reason the hostile media phenomenon cannot explain change over time is that it largely results from the persistence of preexisting attitudes toward the media. It does not explain where these hostile views of the media originated. Also, to the extent that there is an actual reduction in media trust, it tends to be among the most politically engaged. Yet, we see in figure 4-6 that the politically aware have the most negative views of the media among Republicans. Among Democrats, there tends to be a modest increase in media trust among the most aware. For these reasons, it seems unlikely that the hostile media phenomenon is a major cause of the decline in media trust.

Second, while negativity and coverage focusing on the political "game" have increased since the 1960s, these changes can explain only a small part of the decline in press confidence. Negativity and horserace coverage have very modest effects on overall media evaluations, largely because their influence is concentrated among politically aware conservative Republicans. However, as figures 4-5 and 4-6 show, as Republicans' confidence in the press has declined, Democrats' confidence has significantly declined as well, just to a slightly lesser degree.

Third, the evidence also indicates that little of the decline can be explained by direct reactions to news bias. Any direct effect of biased coverage is too small to be detected in my survey experiment, with the lone exception of educated liberal Democrats also receiving Democratic elite media criticism. Moreover, if declining confidence is largely the result of the institutional media becoming increasingly biased in one direction, we would expect the decline to be concentrated on one side of the political spectrum, which is not what has occurred. Moreover, to the extent that news consumption patterns have changed over time, alternative outlets have increased the ability of consumers to choose news sources whose biases do not offend them.

This is not to claim that the news media is free of bias. While there is no consensus in the academic literature on media bias, there is evidence that newspapers have increasingly endorsed Democrats since the mid-1960s (Ansolabehere, Lessem, and Snyder 2006), and two influential quantitative studies find coverage from institutional news organizations to be somewhat more liberal than the mass public (Groseclose and Milyo 2005; Gentzkow and Shapiro 2010b).[26] In addition, several game theorists have demonstrated that it can be rational for news organizations to provide biased news (Baron 2006; Bernhardt, Krasa, and Polborn 2006; Besley and Prat 2006; Gentzkow and Shapiro 2006; but see Bovitz, Druckman, and Lupia 2002).[27] However, while elite rhetoric pointing out bias can reduce media confidence, I find little evidence that directly consuming biased news has this effect.[28]

This leads us to the two most likely sources of the public's increasing antipathy toward the media: tabloid coverage and elite opinion leadership. Like several other styles of news, tabloid coverage has increased over the same period that press confidence has declined. Yet unlike other styles, my experiment indicates that tabloid coverage's effects, while larger among Democrats, are enough to produce significant declines in overall media ratings, which is what we observe in figures 4-4 and 4-5.

The evidence also consistently supports the importance of elite opinion leadership. Criticism of the press has greatly increased over the past 40 years on both sides of the political spectrum. However, criticism among conservatives started earlier and even now appears to be more intense and widespread than criticism from liberals. Thus, if media attitudes are responsive to elite partisan rhetoric, we should expect confidence in the press to decline among everyone over time but with a consistent gap between the parties, with Republicans' confidence being lower. This is the pattern we find in figures 4-4 and 4-5. Furthermore, because conservative media criticism is more intense, at any given point we should expect

---

[26] Consistent with contentions of liberal bias, Baum and Groeling (2010) find that wire service coverage is more similar to coverage on liberal websites than to FoxNews.com coverage. Niven (2002, chap. 3) provides a broader review of the academic literature on media bias.

[27] On the general advantages of providing and receiving biased information, see Patty (2009) and Calvert (1985), respectively.

[28] The frequent tendency of elites to criticize perceived bias likely explains why respondents frequently mention bias among the considerations that come to mind when evaluating the media. People do think about media bias. But they have received influential considerations about bias largely from elite rhetoric, not from whatever biased news they have consumed.

the party gap in media evaluations to be largest among the most politically aware, where the difference in the intensity of elite criticism is most acutely felt. This is the pattern we find in Figure 4-6. Considered together, Democratic elite criticism and Republican elite criticism can reduce media confidence across a broad spectrum of the public. In many ways, Craig Crawford (2006, 15) is correct when he claims that "[p]oliticians won the war against the media with a simple rule: first, attack the messenger."

To reiterate once more, these results do not, in and of themselves, necessarily imply that partisan media criticism and tabloid news are *problems* and other media trends are not. This chapter's aim is very specific: determining what considerations reduce public trust in the media. Just because thinking about negativity, horserace coverage, or media bias does not directly reduce people's trust in the media does not mean those phenomena are not prevalent or not problems. This chapter does not address the question of which media trends have good or bad consequences for the nation overall but focuses on the very specific question of which attributes create media distrust. Negativity, horserace coverage, media bias, and other attributes of the modern media environment may have other important effects on politics or society as a whole that are beyond the scope of this book.

Based only on this chapter, it is also not yet clear whether the distrust created by partisan criticism and tabloid news is problematic. Determining that requires looking at the consequences of media distrust and weighing any undesirable consequences against any benefits of partisan criticism and tabloid news. To that end, the next two chapters investigate the consequences of public antipathy toward the institutional news media. In doing so, they look specifically at how media distrust changes the way people acquire political information and make electoral decisions.

Appendix

QUESTION WORDINGS IN SURVEY EXPERIMENT CONDUCTED BY
KNOWLEDGE NETWORKS, INC., MARCH 15–22, 2007

Question 1

(Respondents are randomly assigned to receive one of six different versions.)

Version A: "We are interested in how well the news media gets information out to the public. There are so many news stories these days that most people have trouble following them all. We want to ask about some stories the news media has reported to see if you happened to hear about them. Recently, the media has reported stories that criticize both President Bush and the Democrats in Congress. Have you heard these stories?"

Version B: "We are interested in how well the news media gets information out to the public. There are so many news stories these days that most people have trouble following them all. We want to ask about some stories the news media has reported to see if you happened to hear about them. Recently, the media has reported on President Bush's standing in opinion polls, especially when his popularity has increased and decreased. Have you heard these stories?"

Version C: "We are interested in how well the news media gets information out to the public. There are so many news stories these days that most people have trouble following them all. We want to ask about a story the news media has reported to see if you happened to hear about it. Recently, the media has reported on the death of Anna Nicole Smith. Have you heard this story?"

Version D: "We are interested in how well the news media gets information out to the public. There are so many news stories these days that most people have trouble following them all. We want to ask about a story the news media has reported to see if you happened to hear about it. Recently, Republican politicians have criticized the media for being overly critical of President Bush. Have you heard this story?"

Version E: "We are interested in how well the news media gets information out to the public. There are so many news stories these days that most people have trouble following them all. We want to ask about a story the news media has reported to see if you happened to hear about it. Recently, Democratic politicians have criticized the media for being too friendly with President Bush. Have you heard this story?"

Version F: "We are interested in how well the news media gets information out to the public. There are so many news stories these days that most people have trouble following them all. Have you been following stories in the news media recently?"

Question 1 Answers

Yes
No

Question 2

(Respondents are shown a number box with range 0–100.)
"We'd like you to rate the news media on a scale we call a 'feeling thermometer.' It runs from 0 to 100 degrees. Ratings between 50 degrees and 100 degrees mean that you feel favorable toward the news media. Ratings between 0 degrees and 50 degrees mean that you feel unfavorable toward the news media. If you don't feel particularly favorable or unfavorable toward the news media, you would rate them at the 50 degree mark. How would you rate the news media on this scale? You can use any number between 0 and 100 to indicate how favorable or unfavorable you feel."

Question 2 Answers

0–100

QUESTION WORDINGS IN SURVEY EXPERIMENT CONDUCTED BY KNOWLEDGE NETWORKS, INC., MARCH 4–11, 2008

Question 1

(Respondents are randomly assigned to receive one of two different versions.)

Version A: "We are interested in how well the news media gets information out to the public. There are so many news stories these days that most people have trouble following them all. We want to ask about some stories the news media has reported to see if you happened to hear about them. Recently, the news media has reported stories critical of President Bush and supportive of the Democratic majority in Congress. Have you seen these stories?"

Version B: "We are interested in how well the news media gets information out to the public. There are so many news stories these days that most people have trouble following them all. We want to ask about some stories the news media has reported to see if you happened to hear about them. Recently, the news media has reported stories supportive of President Bush and critical of the Democratic majority in Congress. Have you seen these stories?"

Version C: "We are interested in how well the news media gets information out to the public. There are so many news stories these days that most people have trouble following them all. We want to ask about some stories the news media has reported to see if you happened to hear about them. Recently, the news media has reported stories about President Bush and the Democratic majority in Congress. Have you seen these stories?"

Question 1 Answers

Yes
No

Question 2

(Respondents are randomly assigned to receive one of three different versions.)

Version A: "Recently, Democratic politicians have criticized the media for being too friendly with President Bush. Have you seen this story?"
Version B: "Recently, Republican politicians have criticized the media for being overly critical of President Bush. Have you seen this story?"
Version C: (Respondents do not receive question 2.)

Question 2 Answers

Yes
No

Question 3

(Respondents are shown a number box with range 0–100.)
"We'd like you to rate the news media on a scale we call a 'feeling thermometer.' It runs from 0 to 100 degrees. Ratings between 50 degrees and 100 degrees mean that you feel favorable toward the news media. Ratings between 0 degrees and 50 degrees mean that you feel unfavorable toward the news media. If you don't feel particularly favorable or unfavorable toward the news media, you would rate them at the 50 degree mark. How would you rate the news media on this scale? You can use any number between 0 and 100 to indicate how favorable or unfavorable you feel."

Question 3 Answers

0–100

TABLE 5-1
Treatment Effects on Media Thermometer Ratings in Survey Experiment

Treatments	All	All Democrats	Educated liberal Democrats	All Republicans	Educated conservative Republicans
Coverage critical of all politicians	−3.8 (2.8)	−3.7 (4.3)	1.1 (8.2)	−4.0 (3.4)	−9.6* (5.3)
Horserace coverage	−1.8 (3.0)	0.0 (4.5)	−0.7 (7.3)	−3.8 (3.6)	−15.5** (4.9)
Tabloid coverage	−7.2** (2.8)	−12.3** (3.9)	−11.0 (7.7)	−2.6 (3.9)	−6.9 (5.1)
Republican elite criticism	−1.7 (3.1)	−0.8 (4.2)	0.04 (8.5)	−2.9 (4.2)	−23.7** (5.1)
Democratic elite criticism	−5.2* (2.9)	−7.6* (4.1)	−17.4** (8.6)	−3.0 (4.0)	−9.2 (5.7)
Intercept	50.1** (2.0)	56.1** (2.9)	52.7** (6.2)	44.8** (2.6)	50.1** (3.9)
R²	0.01	0.04	0.09	0.00	0.13
Standard error of regression	22.3	21.7	21.4	21.7	18.6
n	1,002	467	129	535	187

$**p < .05, *p < .10$

Source: Survey experiment conducted by Knowledge Networks, Inc., March 15–22, 2007.

Note: Entries are ordinary least squares regression coefficients with robust standard errors in parentheses. The explanatory variables, listed in the left-hand column, are coded 1 if the respondent received the treatment and 0 otherwise. All treatments are mutually exclusive. The control condition is the excluded category. The dependent variable is a news media feeling thermometer, which ranges from 0 to 100. Democrats and Republicans include independents who lean toward those parties. Results are substantively similar if leaners are excluded. Pure independents are not analyzed separately because there are too few of them ($n = 76$). Respondents are classified as educated if their level of education is "some college" or higher. Respondents are classified as liberal if they placed themselves at 1, 2, or 3 on the 7-point ideology scale and as conservative if they placed themselves at 5, 6, or 7. Data are weighted by the inverse of their probability of selection into the Knowledge Networks sample.

TABLE 5-2
Treatment Effects of Coverage Bias on Media Thermometer Ratings

		All			Democrats			Republicans		
Treatments	All	Received no media criticism	Received Democratic media criticism	Received Republican media criticism	Received no media criticism	Received Democratic media criticism	Received Republican media criticism	Received no media criticism	Received Democratic media criticism	Received Republican media criticism
Coverage favors Democrats	0.0	2.2	−0.9	−0.9	4.7	1.1	4.1	−1.8	−1.8	−6.5
	(2.1)	(3.6)	(2.9)	(4.1)	(4.8)	(3.2)	(5.6)	(5.8)	(4.2)	(5.4)
Coverage favors Republicans	−1.8	−1.4	−1.2	−2.1	2.0	−4.8	−3.7	−4.6	3.3	1.7
	(2.1)	(3.6)	(3.6)	(3.3)	(4.8)	(4.7)	(4.8)	(5.6)	(5.5)	(4.4)
Intercept	46.6**	49.4**	44.4**	45.9**	49.8**	49.8**	49.1**	48.8**	37.7**	40.4**
	(1.4)	(2.5)	(2.0)	(2.4)	(3.3)	(2.1)	(3.5)	(3.8)	(3.0)	(3.3)
R²	0.002	0.005	0.001	0.002	0.009	0.018	0.021	0.008	0.011	0.029
Standard error of regression	21.4	21.9	21.0	21.0	21.1	19.9	20.1	22.7	20.7	20.3
n	1,000	327	341	332	170	182	175	156	159	156

**p < .05, *p < .10

Source: Survey experiment conducted by Knowledge Networks, Inc., March 4–11, 2008.

Note: Entries are ordinary least squares regression coefficients with robust standard errors in parentheses. The explanatory variables, listed in the left hand column, are coded 1 if the respondent received the treatment and 0 otherwise. The control condition (those who were not told about coverage favoring Democrats or Republicans) is the excluded category. The dependent variable is a news media feeling thermometer, which ranges from 0 to 100. Democrats and Republicans include independents who lean toward those parties. Results are substantively similar if leaners are excluded. Pure independents are not analyzed separately because there are too few of them (n = 50). Data are weighted by the inverse of their probability of selection into the Knowledge Networks sample.

TABLE 5-3
Treatment Effects of Coverage Bias on Media Thermometer Ratings among Educated Ideological Partisans

Treatments	Educated liberal Democrats				Educated conservative Republicans			
	All	Received no media criticism	Received Democratic media criticism	Received Republican media criticism	All	Received no media criticism	Received Democratic media criticism	Received Republican media criticism
Coverage favors Democrats	5.6	2.3	10.4**	4.5	-0.8	4.1	1.4	-4.4
	(4.5)	(7.4)	(4.3)	(8.7)	(3.9)	(6.4)	(5.7)	(7.0)
Coverage favors Republicans	-0.6	-0.2	-1.7	1.3	2.7	6.7	4.4	-4.2
	(4.6)	(5.8)	(8.2)	(6.6)	(4.1)	(7.0)	(5.8)	(5.9)
Intercept	47.8**	50.6**	46.7**	46.2**	37.4**	43.5**	31.6**	36.8**
	(2.6)	(4.1)	(3.1)	(4.4)	(2.5)	(4.5)	(3.8)	(4.2)
R^2	0.016	0.003	0.066	0.008	0.005	0.018	0.008	0.011
Standard error of regression	21.3	21.9	20.8	21.7	21.3	21.4	20.1	20.5
n	246	78	84	84	255	81	91	83

** $p < .05$, * $p < .10$

Source: Survey experiment conducted by Knowledge Networks, Inc., March 4–11, 2008.

Note: For details, see the note to table 5-2, except for the coding of education and ideology, for which see table 5-1.

TABLE 5-4
Relationship between Political Internet Usage and News Media Trust

	All	Politically aware liberal Democrats	Politically unaware liberal Democrats	Independents	Politically aware conservative Republicans	Politically unaware conservative Republicans
Frequency of getting campaign information on the Internet	-0.09	0.34	-0.28	-0.25**	-0.53*	0.06
	(0.07)	(0.31)	(0.20)	(0.13)	(0.32)	(0.18)
Education	0.40**	1.74	0.96	0.54	0.07	0.13
	(0.19)	(3.50)	(0.79)	(0.35)	(3.46)	(0.71)
Income	-0.19*	-0.35	0.27	-0.28	0.27	0.03
	(0.11)	(0.47)	(0.34)	(0.19)	(0.54)	(0.29)
Age	1.80**	2.22	4.85**	2.35	-3.18	-1.05
	(0.82)	(4.87)	(2.48)	(1.48)	(4.54)	(2.15)
Age^2	-1.39*	-1.93	-5.02*	-2.14	4.91	1.00
	(0.82)	(5.13)	(2.60)	(1.53)	(4.44)	(2.13)
Party identification	0.00					
	(0.09)					
Ideology	-0.12			0.01		
	(0.13)			(0.23)		
Log-likelihood	-2065.7	-118.6	-213.4	-637.2	-131.1	-309.7
Pseudo R^2	0.004	0.008	0.023	0.008	0.041	0.001
n	1,906	133	216	599	116	254

**$p < .05$, *$p < .10$

Source: 2008 ANES Time Series Survey.

Note: Table shows ordered probit coefficients with standard errors in parentheses. Estimates of τ cut-point parameters are not reported. In each model, the dependent variable is respondents' trust in the media, with the following response categories: "just about always" (coded as 1), "most of the time" (.67), "only some of the time" (.33), and "just about never" (0). The main explanatory variable is how often respondents "read, watched, or listened to information on the Internet about the campaign for President," with the following response categories: not at all (0), "just one or two" times (.33), "several" times (.67), and "a good many" times (1). Respondents are classified as politically aware if they earned a graduate degree and correctly named the Republicans as the more conservative major American political party. Those who say they lean toward a party are classified as identifying with that party. Other explanatory variables are also coded to range from 0 to 1, with interior categories evenly spaced between these endpoints.

TABLE 5-5
Relationship between Talk Radio Exposure and News Media Trust

	All	Politically aware Democrats	Politically unaware Democrats	Independents	Politically aware Republicans	Politically unaware Republicans
Talk radio exposure	-0.27**	-0.03	0.43**	-0.05	-0.71**	-0.49*
	(0.09)	(0.17)	(0.21)	(0.32)	(0.16)	(0.29)
Education	-0.05	0.09	-0.24	0.19	0.08	0.20
	(0.09)	(0.17)	(0.22)	(0.31)	(0.20)	(0.31)
Income	-0.11	0.09	-0.01	-0.14	-0.02	-0.27
	(0.10)	(0.19)	(0.23)	(0.37)	(0.20)	(0.32)
Age	0.01	0.01	0.00	0.03	-0.03*	0.02
	(0.01)	(0.02)	(0.02)	(0.03)	(0.02)	(0.03)
Age^2	0.00	0.00	0.00	0.00	0.0003*	0.00
	(0.00)	(0.00)	(0.00)	(0.00)	(0.0002)	(0.00)
Ideology	-1.04**	-0.27	-0.50	-0.51	-1.28**	-1.05**
	(0.12)	(0.25)	(0.31)	(0.58)	(0.30)	(0.42)
Log-likelihood	-2149.1	-683.7	-419.2	-197.3	-558.2	-227.1
Pseudo R^2	0.028	0.006	0.013	0.028	0.058	0.026
n	1,967	647	371	176	537	220

$** p < .05, * p < .10$

Source: 1996 and 2000 ANES Time Series Surveys.

Note: Table shows ordered probit coefficients with standard errors in parentheses. All models contain a year fixed effect, which is not reported. Estimates of τ cut-point parameters are also not reported. In each model, the dependent variable is respondents' trust in the media, with the following response categories: "just about always" (coded as 1), "most of the time" (.67), "only some of the time" (.33), and "just about never" (0). The main independent variable is a question asking, "There are a number of programs on radio in which people call in to voice their opinions about politics. Do you ever listen to political talk radio programs of this type?" If they said yes, then they were asked how often they listened. Response categories are "every day" (1), "most days" (.75), "once or twice a week" (.5), "only occasionally" (.25), and "doesn't listen" (0). Other explanatory variables are also coded to range from 0 to 1, with interior categories evenly spaced between these endpoints.

TABLE 5-6
Instrumental Variables Model of the Effect of Talk Radio Exposure on News Media Trust

	All	Politically aware Democrats	Politically unaware Democrats	Independents	Politically aware Republicans	Politically unaware Republicans
Talk radio exposure (instrumented)	-0.31**	-0.11	0.78	1.99	-0.32**	1.23
	(0.16)	(0.23)	(1.20)	(2.74)	(0.15)	(3.93)
Education: Grade 9–12	0.06*	0.08*	0.07	0.47	-0.06	-0.01
	(0.03)	(0.05)	(0.11)	(0.63)	(0.11)	(0.23)
Education: high school or equivalent	0.07**	0.12**	-0.04	0.47	-0.08	-0.15
	(0.03)	(0.05)	(0.21)	(0.66)	(0.11)	(0.39)
Education: some college	0.06*	0.09*	-0.04	0.52	-0.06	-0.02
	(0.03)	(0.05)	(0.19)	(0.66)	(0.11)	(0.20)
Education: BA or equivalent	0.08**	0.12**	-0.04	0.78	-0.06	-0.01
	(0.03)	(0.05)	(0.18)	(1.00)	(0.11)	(0.24)
Income: 17–33 percentile	0.00	0.02	0.04	0.04	-0.02	0.05
	(0.02)	(0.03)	(0.06)	(0.20)	(0.04)	(0.14)
Income: 34–67 percentile	-0.03	0.02	0.05	-0.27	-0.01	0.05
	(0.02)	(0.03)	(0.15)	(0.30)	(0.04)	(0.13)
Income: 68–95 percentile	-0.02	0.02	0.10	-0.22	-0.01	0.00
	(0.02)	(0.03)	(0.12)	(0.25)	(0.04)	(0.15)
Income: 96–100 percentile	-0.01	0.02	0.18	-0.29	0.00	-0.15
	(0.03)	(0.05)	(0.17)	(0.45)	(0.05)	(0.38)
Employed	0.01	0.02	-0.08	-0.25	0.03	-0.15
	(0.02)	(0.03)	(0.08)	(0.41)	(0.03)	(0.22)
Urban	0.01	0.01	-0.06	-0.41	0.00	0.17
	(0.01)	(0.02)	(0.06)	(0.53)	(0.03)	(0.35)
Suburban	-0.01	0.00	-0.05	-0.09	0.01	0.05
	(0.01)	(0.03)	(0.04)	(0.14)	(0.02)	(0.14)

Professional / managerial	0.02	0.00	-0.05	-0.16	0.02	-0.06
	(0.02)	(0.05)	(0.10)	(0.27)	(0.04)	(0.41)
Clerical / sales worker	0.00	-0.02	0.05	-0.10	0.03	0.00
	(0.02)	(0.05)	(0.08)	(0.22)	(0.04)	(0.17)
Service worker	0.01	-0.01	-0.06	-0.14	0.02	-0.01
	(0.02)	(0.04)	(0.08)	(0.21)	(0.04)	(0.28)
Nonfarm laborer	-0.03	0.07	0.02	-0.12	0.04	[a]
	(0.04)	(0.10)	(0.12)	(0.34)	(0.10)	
Farmer	0.00	-0.13	0.00	-0.90	0.04	-0.23
	(0.05)	(0.09)	(0.16)	(1.10)	(0.08)	(0.98)
Age	0.00	0.00	0.00	0.00	0.00	0.01
	(0.00)	(0.00)	(0.01)	(0.02)	(0.00)	(0.01)
Age^2	0.00	0.00	0.00	0.00	0.00	0.00
	(0.00)	(0.00)	(0.00)	(0.00)	(0.00)	(0.00)
Liberal	0.03	0.00	-0.06	-0.45	0.00	0.01
	(0.02)	(0.02)	(0.14)	(0.39)	(0.11)	(0.45)
Conservative	-0.05*	-0.03	-0.05	-0.23	0.00	-0.20
	(0.03)	(0.04)	(0.08)	(0.35)	(0.03)	(0.40)
2000	0.04**	0.03	0.00	0.07	0.05*	-0.01
	(0.01)	(0.03)	(0.05)	(0.13)	(0.03)	(0.08)
Constant	0.55**	0.52**	0.72**	0.15	0.72**	0.40
	(0.05)	(0.09)	(0.28)	(0.57)	(0.14)	(0.35)
Standard error of regression	0.20	0.18	0.27	0.52	0.18	0.40
n	1,634	571	289	141	466	155

** $p < .05$, * $p < .10$

Source: 1996 and 2000 ANES Time Series Surveys.

Note: Table presents coefficient estimates from an instrumental variables regression model with standard errors in parentheses. Talk radio exposure and news media trust are coded as in table 5-5. Talk radio exposure is instrumented with the number of miles the respondent reported driving in "a typical day." Other explanatory variables are also coded to range from 0 to 1, with interior categories evenly spaced between these endpoints.

[a] variable omitted due to multicollinearity

News Media Trust and Political Learning

ATTITUDES TOWARD THE INSTITUTIONAL news media shape how people acquire political information. Those who trust the press are more accepting of new messages about national conditions in major policy areas. In contrast, those who distrust the press are more likely to resist new information that they attribute to the institutional media and seek additional information from more partisan sources. As a result, their beliefs tend to be less accurate and shaped more by partisanship. In this way, declining media trust produces an overall information loss for the citizenry. The public becomes more polarized and less responsive to the results of government policy.

THE MEDIA ARE ESSENTIAL SOURCES OF POLITICAL INFORMATION

In modern democracies, ordinary citizens are called upon to make choices among policies and candidates. Rarely can these citizens directly observe either the behavior of candidates or the macro-level content and consequences of government policies. In order to gain information about the political world, they rely on other entities to transmit information to them. As Zaller (1992, 6) puts it, "To an extent that few like but none can avoid, citizens in large societies are dependent on unseen and usually unknown others for most of their information about the larger world in which they live."

The news media have become the main conduit for transmitting politically relevant information to the mass public. John Petrocik (1995, 136) notes that "[t]he press is consequential because voters need information about candidates in order to make a choice that corresponds to their preferences. Limits on what a person can know and experience make the press the source of that information for most of us."

Even when information originates from another source, it is very often conveyed to the public through the press. Lippmann (1997 [1922]) argues that, to evaluate the performance of elected leaders, citizens must construct "pictures in their heads" of things like overseas wars or macroeconomic conditions. These pictures in their heads constitute what Lippmann calls the "pseudo-environment." It is constructed from secondhand descriptions of world events, primarily from the press. Because people are unable to observe the actual environment, they can only reward and punish politicians for their behavior, acting as a "rational god of vengeance and reward" (Key 1964, 568), based on their pseudo-environments. If people's pseudo-environments are accurate depictions of the world, then modern democracies should work well. Lippmann's primary concern was that the press could create inaccurate pseudo-environments, preventing the public from exercising control over its government.

While the threat of misinformation has not gone away, modern societies' reliance on mass media also creates other potential problems. For instance, if citizens lose faith in the press and decide to ignore its information, they are still unable to observe most political events firsthand. Whether distrust of media messages is justified or not, in the absence of media information there is no guarantee that beliefs will be any closer to the truth. Perhaps there is truth to Fallows's (1996, 1) worry that "[i]gnoring the news leaves people with no way to prepare for trends they don't happen to observe themselves, no sense of what is happening in other countries or even other parts of their own town, no tools with which to make decisions about public leaders or policies." This chapter investigates this question. How does media distrust alter how people learn about the world?

It Is Difficult to Detect Media Effects on Public Opinion

While Lippmann presented an engaging account of how the press shapes the public's view of the world, he did not marshal any quantitative evidence of media power. Lippmann's concern about media influence had been inspired by his observations of World War I. The rise of totalitarian governments in the 1930s and 1940s only increased popular and scholarly concern that modern mass communications allowed elites to lead the public in any direction they desired. But prior to the invention of modern survey sampling, there was no reliable way to measure the views of the entire public. The Gallup, Roper, and Crossly polling organizations were founded in the mid-1930s, but early national polls used unreliable methods such as quota sampling. By the 1940s, academic researchers began using various types of random sampling procedures, which allowed them to estimate the entire population's views with a relatively small sample. By the 1950s, these new methods were widespread (Converse 1987; Sudman and Bradburn 1987; Berinsky 2006).

One of the first things scholars used the new tool of survey research for was investigating the persuasive power of the mass media. Two of the most influential early studies of media influence were conducted by sociologist Paul Lazarsfeld and various colleagues at Columbia University, using panel surveys to track opinion change during the 1940 and 1948 presidential election campaigns (Lazarsfeld, Berelson, and Gaudet 1948; Berelson, Lazarsfeld, and McPhee 1954).[1] Contrary to expectations, they (and other early researchers) found little evidence of media persuasion (see Bartels 2010). Instead, they found, first, that most of the public had preexisting orientations that led them to prefer one of the major parties and its candidate. Second, when preferences did change over the course of a campaign, it was usually what scholars call reinforcement (or partisan activation): the tendency of news exposure, especially during campaigns, to reinforce and intensify existing partisan predispositions. Despite the ubiquity and apparent power of modern mass communications, the consensus among academic researchers for decades asserted that the media had very little persuasive effect beyond reinforcement (e.g. Klapper 1960), a view often called the minimal effects paradigm (Kinder 1998a, 2003; Graber 2010). This disconnect between popular perceptions of media power and the academic view prompted Larry Bartels (1993, 267) to declare that "[t]he state of research on media effects is one of the most notable embarrassments of modern social science."

Several factors prevented quantitative researchers from detecting media effects for so long. First, as early survey research detected, preexisting loyalties are indeed quite stable and shape political preferences in powerful ways (see chapter 7). Except for the few pure independents, any media influence other than partisan reinforcement must overcome these predispositions.[2] Second, researchers were mainly looking for direct media persuasion, where exposure to a message simply leads views to change, rather than less direct effects. Third, not everyone accounted for the fact that, in real-world settings, powerful media messages often offset each other. For instance, in the heat of a presidential campaign, both sides are sending out messages through the media at a high volume. Even if these offsetting messages are very persuasive, if they are of similar intensity there may be minimal net change in public opinion (Bartels 1992, 2006). Fourth, often media messages may be strong and persuasive

[1] Neither survey employed a national sample. The 1940 campaign panel was conducted in Erie County, Ohio (Lazarsfeld, Berelson, and Gaudet 1948), and the 1948 panel was in Elmira, New York (Berelson, Lazarsfeld, and McPhee 1954).

[2] Many people behave as partisans even if they say in survey questions that they are independents who only "lean" toward one of the parties (Keith et al. 1992). Studies of partisan reinforcement since Lazarsfeld, Berelson, and Gaudet (1948) and Berelson, Lazarsfeld, and McPhee (1954) have generally supported the notion that this is a consequence of campaign media exposure (Patterson and McClure 1976; Abramowitz 1978; Finkel 1993; Ansolabehere and Iyengar 1995; but see Bartels 2006).

but show very little variation over time. For instance, if most Americans consistently support a given government policy that most media coverage also supports, it is difficult to say whether the coverage is affecting opinion or vice versa, or whether both are caused by something else. It is much easier if media coverage of the issue dramatically changes at some point, enabling one to check whether opinions move in reaction (Erikson 1976; Zaller 1996).

SCHOLARS DOCUMENT SEVERAL TYPES OF MEDIA EFFECTS

Eventually, scholars developed techniques for overcoming these methodological obstacles and began finding evidence of powerful media effects. By looking for indirect media persuasion, and often employing experiments to manipulate media messages, researchers discovered a variety of ways media can persuade by changing the salience of considerations in people's minds. In studies of actual news coverage and in experimental settings, researchers found that, by devoting heavy attention to a particular issue, the media can cause people to say that that issue is more important to them than others, a phenomenon labeled "agenda-setting" (McCombs and Shaw 1972; Iyengar and Kinder 1987, chap. 3; McCombs and Shaw 2006). Related and even more politically important effects called "priming" occur when the media's focus on an issue leads people to rely more on that issue when making political evaluations. While there are criticisms of this literature (J. Miller and Krosnick 2000; Lenz 2009, 2010a), researchers have found apparent evidence of priming both inside and outside of laboratory experiments (e.g. Krosnick and Kinder 1990; Johnston et al. 1992; Krosnick and Brannon 1993; Iyengar and Simon 1994; Valentino 1999; Gilliam and Iyengar 2000; Ladd 2007). The press can also change opinions by focusing on certain aspects or interpretations of an issue or candidate (e.g. Kahneman and Tversky 1984; Gamson and Modigliani 1989; Iyengar 1991; T. Nelson and Kinder 1996; T. Nelson, Clausen, and Oxley 1997; Kellstedt 2000, 2003; Berinsky and Kinder 2006; Chong and Druckman 2007b). While these effects, known as "framing," do not occur in all contexts (Druckman 2001; Druckman 2004; Sniderman and Theriault 2004; Chong and Druckman 2007a), scholars generally agree that framing can be persuasive in some circumstances (Chong and Druckman 2007b).

Beyond these effects, the media can influence opinions in at least two other ways. The first is by sending a strong message on a particular topic, what we might simply call direct persuasion. To convincingly document these effects, scholars have had to overcome the obstacles mentioned above, particularly lack of variation and offsetting messages. However, a number of (mostly) recent studies have looked at (relatively unusual) instances of historical variations in media messages and found evidence that these messages can strongly shape views of candidates and issues (Veblen 1975; Erikson 1976; Page, Shapiro, and Dempsey 1987; Zaller 1996; DellaVigna and Kaplan 2007; Gabel and Scheve 2007; Huber and Arceneaux 2007; Ladd and Lenz 2009).[3]

Another persuasion effect occurs when the media provide politically relevant information about national conditions and world events, which then becomes the basis of the public's political judgments. This phenomenon is most similar to what Lippmann (1997 [1922]) described when he stated that the press could manipulate people's opinions by controlling their "pictures" of the world. Information about the world is related to political opinions in several ways. People who are more politically knowledgeable have systematically different preferences than others on a range of political topics (Bartels 1996b; Delli Carpini and Keeter 1996; Gilens 2001; Althaus 2003). Furthermore, when survey respondents are provided with specific national statistics, such as the national crime rate or the portion of the federal budget spent on foreign aid, their subsequent opinions, on prison construction and the death penalty in the first instance or on foreign aid in the second, change (Gilens 2001). In addition, election researchers have long found that information about the state of the nation allows voters to make retrospective evaluations of incumbent officeholders (Key 1968; Fiorina 1981), especially the president (e.g., Kinder and Kiewiet 1979; Fiorina 1981; Hibbs 1987; Markus 1988; Erikson 1989; Markus 1992; Hetherington 1996; Hibbs 2000; Bartels and Zaller 2001; Zaller 2004; Hibbs 2007).[4] The news media's role in this process is most clear in years when they send especially strong messages about economic performance. For instance, in 1992, those who reported high levels of news exposure had more negative perceptions of the economy, and those perceptions were associated with a much lower probability of voting to reelect President George H. W. Bush (Hetherington 1996).

---

[3] To my knowledge, Gerber et al. (forthcoming) is the only example of a field experiment testing the persuasive effects of media exposure. That study finds that newspaper exposure influences gubernatorial votes.

On the effect of news coverage on increasing the popularity of incumbent members of Congress, see Prior (2006). Arnold (2004, chap. 8) finds that the quality of local newspaper coverage of a member of Congress is related to the public's knowledgeability about both the member and his or her election opponent. But see also Mondak (1995, chap. 4) for much more mixed results regarding the effect of local newspapers on national political knowledge.

[4] In separate but related work, Alvarez (1997) finds an association between information about the issue positions of candidates and voting preferences. The strength of that association also varies in important ways.

Persuasion Depends on Source Credibility

The new scholarly consensus that the news media can powerfully shape the public's political views has emerged almost at the same time that attitudes toward the institutional press have soured (as outlined in chapter 3). Are those who trust and distrust the press equally influenced by its messages? There are strong reasons to expect that they are not. Because persuasion is central to many social processes, it is an active research topic in several fields, including communication, psychology, economics, and political science. A commonality among persuasion theories across fields is that persuasion depends on the views of the recipient toward the sender (Druckman and Lupia 2000).

For instance, early work by psychologist Carl Hovland and his colleagues on the persuasive effects of communication argued that attitude change depends on perceptions of the sender's expertise, trustworthiness, and similarity to the recipient (Hovland and Weiss 1951–52; Hovland, Janis, and Kelley 1953). Source credibility is also central in the receive-accept-sample model outlined by Zaller (1992), based on work by psychologist William McGuire (1969). According to this theory, people first receive a message, then decide whether to accept the message, then, when they are called upon to express an opinion, sample from the various messages (or considerations) in their heads to construct a response (see also Taylor and Fiske 1978; Tourangeau 1987; Tourangeau and Rasinski 1988; Fischhoff 1991; Zaller and Feldman 1992; Slovic 1995; Tourangeau, Rips, and Rasinski 2000). In this theory, distrust of the message sender induces "partisan resistance," which Zaller classifies as one of three possible reasons people resist messages (Zaller 1992, 121).[5]

Another influential psychological theory of persuasion is the elaboration-likelihood model.[6] It is a "dual-process" theory of persuasion (see Chaiken and Trope 1999), where people respond to messages in one of two ways, depending on the circumstance. When people have the desire or ability to analyze the content of a message, they decide whether to be persuaded based mainly on the quality of the arguments. But when they do not analyze, they use heuristics such as the credibility

---

[5] The other two reasons that Zaller (1992, 121) gives are someone having so much existing information on the topic that anything new cannot overwhelm it (labeled "inertial resistance") and someone also being subject to arguments reinforcing their existing view (labeled "countervalent resistance").

[6] A very similar dual-process theory of persuasion developed by Shelly Chaiken is called the heuristic-systematic model (Chaiken 1980; Eagly and Chaiken 1993). It has predictions very similar to the elaboration-likelihood model, including its predictions regarding when source credibility will be important.

of the speaker as the basis for deciding whether to accept the persuasive message.[7]

Similarly, game theoretic models often used in economics and political science consistently emphasize the importance of source credibility. These types of models, labeled "strategic communication," "cheap talk," or "signaling" models in their various incarnations, almost uniformly predict that the receiver's beliefs about the sender will be a key factor in determining whether he or she accepts an informative message (V. Crawford and Sobel 1982; Sobel 1985; Calvert 1986; Farrell and Gibbons 1989; Gilligan and Krehbiel 1989; Austen-Smith 1994; Lupia and McCubbins 1998; Lupia 2002). Usually, the source criterion is that the recipient must believe the sender has interests (or incentives) that match his or her own. In political science scholarship, having the same interests is often translated to mean holding the same ideology (e.g. McKelvey and Ordeshook 1985, 1986; Gilligan and Krehbiel 1987, 1989; Banks 1991; Lupia and McCubbins 1998; Lupia 2002).

Finally, a substantial political science literature consists of empirical studies of the use of heuristics, or "cue-taking." These studies, which show that ordinary citizens use cues from elites who share their ideology or demographic background or whom they simply like as information shortcuts when forming their opinions, share a similar intellectual lineage and posit similar source credibility criteria as the aforementioned game theoretic models (Camines and Kuklinski 1990; Popkin 1991; Sniderman, Brody, and Tetlock 1991; Mondak 1993; Kuklinski and Hurley 1994; Lupia 1994).

Overall, the only major persuasion theory where source credibility is not always important is the elaboration-likelihood model, where source attributes do not matter when individuals are in "high involvement" situations. Yet Zaller (1992, 46–47) makes a convincing case that, in modern American politics, the vast majority of the population is neither as involved nor as interested as those in Petty and Cacioppo's (1981) experiments who evaluated message content. As he puts it, in American politics, "[t]he stakes are theoretically high, but people find it hard to stay interested" (Zaller 1992, 47).[8] Given this, it is fair to say that, while prominent

---

[7] In experiments testing the elaboration-likelihood model, source credibility is often operationalized by manipulating the expertise of the source. When subjects are not motivated or able to evaluate the content of the arguments, the expertise of the source determines whether they accept the arguments and are persuaded.

[8] On the lack of political engagement by most of the public, see Campbell et al. (1980 [1960], chap. 8), P. Converse (1964), Zaller (1992, chap. 2), and Delli Carpini and Keeter (1996). This lack of interest could be a rational response, considering that any single individual is unlikely to affect national policy (Downs 1957).

theories of persuasion differ in important ways, all predict that the influence of messages will depend on the trustworthiness of the messenger.

One Could Expect Media Trust to Affect Political Learning

Considering that both media persuasion and source credibility have been studied extensively, there has been surprisingly little research connecting the two.[9] This chapter examines the extent to which news media persuasion depends on attitudes toward the news media as an institution. The persuasion literature argues that views toward entire institutions can be consequential. For instance, in describing source credibility effects, Petty and Cacioppo (1981, 61) state that "[t]he originator or *source* of a persuasive communication may be a person (e.g., the president of the United States), a group (e.g., your family), an institution (e.g., Stanford University), and so forth" (italics in the original). In looking at this relationship, I focus on persuasion resulting from information transmission about broad national policy outcomes.

If the reception of politically relevant information depends on people's attitudes toward the news media as an institution, what patterns should we expect to see? One initial complication is that, while most

[9] To my knowledge, nine prior studies have looked at source credibility effects in media persuasion, and none of these have looked at information effects. These all find attitudes toward the media to be influential. In a laboratory experiment, Iyengar and Kinder (1985) found that those who trusted the media were more susceptible to agenda-setting effects from television news. In an experiment embedded in a phone survey, Lupia and McCubbins (1998, chap. 9) found that when respondents were told a media talk-show host's position on an issue they were more likely to adopt that host's position if they believed he was trustworthy or knowledgeable on the topic. In another laboratory experiment, Miller and Krosnick (2000) found that only those who trusted the media (and were politically knowledgeable) were susceptible to priming from newspaper articles. And in another laboratory experiment, Druckman (2001) found that framing in articles from an untrustworthy newspaper did not affect readers' opinions as much as articles from a trustworthy newspaper did. In a similar study, Chong and Druckman (2007a) found not only that frames from more trusted papers have more influence but that, when subjects were exposed to two competing frames, the one in the more trusted newspaper tended to prevail and shape opinions. Tsfati (2002) looked at polls over time and found that those who lacked confidence in the press resisted media agenda setting. Elsewhere, Tsfati (2003) examined people's beliefs about others' opinions, finding that those who trust the media are more likely to accept media messages about the national division of public opinion. Chiang and Knight (2008) combined newspaper endorsement data with presidential vote preference data from the 2000 and 2004 National Annenberg Election Studies. They found, consistent with Calvert's (1985) model, that endorsements were more influential when they went against a newspaper's perceived bias. Finally, also consistent with Calvert's (1985) predictions, Baum and Groeling (2009) found, using an online experiment and observational survey data, that messages on cable news channels were more influential when they contradicted the channel's perceived bias.

theories of persuasion agree that perceived source attributes are important, they differ in identifying what type of attributes are most critical.
While game theoretic models place importance on perceptions of the
sender's similar ideological orientation, expertise, and knowledgeability,
the receive-accept-sample model puts greater emphasis on the former
and the elaboration-likelihood model puts more importance on the latter
two. Yet since the main concern here is the impact of the general lack of
confidence in the institutional news media, my goal is to theorize about
the consequences of having generally negative versus generally positive
attitudes toward the press. There is little indication that the trend toward
distrust of the institutional media in recent decades has been concentrated
on certain dimensions of evaluation. Thus, an attempt to understand the
consequences of this trend should examine press evaluations on a general
negative-to-positive continuum.

Given this, imagine that a person has a prior belief about national
conditions in a given policy area. Then, after receiving a media message
about national conditions in that area, the person's subsequent beliefs
about these conditions are some weighted average of his or her prior
beliefs and the new information. How much weight will people give to
media messages versus prior beliefs? At one extreme, one could imagine
a person who accepts whatever the media tells him or her and gives no
weight to prior beliefs. After encountering media information, this person's new beliefs would perfectly match the information provided. On the
other extreme, one could imagine someone who discounts every media
message he or she encounters. After encountering media information, this
person's beliefs remain what they were before and have no association
with the new information. It is likely that most people fall somewhere
between these two extremes.

What determines the relative weight given to previous beliefs versus new
messages? At the outset, one could intuitively expect at least two things to
be important. First, the more certain a person is about their prior beliefs,
the more influence I would expect these beliefs to have. Second, consistent with the source credibility literature, one could expect those who trust
the news media establishment more to give more weight to information
it provides. As this book is mainly concerned with attitudes toward the
institutional news media, this second prediction will be the main focus of
the rest of this chapter. If attitudes toward the news media do in fact play a
mediating role in information transmission to the public, I expect that: all
else equal, learning from informative media messages is directly related to
the positivity of attitudes toward the institutional news media.[10]

---

[10] Formally, the theory described here can be represented as a Bayesian decision theory
model with normal priors and a normally distributed message. I outline such a model in

Furthermore, if the above statement is true, it also leads to a second, auxiliary prediction involving the tendency of individuals' divergent initial beliefs to converge over time. Imagine two individuals, one a Democrat and the other a Republican. Assume they have different beliefs about economic performance under a Democratic president. Prior to the president taking office, the Democratic individual expects the economy to do well and the Republican expects the economy to do poorly. Then the president serves his or her term, and the news media transmit information about how the economy actually performed during the term. These individuals' new beliefs will be weighted averages of their divergent previous beliefs and the same new information. This will result in their beliefs converging to the extent that each gives weight to the message. In this example, at the conclusion of the presidential term, the Democrat and the Republican will have more similar perceptions of economic performance if they trust the news media than if they distrust the news media. Thus, my second expectation is: all else equal, people with divergent predispositions will have more similar beliefs after receiving media messages if they have more positive attitudes toward the news media.[11]

To test these predictions, I examine how citizens learn about broad national conditions. There are several reasons for this. First, I am interested in attitudes toward the press *as an institution*, which I suspect will most affect informative messages that are prominent in the institutional press and are reported in relatively similar ways by many of these outlets. Second, no previous study has examined the consequences of trust in the institutional news media (or any type of media evaluation) for this type

---

Ladd (2004; 2006, chap. 3). Essentially, in this chapter, I test comparative statics predictions from this type of Bayesian decision theory model, where message precision is a positive function of the recipient's trust in the news media. Comparative statics are necessary because these types of models are very difficult to identify when estimating them directly (Achen 1992; Bartels 1993). Successfully estimating their parameters through a method like maximum likelihood or nonlinear least squares usually requires making restrictive assumptions about quantities in the model. For example, Bartels (1993) estimates a Bayesian voter learning model by assuming prior precision is proportional to message precision. Unfortunately, that approach would not work in this case because the goal here is to look particularly at the effect of variation in message precision. For other examples using Bayesian models to represent voter learning, see Achen (1992; 2002; 2005), Bartels (1993), Calvert (1980; 1986), Calvert and MacKuen (1985), Gerber and Green (1998), Ladd (2004; 2006) and Zechman (1979). Fiorina (1977; 1981, chap. 4) presents a similar mathematical model of party choice that can be easily adapted into a Bayesian framework (Calvert 1980). For examples of apparent deviations from Bayesian learning by voters, see Bartels (2002a). For fully game theoretic models of media persuasion, where media organizations and the mass public behave strategically, see Bovitz, Druckman, and Lupia (2002) and Baron (2005). For work in Bayesian decision theory outside of political science, see Robert (1994), Wald (1950), and Winkler (2003).

[11] For a formalization of this result, see Bartels (2002a, 121–22) and Ladd (2006, 102–5).

of persuasion. Finally, the press's role as an information source is central to our notions of how democracy ought to work. As Lippmann (1997 [1922]) pointed out, if the public is to have control over its elected officeholders, it needs accurate information about the state of the world.

More recent scholars have confirmed Lippmann's assertion that most people acquire their information about the state of the nation from the news media (Zaller 1992; Hetherington 1996; Mutz 1998). Certainly, some citizens also learn through social communication. Still, very often this passes on information originally coming from the press (Lazarsfeld, Berelson, and Gaudet 1948; Katz and Lazarsfeld 1955; Katz 1957; Huckfeldt and Sprague 1995; Schmitt-Beck 2003). So when an individual confronts new information about the state of the economy, war and peace, and so on, whether he or she gets it from the press directly or from other people secondhand, we should expect attitudes toward the press to be paramount.

The remaining four sections of this chapter test these predictions by examining how learning about national conditions depends on attitudes toward the news media as an institution. The first section presents evidence that those who distrust the media have more partisan and less accurate beliefs about the world. The second examines changes in perceptions over time, showing that those who distrust the press are more resistant to new information. The third uses an experiment to illustrate how media distrust causes resistance to informative messages, even when all subjects receive exactly the same message. The last section shows that, in addition to responding differently to the messages they do encounter, those who distrust the media also seek out more partisan sources of news.

LEARNING ABOUT NATIONAL CONDITIONS DEPENDS ON MEDIA TRUST:
CROSS-SECTIONAL SURVEY EVIDENCE

I first turn to the 2000 ANES. In that year, the ANES asked a randomly chosen half of its respondents to report how national conditions had changed since President Bill Clinton was elected in 1992. Almost all of these questions focused on things that most people prefer more or less regardless of their ideology.[12] These policy outcome questions probed change in the federal budget deficit, national economic performance, national security, the moral climate, and crime.[13] The questions directly

[12] Stokes (1966b) labeled these "valence" issues.

[13] The 2000 ANES also asked a sixth question in this battery. It asked for people's perceptions of how the level of government assistance to the poor had changed since 1992. This question is different from the five that I examine because it is not a valence issue. Unlike valence issues, one would not expect everyone in the public to agree whether assistance to the poor should increase or decrease. For example, Democrats may think more aid to the poor

reflected on whether things had gone well or poorly during the Clinton presidency, providing an opportunity to test the convergence prediction. It seems reasonable to assume that, prior to Clinton taking office, Democrats expected national conditions under Clinton to be better than Republicans expected them to be. If Republicans and Democrats received similar media messages about the actual state of the nation over these eight years and media attitudes moderate media influence, one would expect more belief convergence among partisans who trust the media. Fortunately, the 2000 ANES survey obtained respondents' evaluations of the news media by asking, "How much of the time do you think you can trust the media to report the news fairly (just about always, most of the time, only some of the time, or almost never)?"

Figure 6-1 compares the mean perceptions of Democrats and Republicans in these five policy areas, with respondents separated into those who trust the media less ("only some of the time" or "almost never") and those who trust it more ("most of the time" or "just about always"). On the deficit, the economy, national security, and the moral climate partisans who distrust the media have more polarized perceptions than partisans who trust the media.[14] The only area where partisan differences are not greater is crime. Overall, those who distrust the media update their beliefs less in response to events, instead relying more on their partisanship. As illustrated in the statistical results presented in table 6-1 in the appendix, the association between partisan belief polarization and media attitudes in four of five policy areas holds up even when controlling for respondents' level of general political knowledge, which serves as a good proxy for certainty of prior beliefs (Achen 1992, 207; Zaller 1992).[15]

---

is good and that things will go well under Clinton. So they expect that aid to the poor will increase under Clinton. Republicans, on the other hand, may think assistance to the poor is bad and expect that things will go badly under Clinton. Thus, they also expect assistance to the poor to be higher under Clinton. For this reason, we would not expect to find partisan divergence in perceptions of how assistance to the poor changed under Clinton. The data are consistent with this prediction. There is no significant partisan divergence in perceptions of aid to the poor (Bartels 2002a), even among those who distrust the news media.

[14] Bartels examined a similar battery of questions in the 1988 ANES survey that elicited respondents' perceptions of how national conditions had changed during the Reagan presidency. While answers to these questions also exhibit partisan polarization (Bartels 2002a, table 3), one cannot check for these patterns in 1988 because there is no media evaluation question in the 1988 ANES.

[15] Besides crime, the only other exception is economic performance. Here the interaction coefficient between party identification and media trust is not statistically significant at conventional levels ($p < .22$) when general political knowledge is included as a control. While the coefficient is just as large, controlling for political knowledge increases the standard error. Without controlling for the political knowledge interaction, the interaction between party identification and trust in the media is marginally significant at $p < .076$.

Because these questions ask how respondents perceive national conditions, rather than asking about their preferences among policies or candidates, some have objectively correct answers. For the deficit, the national economy, and the crime rate, one can compare national statistics with respondents' perceptions. Assuming that the news media transmits messages that correspond with national conditions, this allows for another test of source credibility effects. In addition to showing more convergence, one should expect that, after receiving a media message, those who trust the media will have beliefs that are closer to the message than those who distrust the media.

In 1992, the federal budget deficit was $290.4 billion, compared to a $236.4 billion surplus in 2000. So the correct answer was that the deficit was "much smaller," coded as 1 on the 0 to 1 scale. In the case of economic performance, in 1992 the U.S. Gross Domestic Product (GDP) grew by 5.6% and the unemployment rate was 7.5%. In 2000, the U.S GDP grew by 5.9% and the unemployment rate was 4.0%. So the most accurate answer regarding the economy was "somewhat better," or possibly "much better," coded as .75 and 1, respectively. In the case of the crime rate, between 1992 and 2000 the crime rate declined 27%, from 5,661 to 4,124 crimes per million people. So the crime rate could be accurately described as either "somewhat better" or "much better," coded as .75 and 1, respectively (U.S. Census Bureau 2002, 305, 417, 367, 183).

Figure 6-1 shows some evidence that partisans' perceptions of these national conditions not only tend to converge when they trust the news media but also get closer to the objectively correct answer when there is one. On perceptions of the deficit, most of the movement is among Republicans, who perceive the deficit as getting better the more they trust the media. Democrats' perceptions change much less because their partisanship already predisposes them to think that the deficit will improve under a Democratic administration. On the subject of the economy, both Democrats and Republicans perceive better performance when they trust the press. On the subject of the crime rate, the movement is predominantly among Democrats. Democrats who trust the media perceive that the crime rate has gotten better than those who distrust the media do. Among Republicans, trust in the media appears to be unrelated to crime perceptions. So the data in these three areas suggest that most people's perceptions of objective national statistics move closer to reality as they trust the media more.

I now turn my attention back to economic perceptions. While perceptions of economic performance during the Clinton presidency showed greater partisan divergence when respondents distrusted the media, there was not enough data in the half of the 2000 ANES sample who were asked this question to determine whether the relationship was statistically significant when controlling for political knowledge. One further way to investigate whether economic perceptions follow the same pattern as

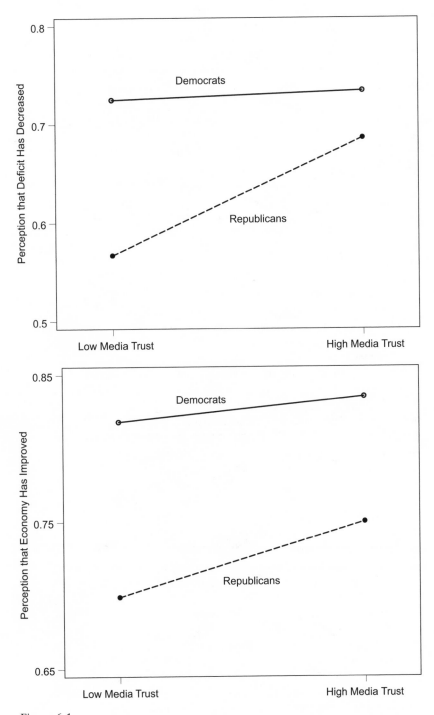

Figure 6-1.

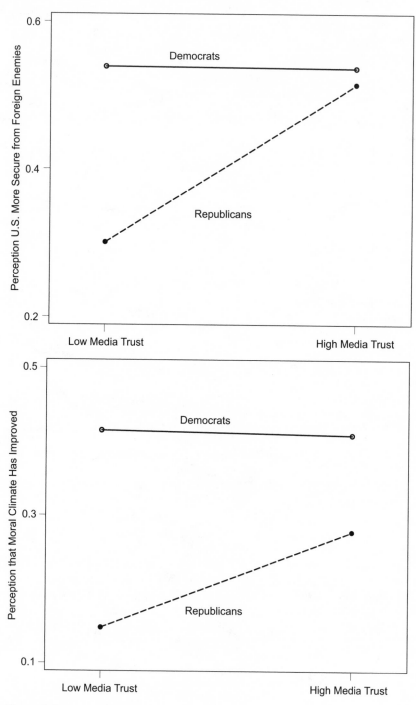

Figure 6-1.

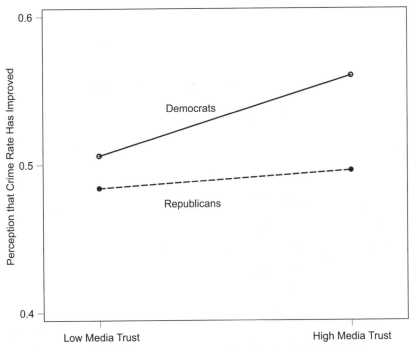

Figure 6-1. Perceptions of change in national conditions, 1992–2000. *Note:* Dots represent mean perceptions for each grouping. All perception variables are coded to range from 0 to 1, with interior categories equally spaced between those endpoints. I collapsed the media trust variable from four into two categories because there are too few respondents in the two extreme categories. The low media trust group includes those who trust the media "only some of the time" or "almost never." The high media trust category includes those who trust the media "most of the time" or "just about always." As a result, the number of respondents represented by each dot in the graphs varies between 110 and 193. For more details, see table 6-1. *Source:* 2000 ANES.

deficit, crime, national security, and moral climate perceptions is to use another retrospective economic perception question that is asked more often. In 1996, 1998, and 2000 the ANES asked its entire sample the following two-part retrospective economic question: "Now thinking about the economy in the country as a whole, would you say that over the past year the nation's economy has gotten better, stayed the same or gotten worse? Would you say much better (worse) or somewhat better (worse)?"[16] My

[16] This question has been asked in similar form in every ANES election survey since 1980. But because trust in the media was not asked until 1996, 1998, and 2000, I use these years in my analysis.

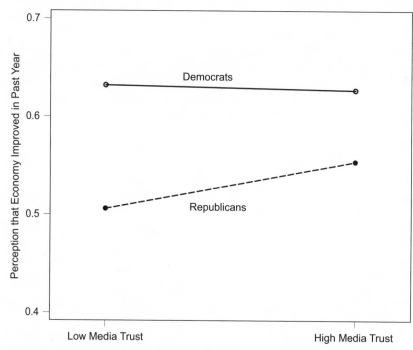

Figure 6-2. Perceptions of the national economy in the past year (1996, 1998, 2000). *Note:* Dots represent mean perceptions for each grouping. Perception and media trust variables are coded as in figure 6-1. The number of respondents represented by each dot varies between 577 and 1,173. For more details, see table 6-1. *Source:* 1996, 1998, and 2000 ANES.

expectations for this question are the same as for perceptions of the whole Clinton presidency. Partisans will expect economic performance to conform to their partisan orientation and then will be influenced to varying degrees by information from the news media reflecting actual economic conditions in the year before the election. Thus, if media evaluations moderate the reception of messages, there should again be greater belief divergence among those who distrust the media. In each of these years, economic performance was very good. Annual change in GDP in 1996, 1998, and 2000 was 5.7%, 5.3%, and 5.9%, respectively (U.S. Census Bureau 2002, 417). Considering that economic conditions were very similar, I pool data from these three years.

Figure 6-2 compares the perceptions of how the economy had performed in the past year among Democrats and Republicans who trust the media more and less. They manifest the same pattern as perceptions of Clinton's entire term. Republicans and Democrats exhibit less partisan divergence when they trust the media. Because these data include the entire sample from three ANES election surveys, one can more precisely estimate whether the association holds up with control variables. The statistical results in column 6 of table 6-1 show that this association is statistically significant even when controlling for general political knowledge. Finally, as with perceptions of Clinton's entire term, those who trust the media more also tend to converge toward the correct answers of "somewhat better" (.75) or "much better" (1). In summary, perceptions of national conditions show patterns quite consistent with the idea that evaluations of the press moderate the influence of media messages on the public's beliefs. In the absence of trusted information, people increasingly fall back on their partisan predispositions to construct beliefs about national conditions.

RESPONSES TO NATIONAL SECURITY CRISES DEPEND ON MEDIA TRUST: PANEL SURVEY EVIDENCE

The data in the previous section measure people's beliefs at a single point in time. Although the patterns are consistent with expectations, it is possible that some other process caused the patterns. One alternative explanation might be that causation goes in the opposite direction: polarized beliefs cause distrust of the institutional media. One way to examine the direction of causation is by looking at temporal order. To gain more confidence that media distrust is a cause of the patterns in the previous section, next I analyze how perceptions change over time using a panel survey.

It is hard to imagine the American national security landscape changing more dramatically over a two-year period than it did between the fall of 2000 and the fall of 2002. In this period, the U.S. experienced the terrorist attacks of September 11, 2001, the initial fighting of the war in Afghanistan, and the buildup to war in Iraq. Yet, as Lippmann (1997 [1922]) describes, relatively few individuals experience events like these directly. The vast majority of the public learned about them through the news media. Luckily for those interested in studying their effects on the public, the ANES interviewed a panel of the same respondents at the time of both the 2000 presidential election and the 2002 congressional election. To see how media coverage of these national security crises affected public beliefs about national security, I examine questions asked of these respondents in both 2000 and 2002 that probed the extent to which they were "worried about conventional war" and "worried about nuclear war."

Between the fall of 2000 and the fall of 2002, people became much more concerned about both types of war. Those "very worried" or "somewhat worried" about conventional war increased from 44% to 84% of respondents, while those "very worried" or "somewhat worried" about nuclear war increased from 43% to 74%. Thus, based on our knowledge of world events and this initial examination of the data, it seems clear that respondents received a message from the media indicating that the threat of war was much larger than they had previously thought. If the reception of informative media messages depends on media attitudes, we should expect those with positive attitudes toward the news media to increase their worry about war more than those with negative media attitudes.

Figure 6-3 compares average perceptions of war in 2000 and 2002 among those with more and less trust in the media. I put respondents' perceptions of the threat of war on a 0 to 1 scale, with 1 indicating "very worried," .5 indicating "somewhat worried," and 0 indicating "not worried at all." On this scale, among all panel respondents, average concern about conventional war increased by .262. Among those who trust the media "most of the time" or "just about always," worry increased by .308. In contrast, among those who trust the media "only sometimes" or "just about never," it increased by just .219. Concern about nuclear war shows a similar pattern. Those who were more trusting of the media increased their worry by .299, while those who were less trusting increased it by just .221. The more elaborate statistical results in table 6-2 in the appendix find that this effect of media trust holds up when controlling for respondents' general political knowledge, strength of party identification, network news exposure, newspaper exposure, talk radio exposure, party identification, and average trust.

These results support the proposition that attitudes toward the press moderate the news media's influence over public perceptions. One benefit of the panel survey is that, because it is measuring real reactions to actual events, we can have more confidence in the generalizability of the results than we would with a laboratory experiment. However, there are also weaknesses. Despite our best efforts, in any real-world setting, one can never control for all possible confounding variables. It is always possible that the control variables I used are insufficient measures of the forces that need to be held constant, allowing a lurking variable to create spurious associations. Of additional concern, even if distrust in the media is causing resistance to new messages, it could be doing so through two possible mechanisms: direct resistance to messages received or exposure to more partisan, less mainstream news sources.

LEARNING ABOUT ONGOING MILITARY CONFLICTS DEPENDS ON MEDIA TRUST: EXPERIMENTAL EVIDENCE

To clear up some of this uncertainty, I conducted an experiment to test how exposure to the exact same message has different effects depending on

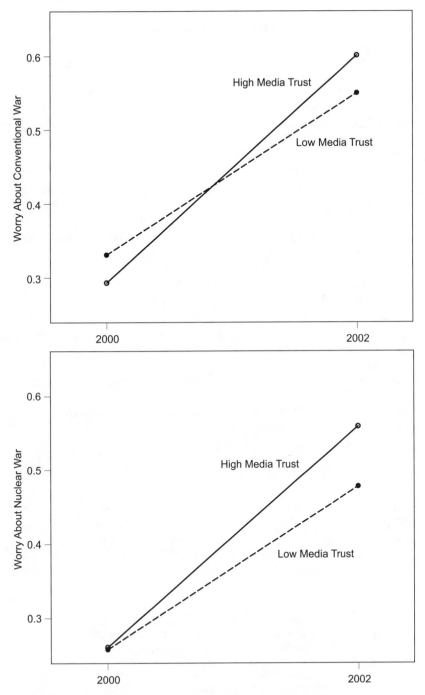

Figure 6-3. Change in worry about war between 2000 and 2002 depends on trust in the news media. *Source:* 2000–2002 ANES Panel Study.

subjects' attitudes toward the media. In this way I can be more confident that the patterns in the two previous sections result from resistance to messages received rather than from spurious variables that were not held constant or entirely from selective exposure. In conducting an experiment, I do sacrifice some realism, raising concerns about generalizability (or external validity). However, in this case I believe the benefits, such as the ability to precisely control message exposure and to assure, through random assignment, that other variables are held constant, outweigh the limitations.[17]

In the experiment, I wish to reproduce the type of circumstance studied above: where individuals are exposed to a media message with new information about an area of national policy.[18] I recruited undergraduates at Princeton University to participate in an Internet survey. Between January 12 and February 2, 2004, 902 students completed the survey. At this time, media messages about American involvement in Iraq were very positive, and most Americans had correspondingly positive views of the Iraq War and occupation. For instance, in a national poll conducted January 6–11, 2004, by the Pew Center for the People and the Press, 70% of respondents thought the Iraq occupation was going either "very well" or "fairly well" and 62% said that using military force in Iraq was "the right decision" (Pew Research Center for the People and the Press 2004). The experiment examines the effect of information about American casualties on these views.

Experimental subjects had a 50% chance of being randomly assigned to be told that recently "the news media has reported that there have been a total of 2,572 American casualties in the U.S. military effort in Iraq." They were then asked whether they had seen the story. This was the most up-to-date casualty statistic at the time the questionnaire was written (Brookings Institution 2003).[19] Those not assigned to receive this message (the control group) were simply told that recently "the news media has reported on the current state of the U.S. military effort in Iraq" and asked if they had seen the story. I expected that, relative to the control group, those given information about the number of U.S. casualties would have more negative perceptions of the U.S. military effort in Iraq. To test this prediction, later in the survey, after a question on an unrelated

[17] On the benefits of experiments generally, see Rubin (1974), Green (2002), and Shadish, Cook, and Campbell (2002).

[18] As with the survey experiments in chapter 5, I again use Gilens's (2001) study of information effects on policy preferences as a model for the design of this study.

[19] When I (and the Brookings Institution) use the term *casualty*, we use it in the conventional sense, meaning a soldier who can no longer serve due to death, injury, or other battlefield incapacitation. *Merriam-Webster's Collegiate Dictionary* (11th ed.) defines *casualty* as "a military person lost through death, wounds, injury, sickness, internment, or capture or through being missing in action."

topic, the students were asked to evaluate how "the U.S. military effort in Iraq is going" and whether they thought the United States "made the right decision or the wrong decision" in going to war.[20] (The complete questionnaire is provided in the appendix.) While I expected this information to alter political beliefs about, and attitudes toward, U.S. involvement in Iraq, the purpose of the experiment was to see if attitudes toward the news media moderate these effects. For this purpose, earlier in the survey, respondents were asked to evaluate the accuracy and unbiasedness of news media coverage on a 100-point scale.

The results, illustrated in figure 6-4, show that subjects did respond differently to the casualty message depending on their attitudes toward the press. The top panel shows the expected effect of receiving the casualties message on beliefs about how the Iraq occupation is going among those who rate the accuracy and fairness of the news media at 20 and 80. The lower panel shows the same comparison, except that the dependent variable is whether one believes that using force in Iraq was the right decision.

Both figures show the same pattern. Among those in the control group, those with positive evaluations of the media have beliefs about Iraq that are much more in line with the general public as a whole. Control group subjects who trusted the media, consistent with the dominant media messages of the time, tended to believe that the Iraq occupation was going better and was not a mistake. However, consistent with my expectations, the new casualty information attributed to the media induced their perceptions of the Iraq occupation to become more negative. While those with positive attitudes toward the press responded to the casualty message, those with negative attitudes toward the press did not. Not only did they resist, but they reacted against the message by becoming slightly more positive in their perceptions of the Iraq occupation. Thus, both prior to and during the experiment, those favorably predisposed to the news media were swayed by media messages, while those unfavorably predisposed were very resistant. Here, attitudes toward the press shape responses to the information, even when individuals are exposed to the same message.[21]

In addition to responding differently to messages they do receive, individuals' attitudes toward the media may change which messages they are exposed to in the first place. To see if this is the case, I look at some survey data measuring exposure to different types of news sources.

---

[20] The unrelated question asks about the construction of a new public library in downtown Princeton, New Jersey. At the time of the survey, the new library was under construction about one block from the university's campus and had been a subject of local controversy for several years because some in town opposed building the new, larger building.

[21] The results in figure 6-4 are based on the regression models presented in table 6-3 in the appendix. The key parameter estimate in these models is the interaction between

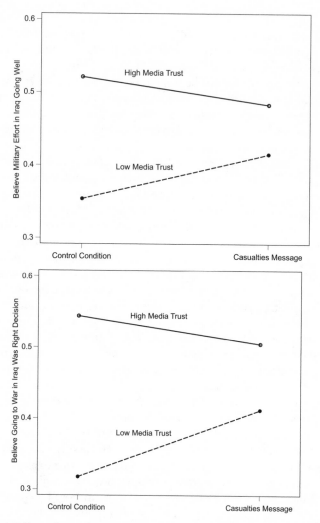

Figure 6-4. Effect of casualty message on opinions about decision to go to war depends on attitudes toward the news media. *Note:* Figure shows predicted values based on the parameter estimates in table 6-3 in the appendix. High media trust represents respondents who give the media a rating of 80 out of 100. Low media trust represents respondents who give the media a rating of 20 out of 100. In the top panel, the dependent variable is a question asking, "How well is the military effort on Iraq going?" Responses are coded "very well" (1), "fairly well" (.67), "not very well" (.33), or "not well at all" (0). In the bottom panel, the dependent variable is a question asking, "Was using force in Iraq the right or wrong decision?" Responses to this question are coded "definitely the right decision" (1), "probably the right decision" (.67), "probably the wrong decision" (.33), or "definitely the wrong decision" (0). For complete question wordings, see the appendix. *Source:* Experiment conducted January 12–February 2, 2004, with Princeton University undergraduates.

Media Distrust Leads People to Utilize Alternative Media Outlets: Cross-Sectional and Panel Survey Evidence

Do those who dislike the institutional news media also seek out different information outlets? In cross-sectional surveys, distrust of the media is correlated with use of alternative news outlets but barely associated at all with exposure to mainstream news sources.[22] The relationship between mainstream news exposure and trust in the press is unclear at best. The correlation between confidence in the press and newspaper readership is a meager .07 in the 2000 GSS, a relationship that is not statistically distinguishable from zero.[23] The 2002 GSS asked respondents how many hours they watched television in an average day, but this only correlated with confidence in the press at .05, also not statistically distinguishable from zero.[24] The ANES shows a positive but very weak connection between trust in the media and mainstream news exposure. In the 2000 ANES, network news exposure and media trust are statistically significantly correlated, but the size of the correlation is relatively small: .07.[25] In contrast, more partisan and less institutional media outlets seem to have larger relationships with media trust. For example, in the 2000 ANES, talk radio exposure is correlated with trust in the media at a statistically significant −.14.[26]

These data hint at a common pattern. The relationship between trust in the news media and exposure to more mainstream news sources (like

---

respondents' rating of the media and whether they received the casualty message. In both cases, the interaction effect is statistically significant and negative, as expected. While the casualties treatment is experimentally manipulated, the other variable used to construct the interaction term (the news media thermometer) is only "quasi-experimental" (Shadish, Cook, and Campbell 2002). Because I rely on real-world variation in news media evaluations, it is possible that these evaluations are serving as a proxy for other attributes. To rule this out, the statistical models in table 6-3 control for the interactions between both party identification and self-reported ideology with the casualty message. Also, because this is a sample of Princeton undergraduates, subjects' level of education and prior political information is held relatively constant.

[22] Tsfati (2002) and Tsfati and Cappella (2003) also find a negative correlation between the use of alternative media sources and trust in the media. However, in at least partial contrast to my results, they also find a positive association between use of mainstream media sources and media attitudes.

[23] Regressing newspaper exposure on confidence produces a coefficient of 0.083 and a standard error of 0.086 when both variables are coded to range from 0 to 1.

[24] Regressing hours of television viewing in an average day on confidence produces a coefficient of 0.015 with a standard error of 0.078 when both variables are coded to range from 0 to 1.

[25] Regressing network news exposure on media trust produces a coefficient of 0.111 with a standard error of 0.041 ($p < .07$) when both variables are coded to range from 0 to 1.

[26] Regressing talk radio exposure on media trust produces a coefficient of −0.159 with a standard error of 0.030 when both variables are coded to range from 0 to 1.

newspapers and network television) tends to be close to zero or only slightly positive. In contrast, there is a clearer relationship between distrust of the media and greater exposure to less institutional, more partisan news formats.

As in so many areas of study, it is difficult to sort out the direction of causation with cross-sectional data. Just as distrust of the institutional media may cause people to search for different sources of news, it is also possible that alternative news outlets merely persuade individuals to dislike the mainstream media with a steady stream of criticism. As chapter 4 documented, criticism of the mainstream press is one of the main topics of partisan media like talk radio, and there is reason to believe these messages do produce media distrust. But does causation also go in the other direction, from media distrust to partisan news exposure?

One way to get greater leverage on the effect of media trust on news exposure is to look over time. Unfortunately, the ANES has never asked its question about talk radio exposure in the same format across different waves of a panel study. However, in 2001, the GSS reinterviewed some of the respondents from its 2000 survey. While confidence in the press was not asked in the 2001 wave, it was asked in 2000, and several questions about news exposure were asked in both waves. These GSS questions probe exposure to various outlets "in the past two years." This means that those asked in the 2000 GSS are reporting media exposure from 1998 through early 2000, while the questions in the 2001 reinterviews cover exposure from 1999 through early 2001. This allows one to see whether the increase in news exposure that comes with a presidential election campaign is affected by confidence in the press. The main (and sometimes serious) limitation of this dataset is that most of the news exposure questions were asked only to subsamples of the reinterviewees. With some questions, the number of respondents is quite small, necessitating more tentative conclusions.

Figure 6-5 illustrates the relationship between newspaper readership (which was asked of all panel participants) in 2000 and 2001 and confidence in the press. While those with more press confidence read newspapers more frequently in both waves, this relationship is not statistically significant, nor is the change in readership over time significantly associated with confidence.

A small subset (about 200) of the panel respondents were randomly selected to be asked whether they used the Internet to search for "government" information. Figure 6-6 shows that change in Internet use for this purpose does seem to be related to confidence in the press. Internet usage increases among those with "hardly any" or "some" confidence in the press but not at all among those with "a great deal" of confidence. The relationship between change in Internet usage for government

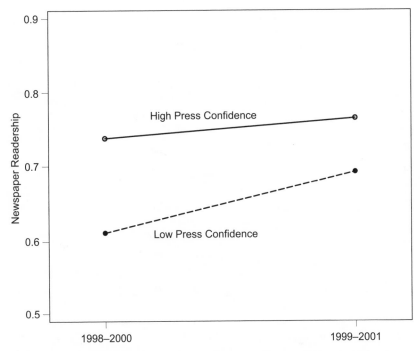

Figure 6-5. Confidence in the press and change in newspaper readership, 2000–2001. *Note:* Newspaper readership is coded from 0 to 1 with the following categories: never (0), less than once a week (.25), once a week (.5), a few times a week (.75), and every day (1). High press confidence includes respondents with "a great deal" or "only some" confidence. Low press confidence includes respondents with "hardly any" confidence. The sample size is 231 for the low press confidence group and 280 for the high press confidence group. There is not a statistically significant association between change in newspaper readership and confidence in the press. *Source:* 2000 GSS and 2001 Reinterviews.

information and press confidence is statistically distinguishable from zero and persists even when controlling for party identification, ideology, education, and average confidence in other institutions (see table 6-4 in the appendix).

All of those interviewed in 2000 and 2001 were also asked (in each wave) whether in the past two years they had "looked for information about the views or background of a candidate for political office." As one might expect, the portion of people reporting searching for information about political candidates increased in the survey after the presidential campaign. However, this increase was not significantly related to press confidence. Among those with "only some" or "a great deal" of

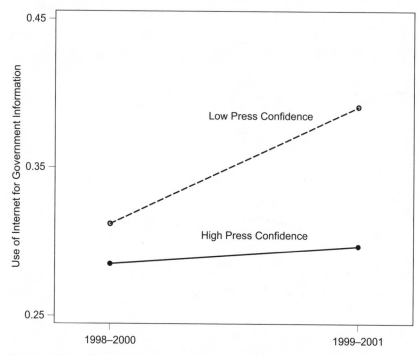

Figure 6-6. Confidence in the press and change in Internet usage for government information, 2000–2001. *Note:* World Wide Web usage in the past 30 days is coded from 0 to 1 with the following categories: never (0), one to two times (.333), two to five times (.666), and more than five times (1). High press confidence and low press confidence groups coded as in figure 6-5. Figure includes respondents who were interviewed in both waves of the panel and were randomly selected to receive the web usage question battery in each wave. The sample size is 92 for the low press confidence group and 118 for the high press confidence group. For more details, see table 6-4 in the appendix. *Source:* 2000 GSS and 2001 Reinterviews.

confidence in the press, the portion looking for candidate information increased 13 percentage points (from 6% to 19%). Among those with "hardly any" confidence, the number looking for candidate information increased by 13 percentage points (from 9% to 22%) (see figure 6-7).

Yet while those without press confidence still search for candidate information, they seem to search in different ways. Among those who did report searching for information about political candidates, a very small subsample (about sixty respondents) of the 2002 reinterviewees were selected to be asked whether they searched in specific places. Of particular interest here, the survey asked whether respondents had searched for

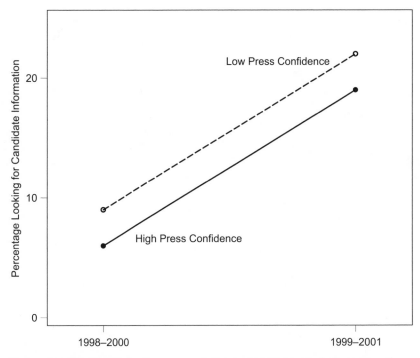

Figure 6-7. Confidence in the press and change in looking for information about candidates for office, 2000–2001. *Note:* Question wording: "Have you looked for information about the views or background of a candidate for office?" There is not a statistically significant association between change in whether one looks for candidate information and confidence in the press. High press confidence and low press confidence groups coded as in figure 6-5. The sample size is 767 for the low press confidence group and 1,070 for the high press confidence group. High press confidence increased 13 percentage points, from 6% to 19%. Low press confidence increased 13 percentage points, from 9% to 22%. *Source:* 2000 GSS and 2001 Reinterviews.

information in "general news magazines like *Time, Newsweek,* and *US News*" and in any "special magazine or newsletter with a particular policy interest or perspective." Figure 6-8 compares the amount of searching for candidate information in both these types of magazines, as reported in 2000 and 2001, broken down by respondents' confidence in the press.

The small sample size makes drawing firm conclusions difficult, yet it seems there is a difference in readers' use of these two types of magazines. There is no significant relationship between confidence in the press and information seeking in mainstream political magazines in either 2000 or 2001. Use of mainstream magazines also increased at comparable rates

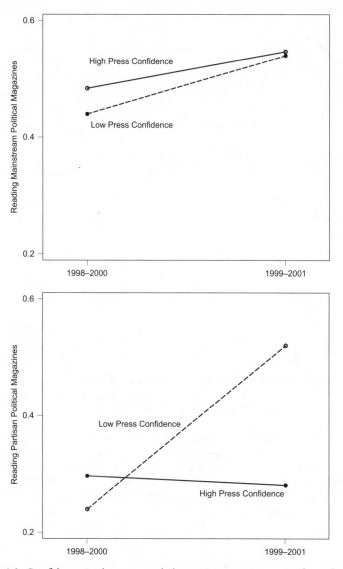

Figure 6-8. Confidence in the press and change in magazine usage for political information, 2000–2001. *Note:* Usage of magazines for information about political candidates in the past two years is coded from 0 to 1, with the following categories: not at all (0), one or two times (.5), and three or more times (1). High press confidence and low press confidence groups coded as in figure 6-5. Figure includes respondents who were interviewed in both waves of the panel, were randomly selected to receive the question battery investigating whether and how they searched for candidate information, and indicated that they had searched for candidate information. The sample size is 25 for the low press confidence group and 32 for the high press confidence group. For more details, see table 6-5 in the appendix. *Source:* 2000 GSS and 2001 Reinterviews.

regardless of media trust during the time period that included the presidential campaign. However, there appears to be a relationship between change in use of magazines with a "policy interest or perspective" and confidence in the press. As the lower panel of figure 6-8 shows, those who had "hardly any" confidence in the press increased their use of these more partisan magazines, while those with "only some" or "a great deal" of confidence slightly decreased their usage.[27] Even with the small sample size, this negative relationship between confidence in the press and the use of partisan political magazines is still statistically distinguishable from zero when controlling for party identification, ideology, education, and average confidence (see table 6-5 in the appendix).

Confidence in the press appears not only to affect whether people accept messages they receive from the mainstream media but also to change their patterns of media exposure. The effect of press confidence on change in exposure resulting from a presidential campaign appears to depend on the nature of the news outlet. For mainstream, institutional sources of news like newspapers and general news magazines, confidence in the press has very little discernable effect on people's usage decisions. What differentiates those with low confidence in the press is that they are more likely to seek out other sources of political information. They are significantly more likely to use the Internet to search for information about government and, when searching for candidate information, to gravitate toward magazines with a clear policy agenda.

ATTITUDES TOWARD THE NEWS MEDIA SHAPE THE PICTURES IN OUR HEADS

This chapter began by reminding us of the problem modern democracies face in ensuring that citizens can hold government accountable: citizens are unable to acquire firsthand the information they need to evaluate the conduct of government officials. Instead, they must rely on the press to construct "pictures" of the world with which to evaluate political leaders. While Lippmann (1997 [1922]) emphasized the danger of the media misleading the public by projecting a distorted vision of reality, it is also clear that without any information, citizens would also have great difficulty controlling a democratic government. This may be why Lippmann, rather than simply condemning journalism, tried to reform it into a more accurate information source for citizens.

This chapter presents evidence that a lack of faith in the institutional press leads to a significant information loss for the citizenry. Those who

---

[27] The latter two categories are combined because only three respondents had "a great deal" of confidence.

distrust the press are more resistant to new information about the state of the nation in major policy areas. This occurs through two different mechanisms. These individuals are both less influenced by the informative messages they receive from the mainstream press and more likely to augment these sources with less conventional, more opinionated sources of news. As a consequence, they are not simply less informed but less informed in systematic ways that reflect and reinforce their partisan predispositions.

Americans tend to choose news sources and interpret messages consistently with their political predispositions. Consequently, they form beliefs about objective facts that reflect those predispositions.[28] Media distrust exacerbates all these tendencies. In this way, increasingly negative attitudes toward the institutional media create a public whose beliefs and preferences are more polarized and more immune to changes in the national landscape. Chapter 7 examines the implications of this for citizens' ability to hold politicians accountable at election time.

Appendix

QUESTIONNAIRE FOR EXPERIMENT CONDUCTED JANUARY 12– FEBRUARY 2, 2004, WITH PRINCETON UNIVERSITY UNDERGRADUATES

Question 1

"We'd like you to rate on a scale from 0 to 100 whether you think the news media reports the news accurately and fairly. Zero means very unfavorable, and 100 means very favorable. Fifty means you do not feel favorable or unfavorable. You may use any number from 0 to 100. Where on this scale would you rate the accuracy and fairness of news media reporting?"

Rating: _____

---

[28] On the tendency to self-select news sources that agree with one's political predispositions, see chapter 3. On partisan biases in the interpretation of information, see Gaines et al. (2007). On partisan differences in beliefs about facts, see Bartels (2002a), Kull, Ramsay, and Lewis (2003/2004), and Kull (2006).

Question 2

(Respondents are randomly assigned to receive one of two different versions.)

> Version A: "We are interested in how well the news media gets information out to the public. There are so many news stories these days that most people have trouble following them all. We want to ask about a story the news media has reported to see if you happened to hear about it. Recently, the news media has reported that there have been a total of 2,572 American casualties in the U.S. military effort in Iraq. Have you seen this story?"

> Version B: "We are interested in how well the news media gets information out to the public. There are so many news stories these days that most people have trouble following them all. We want to ask about a story the news media has reported to see if you happened to hear about it. Recently, the news media has reported on the current state of the U.S. military effort in Iraq. Have you seen this story?"

Question 2 Answers

Yes
No

Question 3

"Do you approve of the recent construction of a new public library in downtown Princeton?"

1. Strongly Approve
2. Approve
3. Disapprove
4. Strongly Disapprove

Question 4

"How well is the United States military effort in Iraq going?"

1. Very Well
2. Fairly Well
3. Not Too Well
4. Not Well at All

Question 5

"Do you think the United States made the right decision or the wrong decision in using military force in Iraq?"

1. Definitely the Right Decision
2. Probably the Right Decision
3. Probably the Wrong Decision
4. Definitely the Wrong Decision

Question 6

"Generally speaking, do you think of yourself as a Republican, a Democrat, an Independent, or what?"

1. Strong Democrat
2. Democrat
3. Lean Towards Democrats
4. Independent
5. Lean Towards Republicans
6. Republican
7. Strong Republican

Question 7

"When it comes to politics, do you usually think of yourself as extremely liberal, liberal, slightly liberal, moderate or middle of the road, slightly conservative, conservative, or extremely conservative?"

1. Extremely Liberal
2. Liberal
3. Slightly Liberal
4. Moderate; Middle of the Road
5. Slightly Conservative
6. Conservative
7. Extremely Conservative

TABLE 6-1
Media Trust Reduces Partisan Polarization in Perceptions of National Conditions

	Deficit (1992–2000)	Economy (1992–2000)	National security (1992–2000)	Moral climate (1992–2000)	Crime (1992–2000)	Economy (past year)
Party identification	−1.00**	−1.06**	−1.84**	−1.86**	−0.29	−1.17**
	(0.31)	(0.31)	(0.32)	(0.32)	(0.30)	(0.17)
Party identification × media trust	1.13**	0.61	2.63**	1.17**	−0.18	0.79**
	(0.50)	(0.50)	(0.52)	(0.50)	(0.48)	(0.24)
Media trust	−0.02	0.10	−0.26	0.11	0.60**	−0.02
	(0.31)	(0.32)	(0.30)	(0.30)	(0.30)	(0.14)
Party identification × political knowledge	−0.69	−0.77*	−0.85**	0.12	0.02	0.06
	(0.42)	(0.46)	(0.39)	(0.42)	(0.39)	(0.16)
Political knowledge	1.48**	1.95**	0.42	−0.29	1.19**	0.48**
	(0.26)	(0.29)	(0.20)	(0.23)	(0.23)	(0.09)
Log-likelihood	−956.0	−859.7	−962.6	−917.3	−1065.8	−5675.2
Pseudo R^2	0.05	0.08	0.07	0.07	0.04	0.03
Number of observations	688	740	721	731	730	4,242

**$p < .05$, * $p < .10$ for two-tailed tests

Source: 2000 ANES Survey (first five columns); pooled 1996, 1998, and 2000 ANES Surveys (sixth column)

Note: Table entries are ordered probit coefficients with standard errors in parentheses. All variables are scaled to range from 0 to 1, with the interior categories evenly spaced between these endpoints. Estimates of τ cut-point parameters are not reported. The sixth column's model contains year fixed effects, whose coefficients are not reported.

TABLE 6-2
Regression Model of the Dynamics of Worry about War

	Predicting "worried about conventional war," 2002			Predicting "worried about nuclear war" '02		
	Simple OLS regression	Errors-in-variables regression	Errors-in-variables regression	Simple OLS regression	Errors-in-variables regression	Errors-in-variables regression
Worried about conventional war 2000 / Worried about nuclear war 2000	0.25** (0.05)	0.58** (0.12)	0.67** (0.14)	0.43** (0.04)	0.79** (0.09)	0.78** (0.09)
Trust in the media	0.18** (0.07)	0.14** (0.08)	0.12ᵃ (0.09)	0.18** (0.06)	0.12** (0.06)	0.11** (0.06)
Political knowledge		0.14 (0.09)	0.12 (0.09)		-0.27** (0.07)	-0.28** (0.07)
Strength of party identification		0.08 (0.08)	0.07 (0.08)		0.13** (0.05)	0.12** (0.06)
Network news exposure		0.02 (0.09)	0.02 (0.09)		0.21** (0.06)	0.22** (0.06)
Newspaper exposure		-0.02 (0.08)	-0.06 (0.08)		-0.02 (0.05)	-0.02 (0.05)
Talk radio exposure		-0.05 (0.06)	-0.07 (0.06)		-0.08* (0.05)	-0.08* (0.05)
Party identification		-0.23** (0.05)	-0.23** (0.05)		-0.11** (0.05)	-0.11** (0.04)
Average trust in government and people			0.22* (0.13)			0.01 (0.09)
Intercept	0.41** (0.04)	0.35** (0.09)	0.25** (0.12)	0.32** (0.03)	0.22** (0.06)	0.23** (0.07)
R²	0.06	0.20	0.21	0.16	0.40	0.40
Standard error of regression	0.34	0.31	0.31	0.33	0.28	0.28
Number of observations	427	418	416	560	550	543

** p < .05, * p < .10, ᵃp < .167 for two-tailed tests

Source: 2000–2004 ANES Panel Study.

Note: All variables are scaled to range from 0 to 1, with interior categories evenly spaced between these endpoints. Simple OLS regression models show coefficients with Huber-White robust standard errors in parentheses. Models with control variables employ errors-in-variables regression models because the worry about war survey questions have an unusually high level of measurement error. These models account for the different reliabilities of the various independent variables. In cases where the reliability of explanatory variables could be estimated using an existing three-wave panel study such as the 1992–96 ANES Panel Study, I use those datasets to calculate the questions' reliabilities using the procedure outlined by Heise (1969) to estimate the reliabilities, which is equivalent to reliability estimates produced by the Wiley and Wiley (1970) method for the second wave of the three-wave panel. No three-wave panel study exists to use to estimate the reliability of trust in the media and talk radio exposure. In these cases, I performed robustness checks to see how the results varied with different assumed reliabilities. The reported results assume a reliability of .9 for these variables. I performed robustness checks, ensuring that the effect of trust in the media was substantively the same if these questions are assumed to have any reliability from .6 to 1. The estimated reliabilities of other variables are as follows: worried about conventional war (.42), worried about nuclear war (.48), political knowledge (.82), strength of party

TABLE 6-3

Regression Model of Experiment Illustrating that Effect of Casualty Information Depends on Media Evaluations

	Dependent variable: "How well is the military effort in Iraq going?"		Dependent variable: "Was using force in Iraq the right decision?"	
Casualty message	0.03	0.00	0.05*	0.01
	(0.02)	(0.02)	(0.03)	(0.02)
Casualty message × media thermometer	−0.21**	−0.16**	−0.28**	−0.22**
	(0.10)	(0.08)	(0.11)	(0.09)
Media thermometer	0.35**	0.28**	0.49**	0.38**
	(0.07)	(0.06)	(0.08)	(0.06)
Casualty message × party identification		0.09		0.10
		(0.09)		(0.11)
Party identification		0.22**		0.23**
		(0.07)		(0.08)
Casualty message × ideology		−0.15		−0.19*
		(0.10)		(0.11)
Ideology		0.36**		0.56**
		(0.07)		(0.08)
Intercept	0.42**	0.49**	0.41**	0.51**
	(0.02)	(0.01)	(0.02)	(0.02)
Standard error of regression	0.26	0.22	0.31	0.25
R^2	0.04	0.28	0.06	0.37
Number of observations	889	882	889	884

**$p < .05$, *$p < .10$

Source: Experiment conducted January 12–February 2, 2004, with Princeton University undergraduates.

Note: Table shows coefficients estimated by ordinary least squares regression with Huber-White robust standard errors in parentheses. All explanatory variables are scaled to range from -.5 to .5, with interior categories evenly spaced between these endpoints. The dependent variable is scaled to range from 0 to 1, with the following four categories: "not well at all" (0), "not very well" (.333), "fairly well" (.667), and "very well" (1).

TABLE 6-4

Dynamics of Internet Usage for Government Information, 2000–2001

	Predicting Internet usage for government information in 2001	
Internet usage in 2000	0.90**	0.74**
	(0.22)	(0.24)**
Confidence in press	−0.27[a]	−0.32*
	(0.18)	(0.19)
Party identification		0.50*
		(0.28)
Ideology		−0.30
		(0.39)
Education		1.35**
		(0.66)
Average confidence		0.45
		(0.41)
Log-likelihood	−259.4	−238.6
Pseudo R^2	0.03	0.05
Number of observations	212	200

**$p < .05$, *$p < .10$, [a]$p < .132$ for two-tailed tests

Source: 2000 GSS and 2001 Reinterviews.

Note: All variables are scaled to range from 0 to 1, with interior categories evenly spaced between these endpoints. Table shows ordered probit coefficients with standard errors in parentheses. Estimates of τ cut-point parameters are not reported.

TABLE 6-5
Dynamics of Magazine Usage for Political Information, 2000–2001

	Mainstream news magazines 2001		Partisan political magazines 2001	
Usage in 2000	1.88**	2.57**	0.90*	0.82
	(0.50)	(0.58)	(0.49)	(0.57)
Confidence in press	−0.38	−0.49	−1.51**	−1.10*
	(0.63)	(0.77)	(0.57)	(0.63)
Party identification		0.26		1.09
		(0.76)		(0.71)
Ideology		0.01		−0.08
		(1.32)		(0.98)
Education		0.01		0.63
		(1.42)		(1.34)
Average confidence		−1.98*		0.32
		(1.05)		(0.67)
Pseudo R²	0.17	0.30	0.09	0.14
Log-likelihood	−47.1	−36.5	−50.6	−44.4
Number of observations	57	53	57	53

**$p < .05$, *$p < .10$ for two-tailed tests
Source: 2000 GSS and 2001 Reinterviews.
Note: All variables are scaled to range from 0 to 1, with interior categories evenly spaced between these endpoints. Table shows ordered probit coefficients with standard errors in parentheses. Estimates of τ cut-point parameters are not reported.

News Media Trust and Voting

> And so I'm very hopeful that [the media] actually will get out
> there, and they actually will spend some time with the people,
> because those same people are the people who voted for George
> Bush and said "screw you, major media."
> —Peter Johnson (*On the Media* from NPR 2004)

THE EFFECTS OF MEDIA DISTRUST on learning carry over into the electoral
realm. Voting requires combining one's partisan predisposition with contemporary information about the candidates. In presidential elections,
among the most important contemporary information is national economic performance, which a voter can use to assess retrospectively the
incumbent party.

Being less responsive to new information, those who distrust the institutional media are more likely to fall back on their party identification as a voting cue. They also appear to change how they incorporate
contemporary messages into their decisions, responding less to economic
conditions in the quarter immediately before the election. In this way,
the effects of media distrust on political learning alter how citizens hold
politicians electorally accountable.

PARTY IDENTIFICATION POWERFULLY SHAPES VOTING

Few aspects of American politics have been studied more extensively than
voting. While political scientists, psychologists, and economists have not
come to agreement on a widely accepted theoretical model of voter decision making, several empirical regularities are quite robust. First, psychological identifications with political parties are relatively stable over time
and serve as powerful starting points for voting decisions. Second, voters
can sometimes be convinced to vote against their party identification when
persuaded by contemporary information about the parties or candidates.

Since the 1950s, survey researchers have consistently observed that psychological attachments to the major political parties serve as influential

baselines for voting decisions. Arguably the most influential book ever written on the psychology of voting is *The American Voter* (A. Campbell et al. 1980 [1960]). It analyzed survey data mainly from the 1952 and 1956 presidential elections, and the power of party attachments was one of its main themes. The authors concluded, "Few factors are of greater importance for our national elections than the lasting attachments of millions of Americans to one of the parties. These loyalties establish the basic division of electoral strength within which the competition of particular campaigns takes place" (Campbell et al. 1980 [1960], 121).[1] Inevitably, a work as influential as this has been the subject of criticism in the 50 years since its publication. However, subsequent researchers have found the strong association between vote choice and party identification to be remarkably consistent (e.g. W. Miller 1991; W. Miller and Shanks 1996; Bartels 2000; Green, Palmquist, and Schickler 2002; Johnston, Hagen, and Jamieson 2004; Johnston 2006; Kaufmann, Petrocik, and Shaw 2008; Lewis-Beck et al. 2008).[2]

Compared to most other survey responses that correlate with vote choice, party identification is more immuné to reverse causation or rationalization. The identification people develop early in life tends to persist or change only gradually (P. Converse 1969; A. Campbell et al. 1980 [1960], 162–63; Jennings and Niemi 1981; P. Beck and Jennings 1991; Cowden and McDermott 2000; Green, Palmquist, and Schickler 2002).[3]

---

[1] On *The American Voter*'s authors' perspective on the role of party identification in the political system, see also Stokes (1966a).

[2] To the degree that there has been variation over time in this relationship, the association declined somewhat from the 1950s to the 1970s before rising again in the 1990s and 2000s to levels that were at least as high as those in the 1950s (Bartels 2000; Bafumi and Shapiro 2009). In this way, it seems to follow overall trends in political polarization (Hetherington 2001).

[3] Along these lines, *The American Voter* describes partisanship as a "firm but not immovable attachment" that is "characterized more by stability than by change—not by rigid, immutable fixation on one party rather than the other, but by a persistent adherence and resistance to contrary influence" (A. Campbell et al. 1980 [1960], 148, 146).

Critics of *The American Voter*'s characterization of party identification's role in vote choice have argued that issue opinions and other new information have larger and more immediate effects on party identification. Models using cross-sectional data produce inconsistent results on this question (A. Goldberg 1966; Jackson 1975; Markus and Converse 1979; Page and Jones 1979; Fiorina 1981; W. Miller and Shanks 1996). However, more powerful research designs, particularly those using panel survey data, tend to support the claim that party identification is more stable and influential than other beliefs and opinions (Jennings and Niemi 1981; Gerber and Green 1998; W. Miller 1999; Green, Palmquist, and Schickler 2002). Gerber, Huber, and Washington (2009) demonstrate the influence of party identification with a field experiment. Johnston's (2006) recent review finds that a preponderance of the evidence supports this view. He concludes, "Party identification, at least in the United States and as measured, is a mover but not entirely unmoved" (347).

Another possible challenge to the claim that party identification is stable and relatively unaffected by short-term forces comes from studies examining aggregate, rather than

It seems to function as, in V. O. Key Jr. and Frank Munger's (1970, 253) famous characterization, a "standing decision" among the parties. People can be persuaded to vote for candidates from the other party, but they need compelling reasons to do so. When confronted with new or unfamiliar election choices, they tend to fall back on their standing decision as a shortcut (Conover and Feldman 1989; Rahn 1993; Snyder and Ting 2002; Jessee 2009).

People can decide to vote for the other party in numerous elections without changing their party attachment. In fact, this was one of the main themes of *The American Voter*, that Eisenhower's decisive wins in the 1952 and 1956 elections had not changed the electorate's basic partisan predispositions, which tended to favor the Democrats. The Youth-Parent Socialization Study asked the same 855 respondents in 1965 and 1982 which party they identified with. Despite the political tumult of the 1960s and 1970s, including the Vietnam War, the Nixon landslide of 1972, the Watergate scandal, Democratic victories in the 1974 congressional election and the 1976 presidential election, the stagflation of the late 1970s, and the victory of Ronald Reagan in 1980, only 5.7% of party identifiers switched to the other party over these seventeen years (Green, Palmquist, and Schickler 2002, 39).

People seem able to distinguish between the party they belong to and their assessments of which party is currently more competent to run the country. A clear example is change in assessments of economic performance in the early 1990s. The ANES interviewed a sample of 405 Democrats in both 1990 and 1992. In these years, the percentage who thought their party was better than the Republicans at handling the economy increased from 39% to 63%. The ANES then interviewed a separate sample of 201 Democrats in both 1992 and 1994. In these years, the percentage who thought their party handled the economy better than Republicans decreased from 64% to 29%. Finally, the ANES interviewed a third sample of 232 Democrats in both 1994 and 1996. Between these interviews, the portion who thought their party handled the economy better increased from 32% to 56% (Green, Palmquist, and Schickler 2002, 128–30).[4]

---

individual-level, data. At the aggregate level, the proportion of the population identifying with the two parties tends to fluctuate, moving in response to perceptions of the economy and evaluations of the president (MacKuen, Erikson, and Stimson 1989; Erikson, MacKuen, and Stimson 2002). However, this movement in response to events tends to be modest in size and relatively slow. Furthermore, aggregate movement in party identification is smaller when measurement error (random fluctuation) is accounted for (Green, Palmquist, and Schickler 1998; 2002, chaps. 3–4).

[4] To say that assessments of the capabilities of parties and candidates are not solely determined by partisanship does not necessarily imply that people do not interpret new information through some partisan filter. A. Campbell et al. (1980 [1960], 133) claim that

Donald P. Green, Bradley Palmquist, and Eric Schickler (2002) theorize that partisanship is stable because it is based on social identity. People identify the Republican and Democratic Parties with certain groups in society. Those who think of themselves as Republicans do so because they identify with the social groups they associate with that party. In Green, Palmquist, and Schickler's words, "Seldom . . . do political events alter the stereotypes of partisan *groups*, and that is why most reversals of political fortune—scandals, diplomatic crises, economic news, legislative outcomes—leave little imprint on the partisan attachments of the adult electorate" (6–7; italics in the original). As a result, "The group affinities of the electorate tend to endure, whereas the special conditions that help propel a candidate to an unusual margin of victory seldom do" (227). In the next section, I explore these "special conditions" that influence voting.

Contemporary Messages Influence Voting Mainly by Sending Messages about National Conditions

Even though most electoral scholars agree that party identification is the largest single influence on each voter's choice, few dispute that information contemporary to that specific election also has some effect. The contemporary variable whose effect has been easiest to document convincingly is recent economic performance. In the aggregate, voters tend to reward the presidential candidate from the party in the White House when the economy is doing well and punish him or her when the economy is sluggish (see, e.g., Tufte 1978; Rosenstone 1983; Lewis-Beck and Rice 1984; Hibbs 1987; Abramowitz 1988; Erikson 1989; Lewis-Beck 1990; Bartels 1992; Lewis-Beck and Rice 1992; Gelman and King 1993; Wlezien and Erikson 1996; Hibbs 2000; Lewis-Beck and Stegmaier 2000; Bartels and Zaller 2001; Hibbs 2007). In addition, statistical models connecting individual-level election survey data over time with objective measures of the economy find a strong relationship between national economic performance and voting decisions (Markus 1988,

---

"identification with a party raises a perceptual screen through which the individual tends to see what is favorable to his partisan orientation. The stronger the party bond, the more exaggerated the process of selection and perceptual distortion will be." Whether partisanship does in fact lead to biased perception of new information is a subject of ongoing scholarly debate (see Gerber and Green 1999; Bartels 2002a; Green, Palmquist, and Schickler 2002, chap. 5; Sniderman and Van Houweling 2005; Taber and Lodge 2006). However, one does not have to agree that people are completely unbiased in their perceptions to acknowledge that in some circumstances messages can persuade voters to vote contrary to their partisanship.

1992; Zaller 2004).[5] An influential study by Gregory B. Markus (1992) found that each one-percentage-point increase in the growth of real disposable income (RDI) per capita in the election year corresponds to a two-percentage-point increase in the probability of an American voter supporting the incumbent party's presidential candidate.

An important caveat, however, is that only recent conditions appear to matter. Analysts who have estimated the weight voters give to economic conditions in different portions of the presidential term find that they heavily weigh conditions right before the election (Hibbs 2000; Achen and Bartels 2004; Bartels 2008b). Specifically, Christopher Achen and Larry Bartels (2004) found that, after accounting for the effects of economic performance in the second and third quarters of the election year, economic performance in the rest of the previous presidential term has no detectable association with election results. But if we acknowledge that the effects are limited to very recent economic performance, the evidence for economic influence is strong.

One piece of corroborating evidence is that, in years when media messages about the economy are especially strong, perceptions of economic performance are correlated with campaign news exposure (Hetherington 1996). Also, studies measuring changes in voter preferences during presidential campaigns tend to find the main influence of the campaign is to make the economy more salient and influential (Bartels 1992; Gelman and King 1993; Holbrook 1994; J. Campbell 2000; Bafumi, Gelman, and Park 2004; Ansolabehere 2006; Bartels 2006). Stephen Ansolabehere (2006, 30) calls this the "reinforcement effect." Thus, a wide variety of evidence indicates that recent economic conditions are an important contemporary factor influencing presidential voting.

Another way that national conditions appear to influence voting is through the effects of unpopular wars. Statistical models of voting and presidential approval ratings find that the Korean and Vietnam Wars reduced retrospective assessments of the president (e.g. Mueller 1973; Kernell 1978; Hibbs 1982; Rosenstone 1983; Hibbs 2000; Bartels and Zaller 2001; Hibbs 2007). Evidence for this type of retrospective voting is thinner than for economic voting because it rests largely on two presidential elections (1952 and 1968) and does not extend to earlier wars that had undivided support from American politicians, like World War II (Berinsky 2007, 2009). Still, based on elections since 1948, after accounting for economic performance, being involved in a costly war reduces the

[5] Some work on this topic relies on self-reports of economic perceptions to estimate individual-level effects (Kinder and Kiewiet 1979; Fiorina 1981), but these can be rationalizations rather than causes of vote choice (Kramer 1983; Wilcox and Wlezien 1993; Wlezien, Franklin, and Twiggs 1997; Bartels 2002a; Gerber and Huber 2009).

incumbent party's share of the presidential vote by about four percentage points (Bartels and Zaller 2001).

Outside of laboratory experiments, convincingly demonstrating the effects of other contemporary factors has been much more difficult (Bartels 1992; Holbrook 1994; Ansolabehere 2006).[6] Quoting Ansolabehere (2006, 37) again, "The inclusion of debates, conventions, and other election-related events adds little to the predictive power of economic models [of voting]." The main difficulty in finding contemporary influences is reverse causation.

Survey reports of voters' issue preferences, perceptions of national conditions, and perceptions of the candidates' positions and personal attributes all tend to be rationalizations, not causes, of vote choice (Berelson, Lazarsfeld, and McPhee 1954; Brody and Page 1972; Page and Brody 1972; Kramer 1983; Rahn, Krosnick, and Breuning 1994; Bartels 2002b; Achen and Bartels 2006; Lenz 2009, 2010a).[7] To take just one example, Gabriel Lenz (2009; 2010a) examined opinion change during the 2000 presidential campaign with panel survey data. He found that, when the campaigns focused on social security, people did not change their votes to be more in line with their social security opinions. Instead, they learned the social security position of the candidate they already preferred and changed their own opinion to match it. Thus, while we cannot rule out the possible effects of other contemporary messages on voting, evidence for them is, at best, inconclusive.[8]

The evidence thus suggests that at least two major factors shape voting decisions: long-term party loyalties and more transitory signals about

---

[6] But see Bartels (1993), who found that those who consumed more news were more likely to change their views of the candidates during the 1980 presidential campaign.

[7] On the general tendency of people to incorporate new information in ways that rationalize their predispositions, see Lord, Ross, and Lepper (1979), Lodge and Taber (2000), Taber and Lodge (2006), and Gaines et al. (2007). On the other hand, aggregate change in voter preferences during campaigns does seem to respond to prominent campaign events (Bartels 1988; Wlezien and Erikson 2002; Hillygus and Jackman 2003). However, another possible research strategy—simply asking survey respondents directly whether candidate attributes influenced their voting decision—is just as problematic as looking at cross-sectional correlations. The problem is that people are notoriously bad at introspecting about what factors affect their decision making (Nisbett and Wilson 1977).

[8] There is some evidence that exposure to campaign coverage from a slanted news outlet can influence voting decisions. For instance, economists DellaVigna and Kaplan (2007) found evidence that exposure to the Fox News Channel made voters more likely to cast Republican votes in 2000. Lenz and I (Ladd and Lenz 2009) found evidence that exposure to partisan newspapers influenced voting decisions in the 1997 British national elections. Gerber, Karlan, and Bergan (forthcoming) found evidence, in a field experiment, that slanted newspaper coverage can influence gubernatorial votes. See also Barker (1999; 2002), Barker and Lawrence (2006), Dalton, Beck, and Huckfeldt (1998), Druckman and Parkin (2005), Erikson (1976), Kahn and Kenney (2002), Lawson and McCann (2004), and Veblen (1975).

the relative quality of the two parties, the most established of the latter being the state of the national economy. In this way, predispositions and contemporary information are combined to form a voting preference.

MEDIA DISTRUST INDUCES PARTISAN VOTING: CROSS-SECTIONAL AND PANEL SURVEY EVIDENCE

Given this, voting provides an opportunity to explore the consequences of media distrust for the political system. We saw in chapter 6 that distrust of the institutional news media led people to resist informative political messages. Those who distrust the media resist messages about the state of the nation in a variety of policy areas, relying instead on their political predispositions to form their beliefs about performance. A potential further consequence is that media distrust alters the bases of voters' decision making. Specifically, we might expect voters who distrust the news media to rely more on their party identification and less on contemporary information like economic conditions.[9]

I test whether the effect of party identification on vote choice depends on voters' media trust using ANES data.[10] As we have seen, both media trust and party identification are relatively stable over time, reducing the danger that reverse causation affects their association with vote choice. However, another danger is that the apparent effects of media trust may actually be produced by other variables that are correlated with it.

To at least partially address this problem, I control for the effects of a series of other variables on partisan voting. To account for political awareness, I control for objective political knowledge.[11] To account for

---

[9] As with the expected effects of media distrust on learning examined in chapter 6, these expectations can be derived from a simple Bayesian decision theory model. Such a model is presented in Ladd (2005; 2006, chap. 4).

[10] In tables 7-1, 7-2, and 7-3, I estimate effects on vote choice with linear probability models. Logit and probit models produce very similar results. However, linear probability models simplify the interpretation of interaction effects, which are a key part if this analysis. On the complexities of interaction terms in logit and probit models, see Ai and Norton (2003) and Brambor, Clark, and Golder (2006).

Angrist and Pischke (2009) recommend using linear regression with binary dependent variables because "the added complexity and extra work required to interpret" logit and probit models are usually not "worth the trouble" (94, 197). Furthermore, linear regression may be more consistent with interpreting the model as a "conditional expectation function" (34–40, 94).

[11] The 2002 and 2004 ANES surveys do not ask a battery of objective political knowledge questions. Instead, I use interviewer ratings of respondents' "general level of information about politics and public affairs." In surveys where both are measured, interviewer ratings and respondents' performance on knowledge questions tend to be strongly correlated

strength of partisanship, I control for the extremity of respondents' stated party identification as well as age, which tends to correlate with stronger party attachment (P. Converse 1969; A. Campbell et al. 1980 [1960], 162–3).[12] To account for other aspects of political engagement, I also control for how frequently people follow public affairs, whether they view television campaign coverage, and how frequently they discuss politics. Finally, because other forms of political trust can also shape political behavior (Hetherington 1998, 1999; Putnam 2000; Hetherington and Globetti 2002; Hetherington 2004), I also control for trust in government and trust in people.

Including these control variables has very little effect on the relationship between media trust and partisan voting. As expected, with or without controls, those who distrust the news media vote based more on their party identification. Figure 7-1 compares the relationship between party identification and vote choice among those trusting the news media "just about always" and those trusting the news media "almost never." (For detailed statistical results, see table 7-1 in the appendix.)[13] Among those trusting the media "just about always," moving from identifying with the Democrats to identifying with the Republicans increases the probability of voting Republican for president by .77.[14] Among those trusting the media "almost never," the same change increases the probability of voting Republican by .88.[15]

The pattern is similar for congressional voting. If one trusts the media "just about always," moving from Democratic to Republican identification increases one's probability of voting for a Republican candidate for the House of Representatives by .56. In contrast, if one trusts the media "almost never," moving from Democratic to Republican identification

---

(Zaller 1985). For that reason, interviewer ratings are often used as substitutes when knowledge questions are not available (e.g. Bartels 1996b).

[12] The extremity of respondents' stated party identification is constructed by folding over the party identification variable so that higher values indicate strong identification with one of the parties and lower values indicate independence.

[13] An alternative statistical approach to examining whether media distrust induces partisan voting is to estimate a model where the dependent variable is a dichotomous indicator for whether the individual voted for his or her own party's candidate. In this type of model, media trust and a series of controls are included as explanatory variables. This approach produces results consistent with those in this chapter. Less media trust is associated with a greater probability of voting for one's own party (Ladd 2010b).

[14] Here and throughout this chapter, I illustrate party identification's effects by showing the change in vote choice that results from moving from "not strong" Democratic identification to "not strong" Republican identification. On the conventional 7-point party identification scale, this is a movement from 2 to 6. When the party identification scale is recoded to range from 0 to 1, as it is in all of the statistical analyses in this book, this is a movement from .167 to .833.

[15] The standard errors for these two effects are 0.03 and 0.02, respectively.

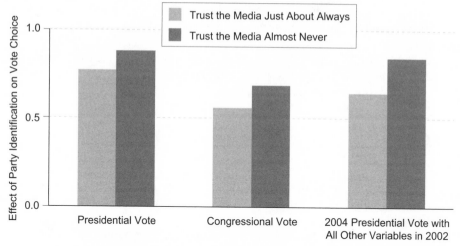

Figure 7-1. Media distrust increases partisan voting. *Note*: The vertical axis represents the effect of moving from weakly identifying with the Democratic Party to weakly identifying with the Republican Party on the probability of voting for the Democratic candidate. Estimates of the effect of party identification on presidential voting are based on the model in the second column of table 7-1. Estimates of the effect on congressional voting are based on the model in the fourth column. Estimates of the effect on 2004 presidential voting, with all other variables measured in 2002, are based on the model in the fifth column. *Source*: 1996, 1998, 2000, and 2004 ANES.

increases one's probability of voting for a Republican House candidate by .68.[16]

An additional way to reduce the likelihood of reverse causation among vote choice, party identification, media trust, and the control variables is to measure the explanatory variables several years before the election.[17] I do this by using the 2000–2004 ANES Panel Study and measuring 2004 vote choice in the 2004 postelection survey and all other variables in 2002. The rightmost bars in figure 7-1 show the results. (For details, see the fifth column of table 7-1.) Compared with the results when all variables are measured in the same year, the effect of media trust on partisan voting is similar, if not a bit stronger. Moving from Democratic to Republican

[16] The standard errors for these effects are 0.04 and 0.03, respectively.

[17] Achen (1992, 208) argues that, given the potential endogeneity of party identification to campaign messages and voting preferences, estimates of the effect of prior party identification on voting should measure identification before the entire campaign, such as several years earlier, rather than in the ANES preelection survey from September and October of the election year.

identification increases one's probability of voting Republican by .64 if one trusts the media "just about always" and by .84 if one trusts the media "almost never."[18]

The same pattern is present in the GSS. The main difference is that, because the GSS contains more questions about sociology and fewer directly about politics, some of the ANES control variables are not available. I control for the effect of education (to account for political awareness), strength of party identification, age, and (to account for general confidence in government) confidence in the executive branch and in Congress.[19] The results, shown in figure 7-2, are similar to those from the ANES. (For details, see table 7-2 in the appendix.) Moving from Democratic to Republican identification increases one's probability of voting Republican by .67 if one has "a great deal" confidence in the press and by .72 if one has "hardly any" confidence in the press.[20]

MEDIA DISTRUST ALTERS ECONOMIC VOTING: POOLED CROSS-SECTIONAL SURVEY EVIDENCE

We can also look for direct evidence that voters who distrust the news media resist contemporary information, in addition to basing their votes more on partisan predispositions. Given that media messages during the campaign both transmit economic information and raise its salience, we might expect recent economic performance to have less impact on those who distrust the media. It is more difficult to test this than it was to test how media trust moderates party identification's influence. The trouble is that estimating economic effects on voting requires data from a substantial number of elections under different economic conditions. For this reason, studies of American economic voting typically use data from

---

[18] The standard errors for these two effects are both 0.08. Data from the 1992–96 ANES Panel Study also indicate that media trust moderates the effect of party identification on voting. Negative attitudes toward the media are associated with a stronger relationship between party identification and 1996 vote choice, even when all explanatory variables are measured in 1994 except media attitudes, which were not asked in 1994 but can instead be measured with a question some panel respondents were asked in the 1993 ANES Pilot Study. However, while the interaction between party identification and media trust is always negative across model specifications, it is usually not statistically significant at conventional levels because sample sizes are less than 350 (Ladd 2005; 2006, chap. 4).

[19] The interaction between confidence in the press and party identification is of very similar size if we also include, as a control, the interaction between trust in people and party identification. The only difference is that this requires us to exclude data on the 1976 and 1980 presidential elections because the 1977 and 1982 GSS did not probe trust in people.

[20] The standard errors for these effects are 0.02 and 0.01, respectively.

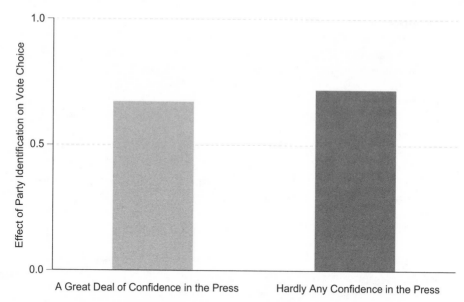

Figure 7-2. More evidence that media distrust increases partisan voting. *Note*: The vertical axis represents the effect of moving from weakly identifying with the Democratic Party to weakly identifying with the Republican Party on the probability of voting for the Democratic presidential candidate. Estimates of the effect of party identification on presidential voting are based on the model in the second column of table 7-2. *Source*: 1973, 1977, 1982, 1986, 1989, 1993, 1998, 2002, and 2006 GSS.

every presidential election from 1952 on.[21] But this analysis necessitates using only years when surveys asked voters for their views on the institutional news media. Given this, one strategy is to use data from the GSS surveys conducted after each presidential election, each of which contains questions about how respondents voted and their confidence in the press. I can then connect these data with economic performance prior to presidential elections from 1972 to the present.[22]

[21] Such as Achen and Bartels (2004), Hibbs (2000), Markus (1988; 1992), and Zaller (2004).

[22] The models in table 7-3 follow the basic setup of those in Markus (1988; 1992) and Zaller (2004) by linking national statistics to individual respondents. The main differences are, first, estimating the effects for different quarters of the election years separately, as Achen and Bartels (2004) do; second, interacting the economic variables with respondents' confidence in the press; and third, using GSS rather than ANES data, which requires including elections since 1972 only rather than since 1952.

The approach of assigning all voters in a given year a certain value on the economic performance variables can produce downwardly biased standard errors, because the disturbances

As I mentioned in the previous section, Christopher Achen and Larry Bartels (2004), using aggregate election returns from 1952 to 2000, found that the entire effect of economic conditions comes from the second and third quarters of the election year. My own analysis, using the GSS and elections from 1972 to 2004, is consistent with their results. I find that better economic performance in the second and third quarters of the election year both significantly increase the probability of voters choosing the incumbent party's candidate.[23] Like Achen and Bartels (2004), I find no positive relationship between first-quarter economic performance and incumbent party voting. In fact, after controlling for the effects of the second and third quarters, I find first-quarter economic performance to be negatively correlated with incumbent party voting. (For details, see table 7-3 in the appendix.)

To see how reception of contemporary information depends on attitudes toward the news media, I estimate how the effects of the second and third quarters each vary across respondents with different amounts of press confidence. As expected, I find that voters with more press confidence are more responsive to very recent economic conditions. Those with high confidence in the press are very responsive to third-quarter economic performance but only modestly responsive to second-quarter performance. In contrast, those with low press confidence are moderately (and about equally) responsive to both the second and third quarters. (For details, see table 7-3.)

To illustrate, figure 7-3 presents the effects of a 7-percentage-point increase in RDI growth in the second and third quarters. This represents the difference between the best and worst third-quarter economic conditions in the dataset: RDI growth of 7.17% in 1972 and 0.17% in 1992. Among those with "a great deal" of press confidence, this change in third-quarter growth increases the probability of voting for the incumbent party by .21.[24] This effect is quite large. For comparison, it is larger

---

will be clustered in each year (Snijders and Bosker 1999; Steenbergen and Jones 2002). I adjust the standard errors in table 7-3 to account for this clustering.

[23] Throughout this chapter, I follow the previous literature (Rosenstone 1983; Markus 1988, 1992; Hibbs 2000; Bartels and Zaller 2001; Achen and Bartels 2004; Zaller 2004) by measuring economic performance with the annualized growth rate of RDI per capita. This tends to be more strongly related to presidential voting than other economic measures such as GDP growth (Bartels and Zaller 2001; Achen and Bartels 2004). The annualized percentage change in RDI per capita is calculated as

$$\Delta RDI = (400/n) \times [\ln(RDI_t) - \ln(RDI_{t-n})],$$

where t is the last quarter of the time period for which economic performance is being calculated and n is the number of quarters in the time period (see Achen and Bartels 2004, 8).

[24] The standard error for this effect is 0.01.

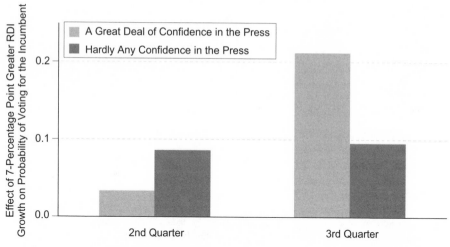

Figure 7-3. The effects of second- and third-quarter election year economic performance depend on confidence in the press. *Note*: The vertical axis represents the effect of increasing the annualized rate of growth in real disposable income (RDI) per capita by seven percentage points. Effect estimates are based on the model in the third column of table 7-3. *Source*: 1973, 1977, 1982, 1986, 1989, 1993, 1998, 2002, and 2006 GSS; quarterly RDI per capita from the Bureau of Economic Analysis, U.S. Department of Commerce.

than the incumbency advantage in House elections, which is estimated at about 6 percentage points in recent decades (Ansolabehere and Snyder 2002),[25] or presidential campaign spending, where Bartels (1992) estimates that a two-to-one advantage, which the Republican Party enjoyed from 1964 to 1972, is associated with a 3-percentage-point increase in votes.[26] It is comparable to the effect of consuming campaign news with a partisan slant, which Gabriel Lenz and I (Ladd and Lenz 2009) estimate at between 10 and 25 percentage points. In contrast, among those with "hardly any" confidence in the press, the same change in third-quarter economic conditions is associated with a much smaller, but still

[25] The literature on the incumbency advantage in congressional elections is vast. In addition to Ansolabehere and Snyder (2002), see, for instance, Ansolabehere et al. (2006), Ansolabehere, Snyder, and Stewart (2000), Cox and Katz (1996), Erikson (1971), Gelman and King (1990), Hirano and Snyder (2009), Mayhew (1974), Prior (2006), and Zaller (1998).

[26] Besides Bartels (1992), there is remarkably little research into the effectiveness of campaign spending in U.S. presidential elections. However, there is a large literature on the effectiveness of campaign spending in congressional elections. See, for instance, Erikson and Palfrey (1998), Gerber (1998), Green and Krasno (1988), Jacobson (1980; 2006), Levitt (1994) and Stratmann (2005).

substantial, .10 increase in the probability of voting for the incumbent party.[27]

Perhaps partially as a consequence of giving so much less weight to very recent economic news, those without press confidence actually give more weight than others do to second-quarter economic performance. A comparable seven-percentage-point increase in second-quarter RDI growth increases the probability of voting for the incumbent party by .03 among those with "a great deal" of press confidence and by .09 among those with "hardly any" confidence in the press.[28]

This chapter shows how the effects of attitudes toward the press on political learning (documented in chapter 6) manifest themselves by changing the bases of Americans' voting decisions. Those with negative attitudes toward the news media as an institution are more resistant to new information and rely more on their predispositions when forming perceptions of the world around them. As a result, they heavily weigh their partisanship when voting and give moderate weight to economic performance, even when it is very close to the election. Voters with positive attitudes toward the media rely less on their partisanship and are much more responsive to economic performance immediately before the election.

---

[27] The standard error for this effect is 0.04.

[28] The standard errors for these two effects are 0.005 and 0.01, respectively.

Appendix

TABLE 7-1
Media Distrust Increases Partisan Voting

	Presidential vote		Congressional vote		2004 Presidential vote with all other variables measured in 2002
Party identification	1.08**	1.96**	0.90**	1.37**	1.67**
	(0.02)	(0.10)	(0.03)	(0.13)	(0.25)
Party identification × trust in the media	−0.14**	−0.16**	−0.16**	−0.19**	−0.30*
	(0.05)	(0.05)	(0.07)	(0.08)	(0.18)
Trust in the media	−0.03	−0.02	0.03	0.01	0.14
	(0.03)	(0.03)	(0.05)	(0.05)	(0.14)
Party identification × political knowledge		0.01		0.03	0.28
		(0.04)		(0.06)	(0.17)
Political knowledge		0.00		−0.01	−0.23*
		(0.03)		(0.04)	(0.12)
Party identification × frequency of following government and public affairs		0.15**		0.09	0.07
		(0.05)		(0.07)	(0.14)
Frequency of following government and public affairs		−0.07**		−0.04	−0.14
		(0.03)		(0.04)	(0.08)
Party identification × strength of partisanship		−1.15**		−0.55**	−1.08**
		(0.08)		(0.11)	(0.19)
Strength of partisanship		0.57**		0.26**	0.56**
		(0.05)		(0.06)	(0.11)
Party identification × campaign television viewing		0.06		0.06	0.10
		(0.05)		(0.06)	(0.09)
Campaign television viewing		−0.02		−0.02	0.02
		(0.03)		(0.04)	(0.05)
Party identification × frequency of political discussion		0.12**		0.01	0.01
		(0.03)		(0.05)	(0.10)
Frequency of political discussion		−0.06**		−0.01	−0.03
		(0.02)		(0.03)	(0.07)
Party identification × age		0.04		−0.12	0.16
		(0.07)		(0.11)	(0.25)
Age		0.04		0.12*	−0.13
		(0.04)		(0.07)	(0.18)
Party identification × trust in government		−0.19**		−0.07	0.01
		(0.07)		(0.11)	(0.18)
Trust in government		0.11**		0.08	0.22*
		(0.05)		(0.07)	(0.13)
Party identification × trust in people		0.01		−0.01	−0.06
		(0.02)		(0.04)	(0.07)
Trust in people		−0.03*		0.06**	−0.01
		(0.02)		(0.02)	(0.05)

continued

TABLE 7-1
(*Continued*)

	Presidential vote		Congressional vote		2004 Presidential vote with all other variables measured in 2002
Year fixed effects	yes	yes	yes	yes	no
Constant	−0.04**	−0.51**	0.11**	−0.20**	−0.30*
	(0.02)	(0.05)	(0.03)	(0.07)	(0.17)
R²	0.61	0.63	0.39	0.42	0.55
Standard error of regression	0.31	0.30	0.39	0.38	0.34
n	2,944	2,908	3,192	2,611	657

**p < .05, *p < .10 for two-tailed tests

Source: Models in the first two columns use the 1996, 2000, and 2004 ANES Time Series Surveys. Models in the third and fourth columns use the 1996, 1998, 2000, and 2004 ANES Time Series Surveys. The ANES did not conduct a survey in 2002. The model in the fifth column uses the 2000–2004 ANES Panel Study.

Note: Table shows results from linear probability models estimated by ordinary least squares (Aldrich and Nelson 1984). Entries are regression coefficients with Huber-White robust standard errors in parentheses. In each model, the dependent variable is 1 if the respondent voted for the Republican and 0 if he or she voted for the Democrat. Explanatory variables are coded to range from 0 to 1, with interior categories evenly spaced between these endpoints. Nonvoters and minor-party voters are excluded.

Table 7-2
Media Distrust Increases Partisan Voting in GSS Data

	Presidential vote	
Party identification	0.99**	1.40**
	(0.01)	(0.08)
Party identification × confidence in the press	−0.09**	−0.07**
	(0.03)	(0.03)
Confidence in the press	0.01	−0.02
	(0.02)	(0.02)
Party identification × education		0.22**
		(0.06)
Education		−0.12**
		(0.04)
Party identification × strength of partisanship		−0.58**
		(0.06)
Strength of partisanship		0.23**
		(0.03)
Party identification × age		0.01
		(0.06)
Age		0.11**
		(0.04)
Party identification × confidence in the executive branch		−0.16**
		(0.03)
Confidence in the executive branch		0.16**
		(0.02)
Party identification × confidence in Congress		−0.02
		(0.03)
Confidence in Congress		0.03
		(0.02)
Year fixed effects	yes	yes
Constant	0.18**	−0.07
	(0.02)	(0.05)
R^2	0.49	0.50
Standard error of regression	0.36	0.35
n	7,819	7,626

**p < .05, *p < .10 for two-tailed tests

Source: 1973, 1977, 1982, 1986, 1989, 1993, 1998, 2002, and 2006 GSS. The 1986 GSS is used for data on the 1984 election because the 1985 GSS did not probe confidence in the press.

Note: Table shows results from linear probability models estimated by ordinary least squares. Entries are regression coefficients with Huber-White robust standard errors in parentheses. In each model, the dependent variable is 1 if the respondent voted for the Republican and 0 if he or she voted for the Democrat. Explanatory variables are coded to range from 0 to 1, with interior categories evenly spaced between these endpoints. Nonvoters and minor-party voters are excluded.

Table 7-3

Effect of Third-Quarter Economic Growth Depends on Confidence in the Press

	Presidential vote		
Party identification	0.967**	0.964**	0.949**
	(0.021)	(0.021)	(0.022)
Economic performance Q1	-0.016*		
	(0.008)		
Economic performance Q2	0.015**	0.009**	0.012**
	(0.004)	(0.002)	(0.002)
Economic performance Q3	0.017**	0.016*	0.014**
	(0.005)	(0.007)	(0.005)
Economic performance Q2 × confidence in the press			-0.008**
			(0.002)
Economic performance Q3 × confidence in the press			0.017**
			(0.006)
Confidence in the press			-0.068**
			(0.015)
Constant	0.055	-0.004	0.026*
	(0.037)	(0.012)	(0.013)
R^2	0.50	0.50	0.48
Standard error of regression	0.35	0.35	0.36
n	11,741	11,741	7,819

**$p < .05$, *$p < .10$ for two-tailed tests

Source: 1973, 1977, 1982, 1986, 1989, 1993, 1998, 2002, and 2006 GSS. The 1986 GSS is used for data on the 1984 election because the 1985 GSS did not probe confidence in the press. The annualized rate of growth in real disposable income (RDI) is calculated based on quarterly RDI data from the Bureau of Economic Analysis of the U.S. Department of Commerce.

Note: Table shows results from linear probability models estimated by ordinary least squares. Entries are regression coefficients with Huber-White robust standard errors in parentheses. All models also adjust standard errors to account for clustering of disturbances by year. In each model, the dependent variable is 1 if the respondent voted for the presidential candidate from the incumbent party and 0 if he or she voted for the candidate of the other major party. Party identification and confidence in the press are coded to range from 0 to 1, with interior categories evenly spaced between these endpoints. Nonvoters and minor-party voters are excluded. Party identification is coded such that higher values indicate greater identification with the incumbent president's party and lower values indicate greater identification with the other major party.

8

The News Media in a Democracy

CHAPTER 1 DESCRIBED the conventional wisdom on the decline of the public's media trust as consisting of two assertions. First, an independent, powerful, trusted news media is a natural part of American politics. Second, widespread media distrust has serious negative consequences for democracy. This book argues that the first claim is inaccurate, yet the second is at least partially true.

Political leaders feel threatened by any form of mass communication they do not control. The press threatens political leaders whenever it provides independent information, which could undermine their popular support. Historically, whether the political system was democratic or not, politicians used available tools to restrict the press's independent power. Earlier, this took the form of censorship and official government newspapers. Later, when democratic institutions proscribed such restrictions, politicians tried to undermine the credibility of independent or hostile media outlets and develop outlets controlled by—or at least highly sympathetic to—their own factions.

The mid-twentieth-century media landscape was unusual. Between the Roosevelt administration's coordinated attacks on the press in the 1930s and the rise in political press criticism in the 1970s, 1980s, and 1990s, an independent, influential, widely respected news media emerged, temporarily unburdened by political attacks. While it is difficult to be certain about public opinion before modern polling, the available evidence suggests that mid-twentieth-century Americans had unusually high media trust. Contemporary observers reported that journalism in the 18th and 19th centuries was generally not a respected form of employment. Despite professionalizing trends in the early twentieth century, the (admittedly thin and unreliable) polling evidence from the 1930s indicates that the press was still held in low esteem. However, by the mid-1950s, the ANES shows that the press was highly trusted. This appears to have lasted into the early 1970s. Yet from that point on, media trust began a steady reversion to historical norms, eventually arriving at its current meager level.

The public's media trust has important consequences for democracy. Chapters 6 and 7 present a variety of evidence that ordinary people interact with the political system differently when they distrust the mainstream media. In general, broad national policy outcomes are the most politically consequential information for people to learn because they shape voting decisions. The most influential outcomes are in economic and national security policy. Those who distrust the institutional media resist new information from the mainstream media on these topics. They are also more likely to utilize alternative, partisan media outlets. As a result, the beliefs of those who distrust the media are less responsive to new events. In the relative absence of information, their beliefs are shaped more by their partisan predispositions. These learning effects carry over into the voting booth. Media distrust leads people to vote based more on partisanship and less on current economic conditions. However, knowing that media distrust alters political learning and vote choice in this way does not necessarily imply that these consequences are entirely or unambiguously negative. Nor does it tell us what a sensible remedy might be.

In this final chapter, I consider the future of the U.S. news media. I argue that, while journalists would generally prefer the media to constitute a trusted national institution, party competition and the economics of the news industry work against this. The mid-twentieth century was atypical because political party competition and economic media competition were both constrained. Both extremely fragmented and extremely institutionalized media environments have potentially negative consequences. As a result, looking to the future, we should not attempt to restore the media environment of the mid-twentieth century but rather seek a balance between these two extremes. I suggest some ways to achieve this balance, each of which has potential benefits and drawbacks.

JOURNALISTS' PREFERENCES PUSH TOWARD MEDIA INSTITUTIONALIZATION

It is fairly uncontroversial to conjecture that journalists would like to achieve social prestige and professional advancement (see Zaller 1999b, especially 21–27). Some journalists undoubtedly have other goals, such as moral or ideological considerations, but social prestige and professional advancement are important motivators. Thus, incentives created by these considerations are likely to be important.

The desire for prestige leads journalists to generally prefer the profession to return to its position in the mid-twentieth century and not to its deeper roots in the 18th and 19th centuries, when newspaper writers were often seen as blue-collar, less educated, partisan hacks. In addition, the professional advancement motive leads to an individual desire to adhere to professional norms. This way, one's work will be regarded by peers as high-quality journalism. As chapter 3 discussed, this entails ex-emplifying "objectivity" as other journalists define it.[1]

If freed from financial and political considerations, this is the news media we should expect to see. But news organizations and individual journalists face constraints, which vary over time. I classify these into two categories: those resulting from economic markets and those re-sulting from party competition. The changing nature of the American news media is shaped by the interaction of journalists' goals and these constraints.

COMPETITIVE ECONOMIC ENVIRONMENTS LEAD TO MORE SOFT NEWS

To produce and disseminate news requires money. No matter what tech-nology they employ, organizations with more money will be better able to pay journalists, research and disseminate news, and thus influence the political process. Early printing was often subsidized by governments, re-ligious authorities, or dissenting political or religious movements. In early American history, newspapers were usually subsidized by governments, political parties, or both. By the mid-nineteenth century, technological advances allowed papers to support themselves through large circula-tions. While outlets relying on governmental, partisan, or personal sub-sidies persist to this day, those relying on consumers (for advertising and subscriptions) predominate.

There is increasing evidence, particularly from the work of Zaller (1999a; 1999b) and Hamilton (2004), that pressure to reach consumers leads to less "objective" (i.e., hard) news and more soft news.[2] Most peo-ple enjoy consuming soft news, even though they often denounce it and it reduces their media trust. For many Americans, soft news appears to be a guilty pleasure. The phenomenon is similar to economist Joel Waldfo-gel's (2007) characterization of television consumption in general: "With perhaps the exception of Homer Simpson, Americans tend to denounce television even as they devour it."

---

[1] This depiction of journalists' goals relies heavily on Zaller's (1999a; 1999b) insights. The main difference between my characterization and Zaller's is that I postulate that journalists prefer to adhere to professional notions of the ideal of objectivity more broadly, while Zaller argues that journalists specifically want to produce "a product rich in journal-istic interpretation and analysis" and in that way "maximize their independent and distinc-tive 'voice' in the news" (Zaller 1999b, 24–25).

[2] See also Arnold (2004, 194–200) and Dunaway (2008). For a dissenting view, see Rosenstiel et al. (2000) and Rosenstiel et al. (2007).

For instance, when Doris Graber (1984) conducted in-depth interviews with a small group of citizens over the course of a presidential campaign, they complained about "the oversimplified treatment of all news" (105) and that "the facts they really wanted to know were ignored by news stories" (103). Yet she found that, "when the debates and other special news programs and newspaper features presented a small opportunity for more extensive exposure to issues, they were unwilling to seize it. For the most part, the panelists would not read and study carefully the more extensive versions of election and other news in newspapers and news magazines. Masses of specific facts and statistics were uniformly characterized as dull, confusing, and unduly detailed" (105). Consumer surveys corroborate that people have little desire to consume serious programs about national policy (W. Bennett 2009, 18).

The irony is that, when given the choice, consumers choose styles of news that cause them to lose respect for the media. A further irony is that, when consuming soft news, they often do absorb information about public affairs (Baum 2002, 2003b, 2003a; Zaller 2003; Baum and Jamison 2006; but see Prior 2003). Yet while soft news can be informative, it indirectly diminishes consumers' future receptivity to information by reducing their media trust. I return to this issue later in this chapter.

As a result, market pressure works against traditional, objective political reporting. Zaller (1999a; 1999b, chap. 3) presents a variety of evidence that news outlets provide more hard news when they are insulated from competition, either by an absence of competitors or by subsidies. Hamilton (2004, chap. 3–4) points out that the minority who do enjoy hard news are not marginal viewers. They are likely to consume news regardless of style. Those on the fence between consuming news or not are less interested in policy debates in Washington and more interested in soft news topics.[3] To compound this, those interested in political coverage also tend to have stronger partisan predispositions (P. Converse 1964; Zaller 1992), making them vulnerable to being stolen away from conventional journalism by partisan news sources. Finally, even setting aside revenue, serious domestic and international political reporting generally costs more than lifestyle and celebrity coverage (W. Bennett 2009, 219). All this supports the notion that competition pushes news organizations to produce more soft news.[4]

---

[3] On general preferences for entertainment versus news, see Prior (2005; 2007).

[4] Zaller (1999b, 28) calls this "The Rule of the Market," which he defines as "the tendency of market competition to force journalists to lower the overall quality and amount of political news."

PARTY COMPETITION GIVES POLITICIANS INCENTIVES TO UNDERMINE THE MEDIA

The news media also face political constraints. In undemocratic systems, government leaders attack independent media because they threaten public support for the regime. But even in democratic systems, politicians have incentives to attack influential and independent information sources.

Just as sellers compete for buyers in economic markets, in competitive democracies parties and their candidates compete for votes. Political scientists conventionally define a party as "an organized attempt to get control of the government" (Schattschneider 1942, ix).[5] The way to get control of the government in a democracy is by gaining public support. Whether parties succeed depends on the public's information about national conditions. As discussed in chapters 6 and 7, voters view the incumbent party as more qualified to hold office when things go well and less when things go poorly.[6]

Yet parties can influence the weight some citizens give to new information about national conditions. A party's media criticism reduces media trust among its supporters. This causes them to discount new information they receive from the institutional media and turn increasingly to alternative (often partisan) news outlets. As a consequence, their beliefs about contemporary national conditions, and their votes, will more reflect their partisan predispositions and less reflect contemporary policy outcomes.

Given this, what incentives do parties face when deciding whether to criticize the news media? First, among those predisposed to support it, a party will tend to do the same or better if supporters ignore contemporary messages and vote based on predispositions. If conditions favor the party, voters predisposed to support it will do so regardless of the weight they give to new information. Their attitudes toward the media will be inconsequential. Yet if conditions are running against the party, voters predisposed to support it will be more likely to do so if they resist new information. Thus, the party generally prefers that its supporters resist new information, and it can achieve that by publicly criticizing the media.

[5] Downs (1957, 96) sees parties' goals similarly, saying, "Our basic hypothesis states that political parties are interested in gaining office *per se*."

[6] As mentioned in chapter 6, in political science these conditions are often called "valence" issues (Stokes 1966b). As discussed in chapter 7 and later in this chapter, the most influential valence issues in the United States are the economy and (to a lesser extent) national security. But thinking about democracies more generally, one could imagine other policy outcomes—crime or pollution, for example—also influencing assessments of parties' capabilities.

A party's rhetoric has little impact on those not predisposed to support it (see, e.g., Zaller 1992). If it did, the party's incentives would change. For those free of party attachments, the party prefers that they respond to new information when conditions favor it and ignore information when conditions do not. For those predisposed to support the opposition, the incentives for the party's own supporters are reversed. When conditions favor it, the party would prefer these individuals to be receptive to new messages. When conditions favor the opposition, these individuals will support the opposition regardless of their responsiveness to information. However, all these incentives will have little impact on the party's rhetoric because such rhetoric has little effect on those not predisposed to support it.

This illustrates how the causes and consequences of media distrust are connected. Because media distrust makes people resist new information and party rhetoric shapes partisans' levels of media trust, parties almost always have an incentive to publicly criticize the press. It allows them to insulate their supporters from future variation in policy outcomes. In this way, party competition leads to media criticism as a strategy for maximizing public support.[7]

Less Competition in the News Industry and Party System Allowed the Institutional News Media to Temporarily Thrive

As I have shown, both economic and political pressures tend to reduce public trust in the institutional news media. Chapter 5 found that soft news and partisan elite criticism can generate media distrust. The former is a consequence of economic incentives, while the latter is a consequence of political incentives.

This helps us better understand both why the press is usually held in low esteem and how that pattern was broken in the 1950s, 1960s, and early 1970s. Party competition and the economic pressures faced by news organization both reached historic lows at this time. As chapter 3 discussed, American party polarization reached a nadir in the 1950s. The Eisenhower administration largely accepted the major liberal policies implemented in the 1930s and 1940s, such as higher taxation, Social Security, greater financial regulation, and an internationalist foreign policy. Racial policy disagreements were still orthogonal to the party divide, while later social controversies, like women's and gay rights, were largely

---

[7] This section's argument can also be presented formally (i.e., mathematically). See Ladd (2006, chap. 5).

off the agenda. Measured quantitatively, the distance in congressional voting patterns between the parties reached its lowest levels in the late 1930s and did not change much before beginning to grow in the late 1970s (McCarty, Poole, and Rosenthal 2006, 29; 2009).

One of the most common explanations for low party polarization in this period is the lack of income inequality. In this view, the "great compression" of wealth in the 1930s and 1940s reduced differences in economic interests, producing less disagreement about redistributive government policies (see McCarty, Poole, and Rosenthal 1997; Poole and Rosenthal 1997; McCarty, Poole, and Rosenthal 2006; Poole and Rosenthal 2007). Yet if this was the driving force, why was wealth evenly distributed in this period? One explanation is the Kuznets Curve, named after economist Simon Kuznets. A simple interpretation of the Kuznets Curve is that industrial development initially causes inequality to increase. Once a society has enough capital, wages rise, profits decline, and wealth equalizes (see Brenner, Kaelble, and Thomas 1991; Krugman 2007, 45). In another explanation, economist Paul Krugman (2007, 44–53) argues that the compression results from changes in federal economic policy. Large increases in inheritance, corporate, and upper-bracket income tax rates; regulations that strengthened unions; and war policies that essentially set wages for large portions of the economy all coincided with the great compression. Also, Claudia Goldin and Robert Margo (1992) point out that World War II greatly increased demand for low-skill laborers, which further contributed to their rising wages.

As for the return of economic inequality late in the century, one explanation is technology. Goldin and economist Lawrence F. Katz (2007, 2008) argue that technological advancement increased demand for highly educated workers. Inequality increased because the American educational system failed to keep pace. Others argue that changing social norms made it more acceptable for executives' salaries to rise and labor unions to be suppressed (Bebchuk and Fried 2004; Krugman 2007, 137–49; Levy and Temin 2007).

Yet changing federal policy is again a prime suspect. Bartels (2008b) and Krugman (2002a, 2005, 2007) argue that conservative policies, such as less enforcement of labor protections and reduced estate and upper-bracket income taxes, are likely causes.[8] As support, Bartels (2008b, 29–42) demonstrates that growth in inequality occurred almost entirely during Republican presidencies.

On the other hand, Nolan McCarty, Keith Poole, and Howard Rosenthal (2006) argue that government policy was conducive to a compressed wealth distribution in the mid-twentieth century not because of simple

[8] See also Levy and Temin (2007).

ideological change but because immigration rates were unusually low. In their view, by increasing the number of poor residents who are ineligible to vote, immigration makes the median voter wealthier than the median resident and therefore less likely to vote for redistribution (chap. 4).

Apart from economic inequality, the partisan ideological divide widened because views on many issues became more correlated with party affiliation. In the 1950s and 1960s, each party included people with liberal and conservative self-identifications, as well as liberal and conservative economic, racial, and gender policy views. This was true both in Congress and in the mass public. Yet now, in these areas and newly prominent ones such as gay rights, liberals and conservatives are almost entirely sorted into the Democratic and Republican Parties, respectively (see, e.g., Mansbridge 1986; Carmines and Stimson 1989; Adams 1997; Abramowitz and Saunders 1998; Green, Palmquist, and Schickler 2002; Fiorina, Abrams, and Pope 2005; Achen and Bartels 2006; Gelman et al. 2008; Bafumi and Shapiro 2009; Karol 2009; Levendusky 2009).

Whatever the ultimate cause, it is clear that the divide between the major parties was unusually narrow in the middle of the last century.[9] This temporary slackening of party competition led to a major reduction in political criticism of the news media and to their acceptance as a powerful, independent, and trusted part of the political process. Tellingly, chapter 2 noted that one of the few other periods when political conflict with the media was muted was the Era of Good Feelings, when party competition eased. It is also revealing that, as criticism increased in the past four decades, it was consistently the more polarized politicians and political activists who were most likely to attempt to discredit the news media.

Yet in addition to political factors, the institutional news media owed its peak of public esteem to unusual changes in the structure of the news industry. Chapter 3 detailed the decline in competitive pressure in the industry in the early twentieth century and its effect on the rise of "objectivity." In brief, newspaper readership was still close to historic highs at midcentury, but the number of newspapers had declined from 1910 on, resulting in most papers facing no competition in their own city. Competitive pressures on news divisions were also minimal in the newer media of radio and television. In both, national news was dominated by a few networks. In most markets, viewers could receive only two or three stations in the 1950s and early 1960s. The stations that were available often

---

[9] While the evidence is overwhelming that elites experienced an unusually low level of ideological polarization in the 1950s, 1960s, and 1970s, it is less clear whether this is true for the mass public. While certainly economic interests have become more polarized as wealth has become more unequal, on many issues asked about in surveys, the public has been more moderate than politicians in recent years (Fiorina, Abrams, and Pope 2005; Bafumi and Herron 2007).

all aired their news programs simultaneously. As a result, over a third of households with televisions watched a network evening newscast.

This environment left journalists largely free to produce content they were proud of (Zaller 1999b, chap. 3). As journalism scholar Arthur J. Kaul (1986, 52) put it, "Professional 'objectivity' emerged as an ideological corollary to commercial noncompetition." While much less colorful than the alternatives that would come later, this style of news helped make the news media socially respected and widely trusted.

In contrast, since the 1970s, institutional news sources have faced increasingly more competitors for the public's time and attention. These include more broadcast channels, entertainment and news cable channels, political talk radio, and an almost endless variety of offerings on the Internet. This increase in competition had several effects. It put much more pressure on all news outlets to draw in customers with soft news (Zaller 1999a; 1999b; Hamilton 2004). It also offered more sensationalist and partisan sources for consumers to turn to when they lost faith in the institutional news media. This situation allowed the decline in media trust to become self-reinforcing: alternative media sources persuade people to trust the institutional media less, resulting in more partisan beliefs and more consumption of alternative news, which persuades people to trust the institutional media less, and so on.

Regulatory changes also increased incentives to produce soft news. In the 1950s and 1960s, FCC regulators regularly checked the number of hours stations devoted to public affairs when reviewing their license renewals (Hamilton 2004, 160; Popkin 2006, 328–30). Because stations could cite news programs as public service content, networks and local stations worried that stations' licenses could be in jeopardy if they strayed from hard news programming. They did not expect the news to make profits because quality news was considered a government requirement for doing business.

However, the regulatory environment changed in the past four decades. In 1984, under Chairman Mark Fowler, the FCC officially dropped the public service programming requirement (Popkin 2006, 330). It now treats television more like an ordinary business, whose primary motivation is expected to be attracting consumers. Fowler memorably summarized this new philosophy, whereby demand dictates content, by saying that "the public's interest . . . defines the public interest" (Hamilton 2004, 32). As described in chapter 4, this allowed soft news to proliferate on local and national news broadcasts free of government restraint.[10]

In sum, anomalous political and economic circumstances in the mid-twentieth century led to less elite political media criticism and more

[10] See Hamilton (2004, chaps. 6–7) and Zaller (1999a; 1999b, chap. 3).

Figure 8-1. Sources of declining media trust.

"objective" hard news coverage, respectively. These phenomena encouraged high levels of media trust. Since then, factors external to the news media have increased party polarization and economic competition in the news industry. These changes resulted in media trust declining.

These processes are summarized in figure 8-1. Importantly, nothing in this depiction precludes direct causal connections between media criticism and the decline in media professionalism. In particular, it is likely that increases in sensationalism and the declining hegemony of the ideal of objectivity provoked politicians (and others) to intensify their attacks on the media. However, the main drivers of the process are political polarization and economic competition.

Yet knowing that the media environment of the 1950s and 1960s was unusual for these reasons still leaves the question of whether it was better. We should judge news media styles not on their historical prevalence but on whether they improve or hinder democratic governance. To answer this question, we must explore the purposes of the news media in a democracy.

What Are the Purposes of the News Media in a Democracy?

Most democratic nations have established protections for the news media. Does democracy really need a free press to function well? The media perform two essential functions in democratic systems.[11] First, they facilitate the formation of party coalitions to structure political conflict. Second, they provide the public with information to enable retrospective voting. Both are more essential to democracy than they may first appear.

---

[11] Different scholars present varying lists of the functions the news media serve in democratic systems. Here I emphasize the two functions that I consider most important. For examples of alternative lists, see Curran (2005), Graber (2010, 5–11), Schudson (2008, chap. 2), and Jamieson, Hardy and Romer (2007).

One of the most consequential advances in mathematical political theory in the past century is its demonstration of majority rule's instability and vulnerability to agenda manipulation. Specifically, Richard McKelvey (1976; 1979) demonstrated that, when voters have preferences over more than one policy dimension, *any* outcome is possible through majority rule voting.[12] The outcome can be determined entirely by the choices presented. This applies to citizens voting on candidates or referenda and to legislators voting on bills.

To reduce instability and ensure that outcomes reflect voters' preferences in some way, the choices available must be structured (i.e., limited). This is called "structure-induced equilibrium" in the political science literature. Committee systems and other parliamentary rules can contribute to structure-induced equilibrium in legislative voting (Shepsle 1979; Shepsle and Weingast 1981). But by reducing the available choices, party systems are another important source of structure-induced equilibrium at both the mass level and in legislatures (Aldrich 1995). Their importance for producing stable policy outcomes is illustrated by the fact that all modern democratic states have parties in some form (Schattschneider 1942, 1; Aldrich 1995, 3).[13]

Creating party coalitions is unusually difficult in the United States because its political institutions are designed to thwart them. The Constitution was written with the intention of suppressing "factions." James Madison famously argued in *Federalist* No. 10 that factions were a threat to the common good (Hofstadter 1969; Madison, Hamilton, and Jay 1987 [1788]). Yet since the beginning, politicians and activists have used the news media to overcome these obstacles and form national coalitions. For example, consider the first party system, which developed in the 1790s. Newspaper writers were prime organizers of that system. Newspapers allowed dispersed supporters to develop a policy agenda and mobilize supporters (see chapter 2; Zaller 2007; M. Cohen et al. 2008, chap. 3). Moreover, Hans Noel (2006) has analyzed the development of ideological coalitions by coding the content of opinion articles throughout American history. He finds that when the ideological coalitions that

---

[12] While there can be an equilibrium in multidimensional settings, this only occurs under the knife-edge condition where a multidimensional median exists, a highly unrealistic circumstance (Plott 1967; Davis, Hinich, and Ordeshook 1970; Kramer 1973). On the instability of majority rule, see also Cox and Shepsle (2007), Riker (1980; 1982), and Schofield (1978; 1983). These results can be seen as a special case of Arrow's (1963a) "general possibility theorem."

[13] To agree that parties are important for structuring democratic decision making does not require agreement on why exactly parties form. For example, Aldrich (1995) argues that the impetus for organizing party coalitions comes from politicians, while Bawn et al. (2006) argue that the impetus comes from policy-demanding groups.

divide American parties change, the new coalitions develop first in opinion articles.

One of the ways American institutions work against strong parties is by denying party officials and activists direct control of nominations. Since the McGovern-Fraser Commission's reforms were implemented in 1972, American presidential nominations have been decided by a series of primaries and caucuses, rather than by delegates representing local party organizations. This lack of structure could potentially produce the type of instability in the nominating process that McKelvey (1976; 1979) described.[14] The media help parties avoid this chaotic outcome. As Marty Cohen and his coauthors (2008) document, before the primaries take place, politicians and party leaders across the country usually settle on a candidate whom most endorse. That candidate usually wins the nomination. Observers often call this competition for endorsements "the invisible primary." As Cohen and his coauthors describe it, party activists engage in long-distance deliberation by publicizing their endorsements in the news media.

Helping politicians organize themselves into party "teams" offering distinctive and coherent policy platforms has additional benefits beyond reducing instability and vulnerability to agenda setting. American political scientists have traditionally argued that these parties are better able to implement coherent policy programs, enhance democratic responsiveness by offering voters clear choices and responsibility for outcomes, and engage people in the political process (Wilson 1885; Schattschneider 1942; Key 1949; Berdahl et al. 1950; Schattschneider 1975 [1960]; Fiorina 1981; Bernhardt, Duggan, and Squintani 2009; Rosenblum 2010; but see Ranney 1975). E. E. Schattschneider (1942, 1, 4) claimed that "modern democracy is unthinkable except in terms of parties. . . . [D]emocracy is a byproduct of party competition."

The second major way the news media improve democratic performance is by informing the public. The most significant thing public opinion research since the 1940s has taught us is that a major portion of the American public has little interest in public affairs (P. Converse 1964; A. Campbell et al. 1980 [1960]; Zaller 1992; Delli Carpini and Keeter 1996; Kinder 1998b, 1998a; Luskin 2002; Achen and Bartels 2006). As Graber's (1984) interviews illustrate, much (though certainly not all) of the public prefers not to follow the day-to-day details of politics. Given this, and the fact that those who do follow politics tend to be committed partisans, national election swings rarely reflect complex assessments of policies and ideologies (see P. Converse 1964; Bartels 2008a).

[14] For a discussion of this problem and how the sequential nature of primaries and caucuses can reduce the instability, see Bartels (1988, chap. 12).

206 • Chapter 8

Instead, as chapter 7 discussed, elections largely respond to policy outcomes. The incumbent coalition is rewarded or punished based on whether the country is in good condition. Political scientists often argue that the ability of the electorate to reward and punish in this way is a primary reason to prefer democracy to other systems (e.g. Downs 1957; Key 1968; Fiorina 1981; Bartels 1992). In support of this view, game theoretic models show that retrospective voting elects higher-quality politicians (Banks and Duggan 2001; Morton 2006) and gives those in office incentives to serve citizens' interests (Ferejohn 1986; Austen-Smith and Banks 1989; Banks and Sundaram 1993; Fearon 1999; Morton 2006).[15] Even though most people do not inform themselves about political details, the news media publicize national conditions loudly enough to enable disengaged voters to hold leaders accountable and reap the resulting benefits.

In sum, the news media facilitate at least two essential democratic functions. They help activists organize party coalitions, so policy making is less prone to instability and agenda manipulation, and they publicize policy outcomes, so disengaged voters can hold politicians accountable. In thinking about the future of the American news media, we should focus on preserving and enhancing their performance of these tasks.

HOW BAD ARE MEDIA DISTRUST'S CONSEQUENCES?

Lippmann's writings in the 1920s—lamenting the uninformed public and urging journalism to provide more accurate information—did not go unchallenged. One of the most forceful dissents came from philosopher John Dewey (1954 [1927]), who saw the role of news media in a democracy very differently. Rather than journalists being scientific information senders and the public passive recipients, Dewey argued that the press should facilitate a conversation among political leaders and diverse factions in the public. Political decisions should emerge from this lively exchange of ideas.[16]

Echoes of Lippmann and Dewey can be heard in today's debates about the media's future (Alterman 2008). On the one hand, there are those who wish that the news media would return to their place in American society in the 1950s, when they were largely a realization of Lippmann's vision of professionalized, "objective" journalism. On the other hand, there are those who welcome recent trends that correspond more to

---

[15] Theorists refer to the former tendency as reducing "adverse selection" and the latter as reducing "moral hazard."

[16] On the debate between Lippmann and Dewey, see Alterman (1999, 288–89; 2008, 53–55).

Dewey's vision, such as less professionalization, more fragmentation, and more diversity.

Declining trust in the institutional media has been an important part of the evolution of the American media environment away from Lippmann's vision and toward Dewey's. Media distrust is both a symptom of this transition and a cause of its further acceleration. Therefore, assessing the consequences of media distrust entails grappling with these claims about the optimal role of mass media in democracy.

There are important advantages to a decentralized, less professional news media. As Dewey describes, this environment is good at fostering lively and open political debate and (as a partial consequence) facilitating the development of partisan coalitions. However, if taken to the extreme, where no sources are widely trusted to provide political information, the public may have no common set of facts on which to base political debate and hold politicians accountable for their performance in office. With public opinion untethered from reality, it may truly become a "phantom public" (in Lippmann's [1927] memorable characterization), responsive only to the balance of media messages.[17]

On the other hand, a media environment dominated by a trusted, professional journalistic establishment also has strengths and weaknesses. By design, this type of "objective" journalism is good at developing an elite consensus on how the country is doing and communicating that to the public. In addition to informing the public, the power of institutional journalism can extend the American system of checks and balances to include another, separate group of elites, in many ways serving as a "fourth branch" of government (e.g. Cater 1959; Stewart 1974–75).

Yet when taken to its extreme, this model can also have serious drawbacks. Primarily, the lack of a decentralized, heterogeneous, permeable media environment restricts society's ability to organize political conflict, including forming strong parties and ideologies. In addition, it limits individual freedom by restricting people's ability to participate in media discourse and consume news in a style they prefer. There is also no guarantee that the messages sent by a homogeneous institutional media will always accurately reflect national conditions. Among the ways highly professionalized journalism could produce inaccurate coverage, it might have cultural ideological bias (e.g. B. Goldberg 2002; Kelly 2002a, 2002b) or its norm of reflecting the balance of messages among official sources might lead it astray (e.g. W. Bennett 1990; Kuklinski and Sigelman 1992). A powerful institutional media will always be vulnerable to the concern that it is using its power inappropriately.

---

[17] But see Zaller (1992, chap. 12) for a normative defense of a world where public opinion is responsive to the balance of elite messages.

Another reason to doubt the benefits of the extreme versions of either the Lipmannian or Deweyian models is that the desirability of soft news, mass partisanship, and economic retrospective voting is, in each case, debatable. As chapter 4 describes, while the institutional media's dominance has declined, the amount of soft news on institutional news outlets has increased, as has the popularity of noninstitutional sources specializing in soft news. However, as noted above and in chapter 5, recent research finds that soft news programming, by mixing political information with more entertaining tabloid topics, can reduce inequalities in political engagement.[18] Matthew Baum finds that exposure to soft news programming increases one's probability of following recent political events, especially for foreign affairs stories and among those who do not usually follow politics (Baum 2002; 2003b, chap. 4). He and Angela Jamison (2006) also find that viewing daytime talk shows helps less politically aware individuals to vote consistently with their issue preferences. As programs featuring soft news have proliferated, they have become important sources of political information for those who do not typically follow politics. We need to balance these significant benefits against the indirect effects of tabloid news, where, by reducing trust in the institutional media, it reduces receptivity to institutional media messages and exacerbates partisanship in beliefs and voting behavior.

Also, it is in dispute whether extreme nonpartisanship in the mass public is preferable to extreme partisanship. While the drawbacks of mass partisanship, such as less responsiveness to information about the performance of officeholders and a more harsh political discourse, are much discussed (e.g. Galston and Nivola 2006; Brownstein 2007; Nivola and Galston 2008), partisanship also has benefits. Strong party ties correlate with more structured political beliefs and greater participation (e.g. P. Converse 1964; A. Campbell et al. 1980 [1960]; Zaller and Feldman 1992; Rosenstone and Hansen 1993; Rosenblum 2010). In addition, having a significant portion of the public holding strong party attachments also enhances democratic stability by preventing wild swings in party strength from election to election (Green, Palmquist, and Schickler 2002, chap. 8).

Finally, while media distrust changes how voters respond to economic conditions, some scholars question the overall usefulness of American patterns of economic voting. Based on their finding that only the last two full quarters influence presidential elections, Achen and Bartels (2004) doubt that economic voting helps elect higher-quality presidents or gives those in office an incentive to govern well. In this view, many idiosyncratic factors might produce short-term variations in economic growth, which

---

[18] Zaller (2003) makes a similar argument but with a greater specific emphasis on "feeding frenzies."

might happen to fall just before an election. Yet to the extent that presidents can intentionally time economic growth, the incentive to produce it immediately before elections regardless of the consequences for other times might not induce the best policies (see Tufte 1978). Voter "myopia" may prevent economic voting from improving democratic governance.[19] In chapter 7, I find that those who trust the media give more weight to the third quarter of the election year and less to the second, while those who distrust the media weight both quarters about equally. Those concerned about voter myopia might doubt the benefits of either of these types of economic voting.

Thus, we should hesitate before embracing Craig Crawford's (2006, 19) claim that "[p]ublic distrust of the news media is one of the most hazardous political challenges now facing America." Declining trust in the news media, and the changing media environment that has accompanied it, have important consequences, at least some of which are arguably negative. However, the type of media environment that existed in the mid-twentieth century has arguably negative consequences as well.

Both Dewey's and Lippmann's preferred styles of journalism have essential benefits, the former helping parties and ideologies to organize and the latter informing the public. Yet, there are drawbacks if the country veers too far in either direction. It is best to find a balance between the two models.

What Policies Can Produce a Middle Ground?

It is difficult to navigate this middle course. If left alone, political and economic incentives consistently push the news media away from Lippmann and toward Dewey. This is why Dewey's model is much more historically typical. Lippmann's style of journalism only became dominant and lasted as long as it did because the intensity of party conflict and competitiveness of the media marketplace were unusually restrained.

Hamilton (2004) describes an informed public as a public good. In economic theory, public goods tend to be underprovided because individuals do not pay the true cost of using them. As a result, society as a whole is worse off. This problem is labeled the "tragedy of the commons" (Hardin 1968). A classic example of a tragedy of the commons is a clean lake. Society as a whole is better off if the lake is kept clean. However, individuals or businesses can all improve their own situations by polluting the lake to make money or for their own recreation. Thus, in the absence

---

[19] On voter myopia, see also Bartels (2008b; 2008a), Healy and Malhotra (2009) and Lenz (2010b).

of government restrictions on water use and pollution, the clean lake will not be preserved.

While the analogy is not perfect, there are similarities between the provision of information to the public through the news media and tragedies of the commons. If the major players—specifically, news organizations and party leaders—pursue their own interests, the public will be underinformed because the news media will move in an extreme Deweyian direction. The standard remedy for a tragedy of the commons is some type of market intervention.[20] Thus, to preserve some balance between Lippmann's and Dewey's visions, market interventions to increase political learning could help. Below, I suggest three possible ways to do this, each with possible benefits and potentially serious limitations.[21]

First, the U.S. could enhance public subsidies for news organizations. While public media are not immune from political criticism, they nevertheless tend to be more trusted than other news outlets (PBS News 2009). The federal government has subsidized television and radio through the Corporation for Public Broadcasting (CPB) since the passage of the Public Broadcasting Act of 1967 (Graber 2010, 29–30).[22] In a complex system, CBP is an independent agency led by a politically appointed board. It is intended to handle general administration, while providing grants to other organizations that produce content, mainly NPR, the Public Broadcasting Service (PBS), and local stations affiliated with these networks. Taken together, this system of stations and networks receives 19% of its revenue from the federal government, 27% from individual donors, 25% from state and local governments, and 15% from business donations.[23]

As one would expect, insulation from market pressure allows these entities to adhere relatively well to standards of journalistic professionalism. The epitome of this may be the PBS NewsHour. Anchor Jim Lehrer explained his broadcasting style this way: "Nothing should be noticed or

[20] But see Ostrom (1999).

[21] Other lists of possible reforms are available. In May 2010, the staff of the Federal Trade Commission circulated a 47-page discussion draft containing proposals to improve the viability of institutional journalism. Reforms presented for discussion included strengthening intellectual property rights over news reports, providing some antitrust exemptions to journalistic organizations, providing various direct or indirect government subsidies, and reducing news-gathering costs by increasing government efforts to disseminate information (Federal Trade Commission 2010). As this chapter makes clear, I am more sympathetic to the latter two suggestions than the others.

[22] In addition, the federal government directly operates the Armed Forces Radio and Television Service as well as several outlets directed at foreign audiences, such as Voice of America (Graber 2010, 29).

[23] The remaining revenue comes from foundations (7%), private colleges and universities (2%), and various other sources (6%). These are 2003 data (Graber 2010, 31).

absorbed except the information. Nothing else should be memorable. . . . Those few seconds while the viewer admires or retches over the gaudy green tie or the red-white-and-blue-flashing map of the drought belt can destroy the whole point of the exercise, the transmitting of information" (Lehrer 1992, 231). Elsewhere, he summarized the *NewsHour*'s journalistic philosophy with 10 principles, which included "[a]ssume personal lives are a private matter, until a legitimate turn in the story absolutely mandates otherwise," "[c]arefully separate opinion and analysis from straight news stories, and clearly label everything," and "I am not in the entertainment business" (*PBS NewsHour* 2009).

Additional funding to improve the depth and prominence of this type of reporting (either through NPR, PBS, or new publicly funded news outlets) could enhance public knowledge of policy outcomes. This could produce a media landscape where outlets produce news with widely varying styles and partisan slants. Yet, like the British Broadcasting Corporation in the United Kingdom, alongside this diverse media marketplace prominent public news organizations would still disseminate news that hewed toward a more informative style (West 2001, 124–25).[24]

Second, government could directly publicize national conditions. Though usually ignored, Lippmann's central recommendation in the last four chapters of *Public Opinion* (1997 [1922]) is for the federal government to operate bureaus devoted to gathering political information and disseminating it to the public. Journalist Eric Alterman (2008, 53) calls this proposal "one of the oddest formulations of [Lippmann's] long career." However, given the politically sensitive tasks many bureaus already perform, it is not impossible to imagine the government aggressively publicizing data on major policy outcomes. The national statistics that citizens use most when retrospectively voting seem to be economic growth and casualties in foreign wars.[25] We already rely on the Department of Commerce's Bureau of Economic Analysis and the Department of Defense, respectively, to compile and release these data. Implementing Lippmann's proposal would entail either giving these bureaus the

---

[24] Hallin and Mancini (2004) classify media systems into three models. The "polarized pluralist" and "democratic corporatist" models are most common in Europe. These entail more government intervention in the media industry. Hallin and Mancini argue that, up to this point, the United States' media system has been a quintessential example of the "liberal model." While they classify the United Kingdom in the liberal model, they acknowledge "substantial differences . . . between the United States—which is a purer example of a liberal system—and Britain, where statist conservatism, liberal corporatism, and social democracy have been stronger than in the United States" (198).

[25] The much greater number of casualties seems to explain why, in the post–World War II era, only the Korean and Vietnam Wars have had detectable effects on presidential election outcomes.

mandate and resources to more aggressively publicize this information or creating a new bureau charged with the task.

While this proposal may strike many as odd, there are some imperfect precedents. It has similarities to the concept of an "organizational report card" in the institutional design literature. William Gormley and David Weimer (1999) define a conventional organizational report card as a "regular effort by an organization to collect data on two or more other organizations, transform the data into information relevant to assessing performance, and transmit the information to some audience external to the organizations themselves" (3). The main goal is for the "collected data to be transformed into information relevant to assessing organizational performance" (4). One use of organizational report cards is improving public knowledge about the performance of private firms, such as health care organizations, child care providers, colleges and universities, and insurance companies, allowing consumers to make more informed choices and these industries to be closer to "perfect" competition. Another use is enhancing public knowledge of the performance of local and state governmental initiatives, such as economic development, employment and training programs, and public schools, to provide citizens with "more and better information to guide them in political activities, such as voting and lobbying" (5–8). In many ways, Lippmann's proposal simply entails charging a federal agency with constructing and publicizing an institutional report card for the federal government's most essential functions: maintaining peace and prosperity.[26]

However, a problem with institutional report cards can be publicizing the results (Gormley and Weimer 1999, chap. 7). A government information bureau would not just have to summarize accessibly economic and national security information but also aggressively disseminate those summaries to the public. This problem is especially thorny because even very accessible websites, news releases, and so on are likely to reach only the most politically aware individuals, who tend to have strong political predispositions. But it is the less politically aware who rely most on contemporary information when voting (Zaller 2004). Unless government-sponsored publicity is extremely widespread—such as billboards and television advertisements about the state of the economy or foreign wars—it is unlikely to reach these voters.

One existing federal bureau that uses these types of methods for an electorally sensitive task is the Bureau of the Census. The decennial census determines the allotment of congressional seats among the states and,

---

[26] This would differ from the standard definition of an organizational report card in that the information bureau would be evaluating only one organization, not two or more, and it would be evaluating an organization (the federal government) of which it was a part.

because districts within states must have equal population, it also determines which substate regions receive more or less representation. In carrying out this delicate task, the Census Bureau conducts a large publicity campaign encouraging people to participate, including television and radio advertisements, billboards, signs on buses, posters in businesses, and so on (Hillygus et al. 2006, chap. 2).

If this type of approach is impractical or insufficient, another strategy would be for the information bureau to engage actively with journalists (see Gormley and Weimer 1999, 190–91). While it could not dictate the amount of attention journalists devote to broad policy outcomes, by following the common public relations technique of packaging the information so that it is, first, interesting, and second, easy for journalists to use, this strategy could have some effect. Given the tendency of journalists to focus on recent specific events rather than broad national trends (Patterson 1993), any increase in attention to the latter would constitute an improvement.

In sum, direct government dissemination of information about broad policy outcomes has potential problems and may be entirely ineffective. My point is merely that this proposal is neither as odd as it initially seems nor necessarily less feasible than other possible reforms.

The main problem with both publicly funded media organizations and government agencies charged with publicizing policy outcomes is the danger of politicization. The danger of partisan manipulation of mechanisms of electoral accountability is not new. Still, in evaluating the government potentially playing a larger role in informing the public, we should consider existing evidence on the government's ability to impartially implement policy, especially when it is media-related or electorally sensitive.

Researchers have found evidence of bureaucratic politicization in a variety of policy areas. The ideology of elected politicians influences bureaus' policy making even absent any statutory changes. This is true for bureaus as diverse as the Equal Employment Opportunity Commission (B. Wood 1990; B. Wood and Waterman 1991), Environmental Protection Agency (B. Wood and Waterman 1991, 1993), Federal Trade Commission (Moe 1982; Weingast and Moran 1983; B. Wood and Waterman 1991), Food and Drug Administration (B. Wood and Waterman 1991), Internal Revenue Service (Scholz and Wood 1998, 1999), National Highway Transportation Safety Administration (B. Wood and Waterman 1991), National Labor Relations Board (Moe 1982, 1985; Brudney 2005), Nuclear Regulatory Commission (B. Wood and Waterman 1991), Office of Surface Mining (B. Wood and Waterman 1991), and Securities and Exchange Commission (Moe 1982).[27] Yet the fact that at least some

---

[27] On electorally motivated congressional influence on bureaucracies' geographic allocation of federal funds, see Arnold (1979). On the responsiveness of state bureaucracies to

politicization of bureaucratic policy making is widespread does not mean it is universal. There is substantial variation in politicization across time and bureaus, with some bureaus achieving substantial, but not complete, autonomy (e.g. Gormley 1986; Arnold 1987; McCubbins, Noll, and Weingast 1987; Gormley 1989; Moe 1989; Woolley 1993; Bawn 1995; Epstein and O'Halloran 1999; Carpenter 2001; Lewis 2003; Gormley and Balla 2004; Lewis 2008).

Turning specifically to media-related bureaus, the record is still mixed at best. In general, bureaus can either be under the control of a cabinet agency or the Executive Office of the President or be organized as independent agencies. Presidents usually appoint the commissions or boards that govern independent agencies, subject to Senate confirmation. But these commissions and boards often contain a certain number of seats guaranteed to each party by statute and their members serve fixed terms and are difficult to remove (even for-cause) (Lewis 2003, 44–49; Devins and Lewis 2008, 462–63).[28] Unlike other bureaus, independent agencies also do not need Office of Management and Budget (OMB) approval of regulatory changes and can often avoid OMB review of their budget requests (Devins and Lewis 2008, 482, 488). The two bureaus currently most directly involved in media policy making, the FCC and the CPB, are both independent agencies.

However, this arrangement has not insulated them from political influence. In most independent agencies, the behavior of Republican and Democratic commissioners has polarized since the 1980s (Devins and Lewis 2008, 477–94). As a result, policy at a given agency increasingly depends on the party affiliation of a majority of appointees (Devins and Lewis 2008). At the FCC, commissioners' voting behavior was already quite partisan in the 1950s, 1960s, and 1970s, a pattern that, following general trends, has intensified from the 1980s to the present. Recently, FCC commissioners have even adopted the practice of issuing separate public statements by party (Gormley 1979; J. Cohen 1986; Devins 1993; Brown and Candeub 2006; Ho 2007; Devins and Lewis 2008, 494).[29]

---

appointed officials, citizen activists, and other interests, see Gormley (1983) and Gormley, Hoadley and Williams (1983).

[28] Lewis (2003, 45) classifies five different types of bureaus in order from least to most politically insulated: (1) those under the Executive Office of the President, (2) those that constitute (or are part of) cabinet departments, (3) independent agencies, (4) independent commissions, and (5) government corporations or "other." I do not disagree with this classification of the degree of political influence. However, for simplicity, here I refer to all bureaus in the final three categories as "independent agencies." See also Gormley and Balla (2004, 4–7).

[29] Ho's (2007) analysis finds that the behavior of FCC commissioners is heavily shaped by their party affiliation, not necessarily the party of the president that appointed them. This dominance of party affiliation over presidential influence has been increased since

The intent of the current public broadcasting system is to prevent politicization by separating the CPB from content-producing organizations. This has been partially, but not entirely, successful. The national news organizations associated with PBS and NPR have developed strong internal news cultures, closely linked to twentieth-century notions of journalistic professionalism. On the one hand, this has produced relative stability in journalistic practice in the face of pressure from political appointees of various ideologies. On the other hand, this stability has not been perfect. The behavior of CPB appointees has been clearly partisan since the early 1970s, even before the overall increase in the partisanship of appointees to independent agencies. Despite a structure designed to prevent political influence, the CPB has often been able use its power over funding to produced politically driven variation in content (Ledbetter 1998). This type of influence leads Graber (2010, 30) to pessimistically conclude, "The attempt to keep CPB from influencing programming has failed. The corporation does not tell public television stations what programs they should feature. Instead, it has guided programming by paying for some types of programs and refusing to pay for others. This has constituted purse-string control of programming by government." Overall, the record of avoiding politicization at existing independent agencies involved in media policy is mixed at best. Government agencies charged with implementing federal policy are almost unavoidably influenced by politics and partisanship. This is especially true in the media policy realm.

Another way to assess the theoretical feasibility of future attempts by government to sponsor public news media or directly publicize policy outcomes without partisan interference is to examine an existing independent agency where the electoral consequences of its work are very high, yet political elites have intensely tried to prevent politicization: the Federal Reserve. Through its control of monetary policy, as well as various other economic regulatory functions, the Federal Reserve regulates the growth of the entire economy. Given economic effects on elections, the Fed's behavior has large political implications.

While incumbent politicians have strong incentives to stimulate growth immediately prior to elections, it is hard to imagine an American government bureau better situated to resist political influence than the Federal Reserve. Monetary policy is primarily set by the Federal Open Market Committee, consisting of the Fed's Board of Governors and five representatives of regional Federal Reserve Banks. Members of the board are appointed by the president and confirmed by the Senate to 14-year

---

1980, meaning that statutory requirements that certain members of commissions be from the opposition party are increasingly consequential.

nonrenewable terms.[30] The Fed is also insulated from the budgeting and appropriations process because it is self-funded (Lewis 2003, 144; Board of Governors of the Federal Reserve System 2008). Furthermore, in Washington, DC, and at its district banks, the Fed's leadership and staff economists are highly professionalized, with loyalty to professional norms of what constitutes sound economic research and policy making. The Fed also benefits from a widespread consensus among economists and other political elites that its independence enhances long-term economic growth (see Shull 2005). Thus, in contemplating government support for public media organizations or bureaus publicizing policy outcomes, the level of politicization at the Fed may be a realistic lower bound. If the Fed cannot be politically insulated, such insulation may not be possible.

Research on the political insulation of Federal Reserve policy making is generally, but not entirely, encouraging. The Fed's statutory mission is to promote "maximum employment, stable prices, and moderate long-term interest rates" without regard to electoral considerations (Woolley 1984, 46). There are several different ways monetary policy could be politicized. First, it could follow a "political business cycle," where monetary policy loosens prior to each presidential election to temporarily increase growth and improve the incumbent party's prospects. Most researchers find no evidence of this, at least after 1980 (N. Beck 1982b, 1987; Alesina, Roubini, and Cohen 1997; Drazen 2000, 86–87).[31] Second, monetary policy could follow a "partisan" model, where it is generally tighter during Republican presidencies and looser during Democratic presidencies, reflecting the parties' different ideological preferences for growth versus stable prices.[32] Some scholars find evidence of this (Hibbs 1987, 145–54; Alesina, Roubini, and Cohen 1997, 95–100; Alesina 2000), but others either disagree (N. Beck 1982a; Sheffrin 1989; Faust and Irons 1999) or find the evidence inconclusive (Drazen 2000, 94–95).[33] In sum, while the results are not entirely unambiguous, the scholarly consensus is that the contemporary Federal Reserve is largely free of political influence, illustrating

[30] The chairmanship is also subject to presidential appointment and Senate confirmation, with four-year renewable terms.

[31] Tufte (1978, 45–51) argues in favor of a partisan business cycle in monetary policy based on pre-1980 evidence, especially the 1972 election.

[32] I am eliding the distinction between Hibbs's (1987, 145–54) more straightforward partisan model and Alesina, Roubini, and Cohen's (1997) "rational partisan model." However, for my purposes, they posit similar politicization of monetary policy making.

[33] A few scholars argue that the Fed engages in more directly partisan behavior, such as looser monetary policy prior to presidential elections when the incumbent president and Fed chairman are of the same party (Abrams and Iossifov 2006), or looser monetary policy prior to presidential elections when the incumbent president is a Republican, regardless of the party affiliation of the Fed chair (Galbraith, Giovannoni, and Russo 2007). But neither of these views is widely accepted by scholars (Drazen 2000; Tempelman 2007).

that under very favorable conditions, government bureaus can carry out electorally sensitive mandates with little political manipulation.[34]

Results of the FCC's, CPB's, and Federal Reserve's attempts to resist politicization suggest that it is very difficult for the government to impartially subsidize news. If the government attempts to inform the public through greater subsidies to public media organizations or government information bureaus, the usual procedures used by independent agencies are insufficient to prevent politicization. The record of the FCC and CPB indicate that parties and politicians can influence the behavior of independent agencies involved in media policy making. The example of the Federal Reserve shows that insulation from political pressure requires long, nonrenewable terms for political appointees, professional norms that are much stronger than current journalistic norms, and a consensus among political elites that the professional aims of the agency are worth protecting. When these conditions hold, insulation from partisan influence is possible, even if a bureau's actions have large electoral consequences. Yet satisfying these conditions in current or future media-related bureaus would be quite difficult.[35]

A third possible way to improve the public's knowledge of major policy outcomes is growth among nonprofit news organizations, which could constitute a sustainable source of more professionalized news.[36] Legal scholar

[34] Drazen (2000) provides a literature review on political influence and the Fed. Other government bureaus that perform politically sensitive tasks include those mentioned above—the Bureau of Economic Analysis, Department of Defense, and Bureau of the Census—as well as the Congressional Budget Office, which makes politically sensitive calculations about the budgetary impact of legislation. However, political influence on these bureaus has not been the subject of as much study as on the Federal Reserve. For a description of political conflict regarding administration of the Census, see Hillygus et al. (2006, especially 30–40).

[35] Ledbetter (1998, 229) endorses Henry Geller's proposal for CPB members to be selected by the president from a list prepared by "leaders in education, culture, broadcasting business, and labor, as well as representatives of women's and minority groups." However, I am skeptical whether this would eliminate politicization or just cause it to flow through the selection of the leaders who produce the list. A more promising suggestion by Ledbetter (1998, 230) is to require that two CPB directors be journalists from within public television or radio, preferably selected by their peers. While not a panacea, this has more potential to increase professional autonomy and insulation from partisanship.

[36] Some examples of nonprofit journalism organizations include the American Independent News Network, the Center for Investigative Reporting, the Huffington Post Investigative Fund, *Inquiry* magazine, MinnPost, ProPublica, the *St. Louis Beacon*, and the *Voice of San Diego* (Shafer 2009a, 2009b). NPR receives both government subsidies and substantial endowment support. Thus, NPR (as well as individual public radio and television stations that rely on contributions) could be considered a hybrid between publicly funded and privately funded nonprofit news organizations. The success of NPR in greatly increasing its audience over the past 30 years, as described in chapter 4, is perhaps the best evidence of the viability of these forms of media. NPR has increased its audience while adhering to a traditional, professionalized style of journalism. Surveys by the Pew Research Center for

Henry B. Hansmann (1980; 1996, chap. 12; 2003) argues that, in a variety of industries, a key advantage of nonprofit firms is their ability to hold the public's trust.[37] This literature primarily focuses not on the consequences of trust for learning and persuasion but on instances of "contract failure" or "asymmetrical information" between firms and the public. An example of this is a market with imperfect competition, where consumers may worry about overpaying for goods from for-profit firms taking excessive rents.

Yet this literature also sees nonprofits' public trust as allowing them to help solve public goods problems. Those who donate to nonprofits that provide public goods are less worried that their donations will be siphoned off for private gain. This, as well as exemption from taxation if they accept an IRS 501(c)(3) designation, may provide enough subsidies to allow nonprofit news organizations to resist market pressure to change their style of news (Swensen and Schmidt 2009).

However, there are also reasons to be skeptical of the benefits of nonprofit journalism. A 501(c)(3) tax status would prevent news organizations from explicitly endorsing candidates for office (Swensen and Schmidt 2009).[38] More worryingly, politicians will still have incentives to undermine trust in these organizations, limiting their ability to inform the public. Also, unlike government, which can reduce public goods problems through coercion (in this case, taxes to support public media or government dissemination of information), nonprofits rely on voluntary donations. While the trust engendered by nonprofit status encourages voluntary donations, collective action problems may still prevent these donations from being sufficient to make nonprofit journalism widespread and influential (Olson 1965; Hansmann 1980, 894–95). As one indicator of the amount of money this would require, supporting the *New York Times* would necessitate an endowment of approximately $5 billion (Swensen and Schmidt 2009). Furthermore, there is no guarantee that news organizations financed by endowments would consistently provide professionalized, "objective" news. Even if this is the intent of the original donors and staff, the uses of endowments sometimes drift away from their original purposes over time (Wooster 2007; Shafer 2009a).

These examples illustrate that it is very difficult to alleviate the problems produced by extreme media distrust and media fragmentation. Each

---

the People and the Press often find it ranked among the most "believable" news sources (Project for Excellence in Journalism 2009). These successes led Craigslist founder Craig Newmark to predict, "I have a feeling that membership models and philanthropy models will be stronger than advertising-supported organizations, because people are willing to pay for trustworthy news. I have a feeling that NPR is going to become a dominant player in the world of media, say, by 2020" (Huffington Post 2010).

[37] See also Arrow (1963b) and R. Nelson and Krashinsky (1973).

[38] On the nature of political restrictions associated with 501(c)(3) status, see Berry (2003).

possible way to increase knowledge of policy outcomes has major weaknesses. Clearly, there is still substantial work to be done developing media policies that contribute to a vibrant and responsive political system in the United States.

In this book, I have assessed the role of the media in American democracy based on their history, evidence regarding the causes and consequences of media trust, assessment of political and economic incentives, and consideration of the media's purposes in a democracy. While I believe this has produced some useful insights and thus revised the conventional wisdom in important ways, I hope that future researchers will fruitfully expand the pool of evidence we apply to this problem. One way for scholars to learn more is to examine patterns of media institutions and media trust cross-nationally.

Two recent studies have followed this approach and found that, while the institutional-versus-noninstitutional divide is central to media trust in the United States, it can be less central elsewhere. In China and post-authoritarian Africa the division between state-controlled and private media is more important to public thinking. However, patterns of trust still differ between these two regions. In China, "commercialized" media are more trusted as information sources, while in postauthoritarian African democracies, public media maintain higher levels of trust, despite their history of political manipulation by dictatorial regimes (Stockmann 2007; Moehler and Singh forthcoming). This type of research can potentially increase our understanding of the nature of media trust, such as why distinctions between institutional and noninstitutional media dominate public opinion in some countries, while in others media trust centers on other considerations. Comparative work may also improve our understanding of the effects of different media reforms, such as those discussed above, on both media trust and the overall news landscape.

Clearly, there is still work to be done in understanding trust in the media in modern nation-states. In doing this, we should idealize neither the highly institutionalized news media environment of mid-twentieth-century America nor the other extreme of a very fragmented, unprofessional news environment toward which the United States has moved recently. Rather, as political and economic pressures continue to push in a Deweyian direction, we should try to find effective ways to alleviate its worst symptom: a less informed and overly partisan public. In designing remedies, we should continue considering both the available empirical evidence and the incentives created by economic and political competition. This type of approach, rather than reflexive nostalgia for the recent past or alarmism about the future, increases the likelihood that our knowledge will grow and reforms will improve democratic governance.

References

Abramowitz, Alan I. 1978. "The Impact of a Presidential Debate on Voter Rationality." *American Journal of Political Science* 22 (3): 680–90.

———. 1988. "An Improved Model for Predicting Presidential Election Outcomes." *PS: Political Science and Politics* 21 (4): 843–46.

Abramowitz, Alan I., and Kyle L. Saunders. 1998. "Ideological Realignment in the U.S. Electorate." *Journal of Politics* 60 (3): 634–52.

Abrams, Burton A., and Plamen Iossifov. 2006. "Does the Fed Contribute to a Political Business Cycle?" *Public Choice* 129 (3–4): 249–62.

Achen, Christopher H. 1992. "Social Psychology, Demographic Variables and Linear Regression: Breaking the Iron Triangle in Voting Research." *Political Behavior* 14 (3): 195–211.

———. 2002. "Parental Socialization and Rational Party Identification." *Political Behavior* 24 (2): 151–70.

———. 2005. "Bayesian Voters and Their Turnout Decisions: Unifying the Behavior Literature." Department of Politics, Princeton University.

Achen, Christopher H., and Larry M. Bartels. 2004. "Musical Chairs: Pocketbook Voting and the Limits of Democratic Accountability." Paper presented at the Annual Meeting of the American Political Science Association, Chicago, IL.

———. 2006. "It Feels Like We're Thinking: The Rationalizing Voter and Electoral Democracy." Paper presented at the Annual Meeting of the American Political Science Association, Philadelphia, PA.

Adams, Greg D. 1997. "Abortion: Evidence of an Issue Evolution." *American Journal of Political Science* 41 (3): 718–37.

Agnew, Spiro. 1989. "Speeches on the Media." In *Killing the Messenger: 100 Years of Media Criticism*, ed. Tom Goldstein. New York: Columbia University Press, 64–85.

Ai, Chunrong, and Edward Norton. 2003. "Interaction Terms in Logit and Probit Models." *Economics Letters* 80 (1): 123–29.

Aldrich, John H. 1995. *Why Parties? The Origin and Transformation of Political Parties*. Chicago: University of Chicago Press.

Aldrich, John H., and Forrest D. Nelson. 1984. *Linear Probability, Logit, and Probit Models*. Newbury Park, CA: Sage.

Alesina, Alberto. 2000. "The Political Business Cycle after 25 Years: Comment." *NBER Macroeconomics Annual* 15: 117–24.

Alesina, Alberto, Nouriel Roubini, and Gerald D. Cohen. 1997. *Political Cycles and the Macroeconomy*. Cambridge, MA: MIT Press.

Allen, Eric W. 1927. "Journalism as Applied Social Science." *Journalism Bulletin* 4 (March): 1–7.

Allen, Mike. 2009. "Fox 'Not Really News,' Says Axelrod." Politico.com October 18. http://www.politico.com/news/stories/1009/28417.html (Accessed April 14, 2010).

Alterman, Eric. 1999. *Sound and Fury: The Making of the Punditocracy.* Rev. ed. Ithaca, NY: Cornell University Press.

———. 2003. *What Liberal Media? The Truth about Bias and the News.* New York: Basic Books.

———. 2008. "Out of Print: The Death and Life of American Newspapers." *New Yorker,* March 31, 48–59.

Althaus, Scott L. 2003. *Collective Preferences in Democratic Politics: Opinion Surveys and the Will of the People.* New York: Cambridge University Press.

Althaus, Scott L., and Young Mie Kim. 2006. "Priming Effects in Complex Information Environments: Reassessing the Impact of News Discourse on Presidential Approval." *Journal of Politics* 68 (4): 960–76.

Alvarez, R. Michael. 1997. *Information and Elections.* Ann Arbor: University of Michigan Press.

Ames, William. 1972. *A History of the National Intelligencer.* Chapel Hill: University of North Carolina Press.

Anand, Bharat, and Rafael Di Tella. 2008. "Perceived Media Bias: Some Evidence on the Impact of Prior Beliefs and Source Awareness." Harvard Business School, Harvard University.

Anderson, Brian C. 2005. *South Park Conservatives: The Revolt against Liberal Media Bias.* Washington, DC: Regnery.

Angrist, Joshua D., Guido W. Imbens, and Donald B. Rubin. 1996. "Identification of Causal Effects Using Instrumental Variables." *Journal of the American Statistical Association* 91 (434): 444–55.

Angrist, Joshua D., and Jörn-Steffen Pischke. 2009. *Mostly Harmless Econometrics: An Empiricist's Companion.* Princeton, NJ: Princeton University Press.

Ansolabehere, Stephen. 2006. "The Paradox of Minimal Effects." In *Capturing Campaign Effects,* ed. Henry E. Brady and Richard Johnston. Ann Arbor: University of Michigan Press, 29–44.

Ansolabehere, Stephen, Shigeo Hirano, James M. Snyder Jr., and Michiko Ueda. 2006. "Party and Incumbency Cues in Voting: Are They Substitutes?" *Quarterly Journal of Political Science* 1 (2): 119–37.

Ansolabehere, Stephen, and Shanto Iyengar. 1995. *Going Negative: How Attack Ads Shrink and Polarize the Electorate.* New York: Free Press.

Ansolabehere, Stephen, Rebecca Lessem, and James M. Snyder Jr. 2006. "The Political Orientation of Newspaper Endorsements in U.S. Elections, 1940–2002." *Quarterly Journal of Political Science* 1 (4): 393–404.

Ansolabehere, Stephen, and James M. Snyder Jr. 2002. "The Incumbency Advantage in U.S. Elections: An Analysis of State and Federal Offices, 1942–2000." *Election Law Journal: Rules, Politics, and Policy* 1 (3): 315–38.

Ansolabehere, Stephen, James M. Snyder Jr., and Charles Stewart III. 2000. "Old Voters, New Voters, and the Personal Vote: Using Redistricting to Measure the Incumbency Advantage." *American Journal of Political Science* 44 (1): 17–34.

Arceneaux, Kevin, and Martin Johnson. 2007. "Channel Surfing: Does Choice Reduce Videomalaise?" Paper presented at the Annual Meeting of the Midwest Political Science Association, Chicago, IL.

Armstrong, Jerome, and Markos Moulitsas. 2006. *Crashing the Gate: Netroots, Grassroots, and the Rise of People-Powered Politics*. White River Junction, VT: Chelsea Green.

Arnold, R. Douglas. 1979. *Congress and the Bureaucracy: A Theory of Influence*. New Haven, CT: Yale University Press.

———. 1987. "Political Control of Administrative Officials." *Journal of Law, Economics, and Organization* 3 (2): 279–86.

———. 2004. *Congress, the Press, and Political Accountability*. New York: Russell Sage Foundation and Princeton University Press.

Arrow, Kenneth J. 1963a. *Social Choice and Individual Values*. 2nd ed. New Haven, CT: Yale University Press.

———. 1963b. "Uncertainty and the Welfare Economics of Medical Care." *American Economic Review* 54 (4): 941–73.

Austen-Smith, David. 1994. "Strategic Transmission of Costly Information." *Econometrica* 62 (4): 955–63.

Austen-Smith, David, and Jeffrey S. Banks. 1989. "Electoral Accountability and Incumbency." In *Models of Strategic Choice in Politics*, ed. Peter C. Ordeshook. Ann Arbor: University of Michigan Press, 121–48.

Bafumi, Joseph, Andrew Gelman, and David K. Park. 2004. "What Does 'Do Campaigns Matter?' Mean?" Department of Political Science, Columbia University.

Bafumi, Joseph, and Michael C. Herron. 2007. "Preference Aggregation, Representation, and Elected American Political Institutions." Department of Political Science, Dartmouth College.

Bafumi, Joseph, and Robert Y. Shapiro. 2009. "A New Partisan Voter." *Journal of Politics* 71 (1): 1–24.

Bai, Matt. 2007. *The Argument: Billionaires, Bloggers, and the Battle to Remake Democratic Politics*. New York: Penguin.

Baldasty, Gerald J. 1992. *The Commercialization of News in the Nineteenth Century*. Madison: University of Wisconsin Press.

Banks, Jeffrey S. 1991. *Signaling Games in Political Science*. Chur, Switzerland: Harwood.

Banks, Jeffrey S., and John Duggan. 2001. "A Multidimensional Model of Repeated Elections." Department of Political Science, University of Rochester.

Banks, Jeffrey S., and Rangaragan K. Sundaram. 1993. "Moral Hazard and Adverse Selection in a Model of Repeated Elections." In *Political Economy: Institutions, Competition, and Representation*, ed. William A. Barnett, Norman Schofield, and Melvin Hinich. New York: Cambridge University Press, 295–311.

Barker, David C. 1999. "Rushed Decisions: Political Talk Radio and Vote Choice." *Journal of Politics* 61 (2): 527–39.

———. 2002. *Rushed to Judgment: Talk Radio, Persuasion, and American Political Behavior*. New York: Columbia University Press.

Barker, David C., and Kathleen Knight. 2000. "Political Talk Radio and Public Opinion." *Public Opinion Quarterly* 64 (2): 149–70.

Barker, David C., and Adam B. Lawrence. 2006. "Media Favoritism and Presidential Nominations." *Political Communication* 23 (1): 41–59.

Baron, David P. 2005. "Competing for the Public through the News Media." *Journal of Economics and Management Strategy* 14 (2): 339–76.

———. 2006. "Persistent Media Bias." *Journal of Public Economics* 90 (1–2): 1–36.

Barr, Andy. 2009. "Palin: Media Sought to Seek, Destroy." Politico.com. February 23. http://www.politico.com/news/stories/0209/19178.html (Accessed February 24, 2009).

Bartels, Larry M. 1988. *Presidential Primaries and the Dynamics of Public Choice*. Princeton, NJ: Princeton University Press.

———. 1992. "The Impact of Electioneering in the United States." In *Electioneering: A Comparative Study of Continuity and Change*, ed. David Butler and Austin Ranney. New York: Clarendon Press and Oxford University Press, 244–77.

———. 1993. "Messages Received: The Political Impact of Media Exposure." *American Political Science Review* 87 (2): 267–85.

———. 1996a. "Politicians and the Press: Who Leads, Who Follows?" Paper presented at the Annual Meeting of the American Political Science Association, San Francisco, CA.

———. 1996b. "Uninformed Votes: Information Effects in Presidential Elections." *American Journal of Political Science* 40 (1): 194–230.

———. 2000. "Partisanship and Voting Behavior, 1952–1996." *American Journal of Political Science* 44 (1): 35–50.

———. 2002a. "Beyond the Running Tally: Partisan Bias in Political Perceptions." *Political Behavior* 24 (2): 117–50.

———. 2002b. "The Impact of Candidate Traits in American Presidential Elections." In *Leaders' Personalities and the Outcomes of Democratic Elections*, ed. Anthony King. Oxford, UK: Oxford University Press, 44–68.

———. 2006. "Priming and Persuasion in Presidential Campaigns." In *Capturing Campaign Effects*, ed. Henry E. Brady and Richard Johnston. Ann Arbor: University of Michigan Press, 78–112.

———. 2008a. "The Irrational Electorate." *Wilson Quarterly* 32 (4): 44–50.

———. 2008b. *Unequal Democracy: The Political Economy of the New Gilded Age*. Princeton, NJ: Russell Sage Foundation and Princeton University Press.

———. 2010. "The Study of Electoral Behavior." In *The Oxford Handbook of American Elections and Political Behavior*, ed. Jan E. Leighley. New York: Oxford University Press, 239–61.

Bartels, Larry M., and Wendy M. Rahn. 2000. "Political Attitudes in the Post-Network Era." Paper presented at the Annual Meeting of the American Political Science Association, Washington, DC.

Bartels, Larry M., and John Zaller. 2001. "Presidential Vote Models: A Recount." *PS: Political Science and Politics* 34 (1): 8–20.

Baum, Matthew A. 2002. "Sex, Lies, and War: How Soft News Brings Foreign Policy to the Inattentive Public." *American Political Science Review* 96 (1): 91–109.

———. 2003a. "Soft News and Political Knowledge: Evidence of Absence or Absence of Evidence?" *Political Communication* 20 (2): 173–90.

———. 2003b. *Soft News Goes to War: Public Opinion and American Foreign Policy in the New Media Age*. Princeton, NJ: Princeton University Press.

Baum, Matthew A., and Tim Groeling. 2009. "Shot by the Messenger: An Experimental Examination of the Effects of Party Cues on Public Opinion Regarding National Security and War." *Political Behavior* 31 (2): 157–86.

———. 2010. *War Stories: The Causes and Consequences of Public Views of War*. Princeton, NJ: Princeton University Press.

Baum, Matthew A., and Phil Gussin. 2008. "In the Eye of the Beholder: How Information Shortcuts Shape Individual Perceptions of Bias in the Media." *Quarterly Journal of Political Science* 3 (1): 1–31.

Baum, Matthew A., and Angela S. Jamison. 2006. "The Oprah Effect: How Soft News Helps Inattentive Citizens Vote Consistently." *Journal of Politics* 68 (4): 946–59.

Bawn, Kathleen. 1995. "Political Control versus Expertise: Congressional Choices about Administrative Procedures." *American Political Science Review* 89 (1): 62–73.

Bawn, Kathleen, Marty Cohen, David Karol, Seth Masket, Hans Noel, and John Zaller. 2006. "A Theory of Parties: Policy Demanders, Long Coalitions, and the Electoral Blind Spot." Department of Political Science, University of California, Los Angeles.

Bebchuk, Lucian, and Jesse Fried. 2004. *Pay without Performance: The Unfulfilled Promise of Executive Compensation*. Cambridge, MA: Harvard University Press.

Beck, Nathaniel. 1982a. "Parties, Administrations, and American Macroeconomic Outcomes." *American Political Science Review* 76 (1): 83–93.

———. 1982b. "Presidential Influence on the Federal Reserve in the 1970s." *American Journal of Political Science* 26 (3): 415–45.

———. 1987. "Elections and the Fed: Is There a Political Monetary Cycle?" *American Journal of Political Science* 31 (1): 194–216.

Beck, Paul Allen, and M. Kent Jennings. 1991. "Family Traditions, Political Periods, and the Development of Partisan Orientations." *Journal of Politics* 53 (3): 742–63.

Bellantoni, Christina. 2008. "Obama Beats Record for Press Conferences." *Washington Times*. November 26. http://www.washingtontimes.com/news/2008/nov/26/obama-beats-record-press-conferences/ (Accessed May 4, 2009).

Bennett, Stephen Earl, Staci L. Rhine, and Richard S. Flickinger. 2001. "Assessing Americans' Opinions about the News Media's Fairness in 1996 and 1998." *Political Communication* 18 (2): 163–82.

Bennett, W. Lance. 1990. "Toward a Theory of Press-State Relations in the United States." *Journal of Communication* 40 (2): 103–25.

———. 2009. *News: The Politics of Illusion*. 8th ed. New York: Pearson Longman.

Bennett, W. Lance, Regina G. Lawrence, and Steven Livingston. 2007. *When the Press Fails: Political Power and the News Media from Iraq to Katrina*. Chicago: University of Chicago Press.

Bennett, W. Lance, and Steven Livingston. 2003. "A Semi-Independent Press: Government Control and Journalistic Autonomy in the Political Construction of News." *Journal of Communication* 20 (4): 359–62.

Berdahl, Clarence A., Bertram M. Gross, Louise Overacker, E. E. Schattschneider, and Fritz Morstein Marx. 1950. "Toward a More Responsible Two-Party

System: A Report of the Committee on Political Parties, American Political Science Association." *American Political Science Review* 44 (3, pt. 2): i–99.

Berelson, Bernard, Paul F. Lazarsfeld, and William N. McPhee. 1954. *Voting: A Study of Opinion Formation in a Presidential Campaign.* Chicago: University of Chicago Press.

Berinsky, Adam J. 2006. "Public Opinion in the 1930s and 1940s: The Analysis of Quota Controlled Sample Survey Data." *Public Opinion Quarterly* 70 (4): 530–64.

———. 2007. "Assuming the Costs of War." *Journal of Politics* 69 (4): 975–97.

———. 2009. *In Time of War: Understanding American Public Opinion from World War II to Iraq.* Chicago: University of Chicago Press.

Berinsky, Adam J., and Donald R. Kinder. 2006. "Making Sense of Issues through Media Frames: Understanding the Kosovo Crisis." *Journal of Politics* 68 (3): 640–56.

Bernhardt, Dan, John Duggan, and Francesco Squintani. 2009. "The Case for Responsible Parties." *American Political Science Review* 103 (4): 570–87.

Bernhardt, Dan, Stefan Krasa, and Mattias Polborn. 2006. "Political Polarization and the Electoral Effects of Media Bias." *Journal of Public Economics* 92 (5–6): 1092–104.

Bernstein, Carl, and Bob Woodward. 1974. *All the President's Men.* New York: Simon and Schuster.

Berry, Jeffrey M. 2003. *A Voice for Nonprofits.* Washington, DC: Brookings Institution.

Besley, Timothy, and Andrea Prat. 2006. "Handcuffs for the Grabbing Hand? Media Capture and Government Accountability." *American Economic Review* 96 (3): 720–36.

Board of Governors of the Federal Reserve System. 2008. "Annual Report: Budget Review." Washington, DC.

Boehlert, Eric. 2006. *Lapdogs: How the Press Rolled Over for Bush.* New York: Free Press.

Bovitz, Gregory L., James N. Druckman, and Arthur Lupia. 2002. "When Can a News Organization Lead Public Opinion? Ideology versus Market Forces in Decisions to Make News." *Public Choice* 113 (1–2): 127–55.

Bower, Robert T. 1973. *Television and the Public.* New York: Holt, Rinehart and Winston.

Bozell, L. Brent. 2004. *Weapons of Mass Distortion: The Coming Meltdown of the Liberal Media.* New York: Crown Forum.

Brady, Henry E., and Paul M. Sniderman. 1985. "Attitude Attribution: A Group Basis for Political Reasoning." *American Political Science Review* 79 (4): 1061–78.

Brambor, Thomas, William Roberts Clark, and Matt Golder. 2006. "Understanding Interaction Models: Improving Empirical Analysis." *Political Analysis* 14 (1): 63–82.

Brenner, Y. S., Hartmut Kaelble, and Mark Thomas, eds. 1991. *Income Distribution in Historical Perspective.* New York: Cambridge University Press.

Broadcasting Publications. 1969. *Broadcasting Yearbook 1969.* Washington, DC: Broadcasting Publications.

Brock, David. 2004. *The Republican Noise Machine: Right-Wing Media and How It Corrupts Democracy*. New York: Crown.

Brock, Timothy C. 1965. "Commitment to Exposure as a Determination of Information Receptivity." *Journal of Personality and Social Psychology* 2 (1): 10–19.

Broder, David S. 2006. "A Lonely Warning on Debt," *Washington Post*, May 14, B7.

Brody, Richard A., and Benjamin I. Page. 1972. "Comment: The Assessment of Policy Voting." *American Political Science Review* 66 (2): 450–58.

Brookings Institution. 2003. "Iraq Index: Tracking Reconstruction and Security in Post-Saddam Iraq." http://www.brookings.org/iraqindex (Accessed December 20, 2003).

Brown, Keith S., and Adam Candeub. 2006. "Ideology versus Partisanship: Regulatory Behavior and Cyclical Political Influence." Michigan State University Legal Studies Research Paper no. 04-10.

Brownstein, Ronald. 2007. *The Second Civil War: How Extreme Partisanship Has Paralyzed Washington and Polarized America*. New York: Penguin.

Brudney, James J. 2005. "Isolated and Politicized: The N.L.R.B.'s Uncertain Future." *Comparative Labor Law and Policy Journal* 26 (2): 221–60.

Calvert, Randall L. 1980. "The Role of Imperfect Information in Electoral Politics." PhD diss. Division of the Humanities and Social Sciences, California Institute of Technology.

———. 1985. "The Value of Biased Information." *Journal of Politics* 47 (2): 530–55.

———. 1986. *Models of Imperfect Information in Politics*. Chur, Switzerland: Harwood Academic.

Calvert, Randall, and Michael B. MacKuen. 1985. "Bayesian Learning and the Dynamics of Public Opinion." Paper presented at the Annual Meeting of the Midwest Political Science Association, Chicago, IL.

Camines, Edward G., and James H. Kuklinski. 1990. "Incentives, Opportunities, and the Logic of Public Opinion in American Political Representation." In *Information and Democratic Processes*, ed. John A. Ferejohn and James H. Kuklinski. Urbana: University of Illinois Press, 240–68.

Campbell, Angus, Philip E. Converse, Warren E. Miller, and Donald E. Stokes. 1980 [1960]. *The American Voter*. Chicago: University of Chicago Press / Midway Reprint.

Campbell, James E. 2000. *American Campaign: U.S. Presidential Campaigns and the National Vote*. College Station: Texas A&M University Press.

Campbell, W. Joseph. 2001. *Yellow Journalism: Puncturing the Myths, Defining the Legacies*. Westport, CT: Praeger.

———. 2006. *The Year That Defined American Journalism: 1897 and the Clash of Paradigms*. New York: Routledge.

Cannon, Lou. 1991. *President Reagan: The Role of a Lifetime*. New York: Public Affairs.

Cappella, Joseph N., and Kathleen Hall Jamieson. 1997. *Spiral of Cynicism*. New York: Oxford University Press.

Carmines, Edward, and James Stimson. 1989. *Issue Evolution: Race and the Transformation of American Politics*. Princeton, NJ: Princeton University Press.

Carpenter, Daniel P. 2001. *The Forging of Bureaucratic Autonomy: Reputations, Networks, and Policy Innovation in Executive Agencies, 1862–1928*. Princeton, NJ: Princeton University Press.

Cater, Douglass. 1959. *The Fourth Branch of Government*. Boston: Houghton Mifflin.

Chaiken, Shelly. 1980. "Heuristic versus Systematic Information Processing and the Use of Source versus Message Cues and Persuasion." *Journal of Personality and Social Psychology* 39 (5): 752–66.

Chaiken, Shelly, and Yaacov Trope, eds. 1999. *Dual-Process Theories of Social Psychology*. New York: Guilford.

Chait, Jonathan. 2007. "The Left's New Machine: How the Netroots Became the Most Important Mass Movement in U.S. Politics." *New Republic*, May 7, 18–26.

Chia, Stella C., Shing Yew Joel Yong, Zi Wen Diana Wong, and Wei Ling Koh. 2007. "Personal Bias or Government Bias? Testing the Hostile Media Effect in a Regulated Press System." *International Journal of Public Opinion Research* 19 (3): 313–30.

Chiang, Chun Fang, and Brian Knight. 2008. "Media Bias and Influence: Evidence from Newspaper Endorsements." National Bureau of Economic Research, Working Paper no. 14445.

Chomsky, Noam. 1989. *Necessary Illusions: Thought Control in Democratic Societies*. Boston: South End Press.

Chong, Dennis, and James Druckman. 2007a. "Framing Public Opinion in Competitive Democracies." *American Political Science Review* 101 (4): 637–55.

———. 2007b. "Framing Theory." *Annual Review of Political Science* 10: 103–26.

Christen, Cindy T., Prathana Kannaovakun, and Albert C. Gunther. 2002. "Hostile Media Perceptions: Partisan Assessments of Press and Public during the 1997 United Parcel Service Strike." *Political Communication* 19 (4): 423–36.

Chronicle of Higher Education. 2004. "The Chronicle Survey of Public Opinion on Higher Education" 51 (1): 35–36.

Clark, Charles E. 2005. "The Press the Founders Knew." In *Freeing the Presses: The First Amendment in Action*, ed. Timothy E. Cook. Baton Rouge: Louisiana State University Press, 33–50.

Clegg, Cyndia Susan. 1997. *Press Censorship in Elizabethan England*. New York: Cambridge University Press.

———. 2008. *Press Censorship in Caroline England*. New York: Cambridge University Press.

Clinton, Joshua D. 2006. "Representation in Congress: Constituents and Roll Calls in the 106th House." *Journal of Politics* 68 (2): 397–409.

Clinton, Joshua D., and John Lapinski. 2004. "An Experimental Study of Political Advertising Effects in the 2000 Presidential Election." *Journal of Politics* 66 (1): 67–96.

Cohen, Geoffrey L. 2003. "Party over Policy: The Dominating Impact of Group Influence on Political Beliefs." *Journal of Personality and Social Psychology* 85 (5): 808–22.

Cohen, Jeff, and Norman Sullivan. 1995. *Through the Media Looking Glass: Decoding Bias and Blather in the News*. Monroe, ME: Common Courage Press.

Cohen, Jeffrey E. 1986. "The Dynamics of the 'Revolving Door' on the F.C.C." *American Journal of Political Science* 30 (4): 689–708.

Cohen, Marty, David Karol, Hans Noel, and John Zaller. 2008. *The Party Decides: Presidential Nominations before and after Reform*. Chicago: University of Chicago Press.

Commission on Presidential Debates. 2004. "Debate Transcript: The Third Bush–Kerry Presidential Debate." http://www.debates.org/pages/trans2004d.html (Accessed November 23, 2004).

Conason, Joe. 2003. *Big Lies: The Right-Wing Propaganda Machine and How It Distorts the Truth*. New York: Thomas Dunne.

Conover, Pamela Johnston, and Stanley Feldman. 1989. "Candidate Perception in an Ambiguous World: Campaigns, Cues and Inference Processes." *American Journal of Political Science* 33 (4): 912–40.

Converse, Jean M. 1987. *Survey Research in the United States: Roots and Emergence, 1890–1960*. Berkeley: University of California Press.

Converse, Philip E. 1962. "Information Flow and the Stability of Partisan Attitudes." *Public Opinion Quarterly* 26 (4): 578–99.

———. 1964. "The Nature of Belief Systems in Mass Publics." In *Ideology and Discontent*, ed. David E. Apter. New York: Free Press, 206–61.

———. 1969. "Of Time and Partisan Stability." *Comparative Political Studies* 2 (2): 139–71.

Cook, Timothy E. 1998. *Governing with the News: The News Media as a Political Institution*. Chicago: University of Chicago Press.

———. 2005. "Freeing the Presses: An Introductory Essay." In *Freeing the Presses: The First Amendment in Action*, ed. Timothy E. Cook. Baton Rouge: Louisiana State University Press, 1–26.

Cooper, James Fenimore. 1969 [1838]. *The American Democrat*. Baltimore: Penguin.

Copeland, David A. 1997. *Colonial American Newspapers: Character and Content*. Newark: University of Delaware Press.

———. 2006. *The Idea of a Free Press: The Enlightenment and Its Unruly Legacy*. Evanston, IL: Northwestern University Press.

Cowden, Jonathan A., and Rose M. McDermott. 2000. "Short-Term Forces and Partisanship." *Political Behavior* 22 (3): 197–222.

Cox, Gary W., and Jonathan N. Katz. 1996. "Why Did the Incumbency Advantage in U.S. House Elections Grow?" *American Journal of Political Science* 40 (2): 478–97.

Cox, Gary W., and Kenneth A. Shepsle. 2007. "Majority Cycling and Agenda Manipulation: Richard McKelvey's Contributions and Legacy." In *Positive Changes in Political Science: The Legacy of Richard D. McKelvey's Most Influential Writings*, ed. John H. Aldrich, James E. Alt, and Arthur Lupia. Ann Arbor: University of Michigan Press.

Coyne, John R., Jr. 1972. *The Impudent Snobs: Agnew vs. the Intellectual Establishment*. New Rochelle, NY: Arlington House.

Crano, William D., and Radmila Prislin. 2006. "Attitudes and Persuasion." *Annual Review of Psychology* 57: 345–74.

Crawford, Craig. 2006. *Attack the Messenger: How Politicians Turn You against the Media*. Lanham, MD: Rowman and Littlefield.

Crawford, Nelson Antrim. 1924. *The Ethics of Journalism*. New York: Alfred A. Knopf.

Crawford, Vincent, and Joel Sobel. 1982. "Strategic Information Transmission." *Econometrica* 50 (6): 1431–51.

Crouse, Timothy. 1973. *The Boys on the Bus*. New York: Ballantine.

Curran, James. 2005. "What Democracy Requires of the Media." In *The Press*, ed. Geneva Overholsen and Kathleen Hall Jamieson. Oxford, UK: Oxford University Press, 120–40.

Dalton, Russell J., Paul A. Beck, and Robert Huckfeldt. 1998. "Partisan Cues and the Media: Information Flows in the 1992 Presidential Election." *American Political Science Review* 92 (1): 111–26.

Dautrich, Kenneth, and Thomas H. Hartley. 1999. *How the News Media Fail American Voters*. New York: Columbia University Press.

Davidson, Philip. 1941. *Propaganda and the American Revolution, 1763–1783*. Chapel Hill: University of North Carolina Press.

Davis, Otto, Melvin Hinich, and Peter Ordeshook. 1970. "An Expository Development of a Mathematical Model of the Electoral Process." *American Political Science Review* 64 (2): 426–48.

Davis, Richard, and Diana Owen. 1998. *New Media and American Politics*. New York: Oxford University Press.

DellaVigna, Stefano, and Ethan Kaplan. 2007. "The Fox News Effect: Media Bias and Voting." *Quarterly Journal of Economics* 122 (3): 1187–234.

Delli Carpini, Michael X., and Scott Keeter. 1996. *What Americans Know about Politics and Why It Matters*. New Haven, CT: Yale University Press.

de Tocqueville, Alexis. 2000 [1835–40]. *Democracy in America*. Translated by George Lawrence. New York: Perennial Classics.

Devins, Neal. 1993. "Congress, the F.C.C., and the Search for the Public Trustee." *Law and Contemporary Problems* 56 (4): 145–88.

Devins, Neal, and David E. Lewis. 2008. "Not-So Independent Agencies: Party Polarization and the Limits of Institutional Design." *Boston University Law Review* 88 (2): 459–98.

Dewey, John. 1954 [1927]. *The Public and Its Problems*. Athens, OH: Swallow Press.

Dickerson, John. 2006. "The Good News from Iraq: We Can't Hear It—the Bombs Are Too Loud." Slate.com. March 26. http://www.slate.com/id/2138622/ (Accessed April 26, 2009).

Dionne, E. J., Jr. 1992. *Why Americans Hate Politics*. New York: Simon and Schuster.

———. 2002. "The Rightward Press." *Washington Post*, Dec. 6, A45.

Domke, David, Mark D. Watts, Dhavan V. Shah, and David P. Fan. 1999. "The Politics of Conservative Elites and the 'Liberal Media' Argument." *Journal of Communication* 49 (4): 35–58.

Downie, Leonard, Jr., and Robert G. Kaiser. 2003. *The News about the News: American Journalism in Peril.* New York: Vintage.

Downs, Anthony. 1957. *An Economic Theory of Democracy.* New York: Harper.

Drazen, Allan. 2000. "The Political Business Cycle after 25 Years." *NBER Macroeconomics Annual* 15: 75–117.

Druckman, James N. 2001. "On the Limits of Framing Effects: Who Can Frame?" *Journal of Politics* 63 (4): 1041–66.

———. 2004. "Political Preference Formation: Competition, Deliberation, and the (Ir)Relevance of Framing Effects." *American Political Science Review* 98 (4): 671–86.

Druckman, James N., and Arthur Lupia. 2000. "Preference Formation." *Annual Review of Political Science* 3: 1–24.

Druckman, James N., and Michael Parkin. 2005. "The Impact of Media Bias." *Journal of Politics* 67 (4): 1030–142.

Dunaway, Johanna. 2008. "Markets, Ownership, and the Quality of Campaign News Coverage." *Journal of Politics* 70 (4): 1193–202.

Eagly, Alice H., and Shelley Chaiken. 1993. *The Psychology of Attitudes.* New York: Harcourt College.

Edwards, George C., III, and B. Dan Wood. 1999. "Who Influences Whom? The President, Congress, and the Media." *American Political Science Review* 93 (2): 327–44.

Efron, Edith. 1971. *The News Twisters.* Los Angeles: Nash.

Eisenstein, Elizabeth L. 1979. *The Printing Press as an Agent of Change: Communications and Cultural Transformations in Early Modern Europe.* New York: Cambridge University Press.

Emery, Michael, Edwin Emery, and Nancy L. Roberts. 2000. *The Press and America: An Interpretive History of the Mass Media.* 9th ed. Boston: Allyn and Bacon.

Entman, Robert M., and Benjamin I. Page. 1994. "The News before the Storm: The Iraq War Debate and Limits to Media Independence." In *Taken by Storm: The Media, Public Opinion, and U.S. Foreign Policy in the Gulf War,* ed. W. Lance Bennett and David L. Paletz. Chicago: University of Chicago Press, 82–101.

Epstein, David, and Sharyn O'Halloran. 1999. *Delegating Powers: A Transaction Cost Politics Approach to Policy Making under Separate Powers.* New York: Cambridge University Press.

Erikson, Robert S. 1971. "The Advantage of Incumbency in Congressional Elections." *Polity* 3 (3): 395–405.

———. 1976. "Influence of Newspaper Endorsements in Presidential Elections: Case of 1964." *American Journal of Political Science* 20 (2): 207–33.

———. 1989. "Economic Conditions and the Presidential Vote." *American Political Science Review* 83 (2): 567–73.

Erikson, Robert S., Michael MacKuen, and James A. Stimson. 2002. *The Macro Polity.* New York: Cambridge University Press.

Erikson, Robert S., and Thomas R. Palfrey. 1998. "Campaign Spending and Incumbency: An Alternative Simultaneous Equations Approach." *Journal of Politics* 60 (2): 355–73.

Erskine, Hazel. 1970–71. "The Polls: Opinion of the News Media." *Public Opinion Quarterly* 34 (4): 630–43.

Eveland, William P., and Dhavan V. Shah. 2003. "The Impact of Individual and Interpersonal Factors on Perceived News Media Bias." *Political Psychology* 24 (1): 101–17.

Evensen, Bruce E. 2002. "Objectivity." In *American Journalism: History, Principles, Practices*, ed. W. David Sloan and Lisa Mullikin Parcell. Jefferson, NC: McFarland.

Fallows, James. 1996. *Breaking the News: How the Media Undermine American Democracy*. New York: Pantheon.

———. 2010. "How to Save the News." *Atlantic*, June 1, 44–56.

Farrell, Joseph, and Robert Gibbons. 1989. "Cheap Talk with Two Audiences." *American Economic Review* 79 (5): 1214–23.

Faust, Jon, and John S. Irons. 1999. "Money, Politics and the Post-War Business Cycle." *Journal of Monetary Economics* 43 (1): 61–89.

Fearon, James. 1999. "Electoral Accountability and the Control of Politicians: Selecting Good Types versus Sanctioning Poor Performance." In *Democracy, Accountability, and Representation*, ed. Susan C. Stokes, Adam Przeworski, and Bernard Manin. New York: Cambridge University Press, 55–96.

Febvre, Lucien, and Henri-Jean Martin. 1976 [1958]. *The Coming of the Book: The Impact of Printing 1450–1800*. Translated by David Gerard. London: N.L.B.

Federal Trade Commission. 2010. "Federal Trade Commission Staff Discussion Draft: Potential Policy Recommendations to Support the Reinvention of Journalism." Washington, DC.

Ferejohn, John. 1986. "Incumbent Performance and Electoral Control." *Public Choice* 50 (1): 5–25.

Fineman, Howard. 2005. "The 'Media Party' Is Over." MSNBC.com. January 13. http://msnbc.msn.com/id/6813945/ (Accessed February 1, 2007).

Finkel, Steven E. 1993. "Reexamining the 'Minimal Effects' Model in Recent Presidential Elections." *Journal of Politics* 55 (1): 1–21.

Fiorina, Morris P. 1977. "An Outline for a Model of Party Choice." *American Journal of Political Science* 21 (3): 601–25.

———. 1981. *Retrospective Voting in American National Elections*. New Haven, CT: Yale University Press.

Fiorina, Morris P., Samuel J. Abrams, and Jeremy C. Pope. 2005. *Culture War? The Myth of a Polarized America*. 2nd ed. New York: Pearson Longman.

Fischhoff, Baruch. 1991. "Value Elicitation: Is There Anything in There?" *American Psychologist* 46 (8): 835–47.

Foer, Franklin. 2005. "Bad News." *New Republic*, December 26, 6.

Gabel, Matthew, and Kenneth Scheve. 2007. "Estimating the Effect of Elite Communications on Public Opinion Using Instrumental Variables." *American Journal of Political Science* 51 (4): 1013–28.

Gaines, Brian J., James H. Kuklinski, Paul J. Quirk, Buddy Peyton, and Jay Verkuilen. 2007. "Same Facts, Different Interpretations: Partisan Motivation and Opinion on Iraq." *Journal of Politics* 69 (4): 957–74.

Galbraith, James K., Olivier Giovannoni, and Ann J. Russo. 2007. "The Fed's Real Reaction Function: Monetary Policy, Inflation, Unemployment,

Inequality—and Presidential Politics." Levy Institute of Bard College, Working Paper no. 511.

Galston, William A., and Pietro S. Nivola. 2006. "Delineating the Problem." In *Red and Blue Nation?* Vol. 1. *Characteristics and Causes of America's Polarized Politics*, ed. David W. Brady and Pietro S. Nivola. Washington, DC: Brookings Institution Press; Stanford, CA: Hoover Institution, 1–47.

Gamson, William A., and Andre Modigliani. 1989. "Media Discourse and Public Opinion on Nuclear Power: A Constructionist Approach." *American Journal of Sociology* 95 (1): 1–37.

Gelman, Andrew, and Gary King. 1990. "Estimating Incumbency Advantage without Bias." *American Journal of Political Science* 34 (4): 1142–64.

———. 1993. "Why Are American Presidential Election Campaign Polls So Variable When Votes Are So Predictable?" *British Journal of Political Science* 23 (1): 409–51.

Gelman, Andrew, David K. Park, Boris Shor, Joseph Bafumi, and Jeronimo Cortina. 2008. *Red State, Blue State, Rich State, Poor State: Why Americans Vote the Way They Do.* Princeton, NJ: Princeton University Press.

Gentzkow, Matthew, Edward L. Glaeser, and Claudia Goldin. 2006. "The Rise of the Fourth Estate: How Newspapers Became Informative and Why It Mattered." In *Corruption and Reform: Lessons from America's Economic History*, ed. Edward L. Glaeser and Claudia Goldin. Cambridge, MA: National Bureau of Economic Research, 187–230.

Gentzkow, Matthew, and Jesse M. Shapiro. 2006. "Media Bias and Reputation." *Journal of Political Economy* 114 (2): 280–316.

———. 2010a. "Ideological Segregation Online and Offline." Booth School of Business, University of Chicago.

———. 2010b. "What Drives Media Slant? Evidence from U.S. Daily Newspapers." *Econometrica* 78 (1): 35–71.

Gerber, Alan S. 1998. "Estimating the Effect of Campaign Spending on Senate Election Outcomes Using Instrumental Variables." *American Political Science Review* 92 (2): 401–11.

Gerber, Alan S., and Donald P. Green. 1998. "Rational Learning and Partisan Attitudes." *American Journal of Political Science* 42 (3): 794–818.

———. 1999. "Misperceptions about Perceptual Bias." *Annual Review of Political Science* 2: 189–210.

Gerber, Alan S., and Gregory A. Huber. 2009. "Partisanship and Economic Behavior: Do Partisan Differences in Economic Forecasts Predict Real Economic Behavior?" *American Political Science Review* 103 (3): 407–26.

Gerber, Alan S., Dean Karlan, and Daniel Bergan. Forthcoming. "Does the Media Matter? A Field Experiment Measuring the Effect of Newspapers on Voting Behavior and Political Opinions." *American Economic Journal: Applied Economics.*

Gerber, Alan S., Gregory A. Huber, and Ebonya Washington. 2009. "Party Affiliation, Partisanship, and Political Beliefs: A Field Experiment." National Bureau of Economic Research, Working Paper no. 15365.

Gerstein, Josh, and Patrick Gavin. 2010. "Why Reporters Are Down on Obama." Politico.com. April 28. http://www.politico.com/news/stories/0410/36454.html (Accessed April 30, 2010).

Gilens, Martin. 2001. "Political Ignorance and Collective Policy Preferences." *American Political Science Review* 95 (2): 379–96.

Gilens, Martin, and Craig Hertzman. 2000. "Corporate Ownership and News Bias: Newspaper Coverage of the 1996 Telecommunications Act." *Journal of Politics* 62 (2): 369–86.

Gilliam, Franklin D., Jr., and Shanto Iyengar. 2000. "Prime Suspects: The Influence of Local Television News on the Viewing Public." *American Journal of Political Science* 44 (3): 560–73.

Gilligan, Thomas W., and Keith Krehbiel. 1987. "Collective Decision-Making and Standing Committees: An Informational Rationale for Restrictive Amendment Procedures." *Journal of Law, Economics, and Organization* 3 (2): 287–335.

———. 1989. "Asymmetric Information and Legislative Rules with a Heterogeneous Committee." *American Journal of Political Science* 33 (2): 459–90.

Giner-Sorolla, Roger, and Shelley Chaiken. 1993. "The Causes of Hostile Media Judgments." *Journal of Experimental Social Psychology* 30 (1): 165–80.

Gitlow v. New York. 1925. 268 U.S. 652.

Goldberg, Arthur S. 1966. "Discerning a Causal Pattern among Data on Voting Behavior." *American Journal of Political Science* 60 (4): 913–22.

Goldberg, Bernard. 2002. *Bias: A CBS Insider Exposes How the Media Distort the News*. Washington, DC: Regnery.

———. 2009. *A Slobbering Love Affair: The True (and Pathetic) Story of the Torrid Romance between Barack Obama and the Mainstream Media*. Washington, DC: Regnery.

Goldin, Claudia, and Lawrence F. Katz. 2007. "The Race between Education and Technology: The Evolution of U.S. Educational Wage Differentials, 1890 to 2005." National Bureau of Economic Research, Working Paper no. 12984.

———. 2008. *The Race between Education and Technology*. Cambridge, MA: Belknap Press of Harvard University Press.

Goldin, Claudia, and Robert A. Margo. 1992. "The Great Compression: The Wage Structure in the United States at Mid-Century." *Quarterly Journal of Economics* 107 (1): 1–34.

Goldstone, Jack A. 1991. *Revolution and Rebellion in the Early Modern World*. Berkeley: University of California Press.

Goodman, Amy. 2004. *The Exception to the Rulers: Exposing Oily Politicians, War Profiteers, and the Media That Love Them*. New York: Hyperion.

Gormley, William, John Hoadley, and Charles Williams. 1983. "Potential Responsiveness in the Bureaucracy: Views of Public Utility Regulation." *American Political Science Review* 77 (3): 704–17.

Gormley, William T., Jr. 1979. "A Test of the Revolving Door Hypothesis at the F.C.C." *American Journal of Political Science* 23 (4): 665–83.

———. 1983. "Policy, Politics, and Public Utility Regulation." *American Journal of Political Science* 27 (1): 86–105.

———. 1986. "Regulatory Issue Networks in a Federal System." *Polity* 18 (4): 595–620.

———. 1989. *Taming the Bureaucracy: Muscles, Prayers, and Other Strategies*. Princeton, NJ: Princeton University Press.

Gormley, William T., Jr., and Steven J. Balla. 2004. *Bureaucracy and Democracy: Accountability and Performance*. Washington, DC: CQ Press.

Gormley, William T., Jr., and David L. Weimer. 1999. *Organizational Report Cards*. Cambridge, MA: Harvard University Press.

Gould, Lewis L. 2003. *Grand Old Party: A History of the Republicans*. New York: Random House.

Graber, Doris A. 1984. *Processing the News: How People Tame the Information Tide*. New York: Longman.

———. 2010. *Mass Media and American Politics*. 8th ed. Washington, DC: CQ Press.

Green, Donald P., and Alan S. Gerber. 2002. "Reclaiming the Experimental Tradition in Political Science." In *Political Science: The State of the Discipline*, ed. Helen V. Milner and Ira Katznelson. New York: W. W. Norton, 805–32.

Green, Donald P., Bradley Palmquist, and Eric Schickler. 1998. "Macropartisanship: A Replication and Critique." *American Political Science Review* 92 (4): 883–99.

———. 2002. *Partisan Hearts and Minds: Political Parties and the Social Identity of Voters*. New Haven, CT: Yale University Press.

Green, Donald P., and Jonathan S. Krasno. 1988. "Salvation for the Spendthrift Incumbent: Reestimating the Effects of Campaign Spending in House Elections." *American Journal of Political Science* 32 (4): 884–907.

Grendler, Paul F. 2004. *Encyclopedia of the Renaissance*. New York: Charles Scribner's Sons.

Gronke, Paul, and Timothy E. Cook. 2002. "Disdaining the Media in the Post 9/11 World." Paper presented at the Annual Meeting of the American Political Science Association, Boston, MA.

Groseclose, Timothy, and Jeff Milyo. 2005. "A Measure of Media Bias." *Quarterly Journal of Economics* 120 (4): 1191–237.

Gunther, Albert C. 1992. "Biased Press or Biased Public? Attitudes toward Media Coverage of Social Groups." *Public Opinion Quarterly* 56 (2): 147–67.

Halberstam, David. 1979. *The Powers That Be*. New York: Knopf.

Hallin, Daniel C., and Paolo Mancini. 2004. *Comparing Media Systems: Three Models of Media and Politics*. Cambridge, UK: Cambridge University Press.

Hamilton, James T. 2004. *All the News That's Fit to Sell: How the Market Transforms Information into News*. Princeton, NJ: Princeton University Press.

Hannity, Sean. 2009. "George W. Bush Reflects on Presidency in Premiere of 'Hannity.'" FoxNews.com. January 13. http://www.foxnews.com/story/0,2933,479805,00.html (Accessed May 3, 2009).

Hansmann, Henry B. 1980. "The Role of Nonprofit Enterprise." *Yale Law Journal* 89 (5): 835–901.

———. 1996. *The Ownership of Enterprise*. Cambridge, MA: Belknap Press of Harvard University Press.

———. 2003. "The Role of Trust in Nonprofit Enterprise." In *The Study of the Nonprofit Enterprise: Theories and Approaches*, ed. Helmut K. Anheier and Avner Ben-Ner. New York: Kluwer Academic / Plenum.

Hanushek, Eric A., and John E. Jackson. 1977. *Statistical Methods for Social Scientists*. New York: Academic Press.

Hardin, Garrett. 1968. "The Tragedy of the Commons." *Science* 162 (3859): 1243–48.

Harris, John F. 2005. *The Survivor: Bill Clinton in the White House*. New York: Random House.

Hazlett, Thomas W., and David W. Sosa. 1997. "Was the Fairness Doctrine a 'Chilling Effect'? Evidence from the Postderegulation Radio Market." *Journal of Legal Studies* 26 (1): 279–301.

Healy, Andrew, and Neil Malhotra. 2009. "Myopic Voters and Natural Disaster Policy." *American Political Science Review* 103 (3): 387–406.

Heise, David. 1969. "Separating Reliability and Stability in Test-Retest Correlation." *American Sociological Review* 34 (1): 93–101.

Herman, Edward S., and Noam Chomsky. 1988. *Manufacturing Consent: The Political Economy of the Mass Media*. New York: Pantheon.

Hertsgaard, Mark. 1988. *On Bended Knee: The Press and the Reagan Presidency*. New York: Farrar, Straus and Giroux.

Hess, Stephen. 1981. *The Washington Reporters*. Washington, DC: Brookings Institution Press.

Hetherington, Marc J. 1996. "The Media's Role in Forming Voters' National Economic Evaluations in 1992." *American Journal of Political Science* 40 (2): 372–95.

———. 1998. "The Political Relevance of Political Trust." *American Political Science Review* 92 (4): 791–808.

———. 1999. "The Effect of Political Trust on the Presidential Vote, 1968–96." *American Political Science Review* 93 (2): 311–26.

———. 2001. "Resurgent Mass Partisanship: The Role of Elite Polarization." *American Political Science Review* 95 (3): 619–31.

———. 2004. *Why Trust Matters: Declining Political Trust and the Demise of American Liberalism*. Princeton, NJ: Princeton University Press.

Hetherington, Marc J., and Suzanne Globetti. 2002. "Political Trust and Racial Policy Preferences." *American Journal of Political Science* 46 (2): 253–75.

Hibbing, John R., and Elizabeth Theiss-Morse. 1995. *Congress as Public Enemy: Public Attitudes toward American Political Institutions*. New York: Cambridge University Press.

———. 2002. *Stealth Democracy: Americans' Beliefs about How Government Should Work*. New York: Cambridge University Press.

Hibbs, Douglas A., Jr. 1982. "The Dynamics of Political Support for American Presidents among Occupational and Partisan Groups." *American Journal of Political Science* 26 (2): 312–32.

———. 1987. *The American Political Economy: Macroeconomics and Electoral Politics*. Cambridge, MA: Harvard University Press.

———. 2000. "Bread and Peace Voting in U.S. Presidential Elections." *Public Choice* 104 (1–2): 149–80.

———. 2007. "Voting and the Macroeconomy." In *Oxford Handbook of Political Economy*, ed. Barry R. Weingast and Donald Wittman. Oxford, UK: Oxford University Press, 565–86.

Hillygus, D. Sunshine. 2005. "The Dynamics of Turnout Intention in Election 2000." *Journal of Politics* 67 (1): 50–68.

Hillygus, D. Sunshine, and Simon Jackman. 2003. "Voter Decision Making in Election 2000: Campaign Effects, Partisan Activation, and the Clinton Legacy." *American Journal of Political Science* 47 (4): 583–96.

Hillygus, D. Sunshine, Norman H. Nie, Kenneth Prewitt, and Heili Pals. 2006. *The Hard Count: The Political and Social Challenges of Census Mobilization.* New York: Russell Sage Foundation.

Hindman, Matthew. 2009. *The Myth of Digital Democracy.* Princeton, NJ: Princeton University Press.

Hirano, Shigeo, and James M. Snyder, Jr. 2009. "Using Multi-Member Districts to Decompose the Incumbency Advantage." *American Journal of Political Science* 53 (2): 292–306.

Hirsch, Rudolf. 1974. *Printing, Selling and Reading, 1450–1550.* 2nd ed. Wiesbaden, Germany: Harrassowitz.

Ho, Daniel E. 2007. "Congressional Agency Control: The Impact of Statutory Partisan Requirements on Regulation." Stanford Law School, Stanford University.

Hofstadter, Richard. 1969. *The Idea of a Party System: The Rise of Legitimate Opposition in the United States, 1780–1840.* Berkeley: University of California Press.

Hofstetter, C. Richard. 1976. *Bias in the News: Network Television Coverage of the 1972 Election Campaign.* Columbus: Ohio State University Press.

Holbrook, Thomas M. 1994. "Campaigns, National Conditions, and U.S. Presidential Elections." *American Journal of Political Science* 38 (4): 973–98.

Holland, Paul W. 1986. "Statistics and Causal Inference." *Journal of the American Statistical Association* 81 (396): 945–60.

Hovland, Carl I., Irving Lester Janis, and Harold H. Kelley. 1953. *Communication and Persuasion: Psychological Studies of Opinion Change.* New Haven, CT: Yale University Press.

Hovland, Carl I., and Walter Weiss. 1951–52. "The Influence of Source Credibility on Communication Effectiveness." *Public Opinion Quarterly* 15 (4): 635–50.

Huber, Gregory A., and Kevin Arceneaux. 2007. "Identifying the Persuasive Effects of Presidential Advertising." *American Journal of Political Science* 51 (4): 957–77.

Huckfeldt, Robert, and John Sprague. 1995. *Citizens, Politics and Social Communication: Information and Influence in an Election Campaign.* New York: Cambridge University Press.

Huffington Post. 2010. "Craig Newmark: NPR Will Be a Dominant News Force in Ten Years." HuffingtonPost.com. October 1. http://www.huffingtonpost .com/2010/10/01/craig-newmark-npr-will-be_n_746027.html (Accessed October 3, 2010).

Ickes, Harold L. 1939. *America's House of Lords.* New York: Harcourt, Brace.

Iyengar, Shanto. 1991. *Is Anyone Responsible? How Television Frames Political Issues.* Chicago: University of Chicago Press.

Iyengar, Shanto, Kyu Hahn, and Markus Prior. 2001. "Has Technology Made Attention to Political Campaigns More Selective? An Experimental Study of the 2000 Presidential Campaign." Paper presented at the Annual Meeting of the American Political Science Association, San Francisco, CA.

Iyengar, Shanto, and Kyu S. Hahn. 2007. "Red Media, Blue Media: Evidence of Ideological Selectivity in Media Use." *Journal of Communication* 59 (1): 19–39.

Iyengar, Shanto, and Donald R. Kinder. 1985. "Psychological Accounts of Agenda-Setting." In *Mass Media and Political Thought: An Information Processing Approach*, ed. Sidney Kraus and Richard M. Perloff. Beverly Hills, CA: Sage, 117–40.

———. 1987. *News That Matters: Television and American Opinion*. Chicago: University of Chicago Press.

Iyengar, Shanto, and Adam Simon. 1994. "News Coverage of the Gulf Crisis and Public Opinion: A Study of Agenda Setting, Priming, and Framing." In *Taken by Storm: The Media, Public Opinion, and U.S. Foreign Policy in the Gulf War*, ed. W. Lance Bennett and David L. Paletz. Chicago: University of Chicago Press, 186–209.

Jackson, John. E. 1975. "Issues, Party Choices, and Presidential Votes." *American Journal of Political Science* 19 (2): 161–85.

Jacobson, Gary C. 1980. *Money in Congressional Elections*. New Haven, CT: Yale University Press.

———. 2006. "Campaign Spending Effects in U.S. Senate Elections: Evidence from the National Annenberg Election Survey." *Electoral Studies* 25 (2): 195–226.

———. 2007. *A Divider, Not a Uniter: George W. Bush and the American People*. New York: Pearson Longman.

Jamieson, Kathleen Hall. 1992. *Dirty Politics: Deception, Distraction, and Democracy*. New York: Oxford University Press.

Jamieson, Kathleen Hall, and Joseph N. Cappella. 2008. *Echo Chamber: Rush Limbaugh and the Conservative Media Establishment*. New York: Oxford University Press.

Jamieson, Kathleen Hall, Bruce W. Hardy, and Daniel Romer. 2007. "The Effectiveness of the Press in Serving the Needs of Democracy." In *A Republic Divided: The Annenberg Democracy Project*, ed. Kathleen Hall Jamieson. New York: Oxford University Press.

Janowitz, Morris. 1975. "Professional Models in Journalism: The Gatekeeper and the Advocate." *Journalism Quarterly* 52 (4): 618–26.

Jennings, M. Kent, and Richard G. Niemi. 1981. *Generations and Politics: A Panel Study of Young Adults and Their Parents*. Princeton, NJ: Princeton University Press.

Jessee, Stephen A. 2009. "Spatial Voting in the 2004 Presidential Election." *American Political Science Review* 103 (1): 59–81.

Johnston, Richard. 2006. "Party Identification: Unmoved Mover or Sum of Preferences?" *Annual Review of Political Science* 9: 329–51.

Johnston, Richard, Andre Blais, Henry Brady, and Jean Crete. 1992. *Letting the People Decide: Dynamics of a Canadian Election*. Stanford, CA: Stanford University Press.

Johnston, Richard, Michael G. Hagen, and Kathleen Hall Jamieson. 2004. *The 2000 Presidential Election and the Foundations of Party Politics*. New York: Cambridge University Press.

Jones, David A. 2004. "Why Americans Don't Trust the Media: A Preliminary Analysis." *Harvard International Journal of Press/Politics* 9 (2): 60–75.

Just, Marion R., Ann N. Crigler, Dean E. Alger, Timothy E. Cook, Montague Kern, and Darrell M. West. 1996. *Crosstalk: Citizens, Candidates, and the Media in a Presidential Campaign.* Chicago: University of Chicago Press.

Kahn, Kim Fridkin, and Patrick J. Kenney. 2002. "The Slant of the News: How Editorial Endorsements Influence Campaign Coverage and Citizens' Views of Candidates." *American Political Science Review* 96 (2): 381–94.

Kahneman, Daniel, and Amos Tversky. 1984. "Choices, Values and Frames." *American Psychologist* 39 (4): 341–50.

Karol, David. 2009. *Party Position Change in American Politics: Coalition Management.* New York: Cambridge University Press.

Karpowitz, Christopher. 2009. "What Can a President Learn from the News Media? The Instructive Case of Richard Nixon." *British Journal of Political Science* 39 (3): 755–80.

Katz, Elihu. 1957. "The Two-Step Flow of Communication: An Up-to-Date Report on a Hypothesis." *Public Opinion Quarterly* 21 (1): 61–78.

Katz, Elihu, and Paul F. Lazarsfeld. 1955. *Personal Influence: The Part Played by People in the Flow of Mass Communication.* Glencoe, IL: Free Press.

Kaufmann, Karen M., John R. Petrocik, and Daron R. Shaw. 2008. *Unconventional Wisdom: Facts and Myths about American Voters.* New York: Oxford University Press.

Kaul, Arthur J. 1986. "The Proletarian Journalist: A Critique of Professionalism." *Journal of Mass Media Ethics* 1 (2): 47–55.

Keith, Bruce E., David B. Magleby, Candice J. Nelson, and Elizabeth Orr. 1992. *The Myth of the Independent Voter.* Berkeley: University of California Press.

Keller, Allan. 1969. *The Spanish-American War: A Compact History.* New York: Hawthorn.

Kellstedt, Paul M. 2000. "Media Framing and the Dynamics of Racial Policy Preferences." *American Journal of Political Science* 44 (2): 239–55.

———. 2003. *The Mass Media and the Dynamics of American Racial Attitudes.* New York: Cambridge University Press.

Kelly, Michael. 2002a. "Left Everlasting," *Washington Post,* December 11, A33.

———. 2002b. "Left Everlasting (Con't)," *Washington Post,* December 18, A35.

Kennedy, Peter. 2003. *A Guide to Econometrics.* 5th ed. Cambridge, MA: MIT Press.

Kernell, Samuel. 1978. "Explaining Presidential Popularity." *American Political Science Review* 72 (2): 506–22.

Kessler, Ronald. 2009. "G.O.P. House Members Form Caucus to Fight Media Bias." Newsmax.com. June 3. http://www.newsmax.com/kessler/media_bias_House_caucus/2009/06/03/221014.html (Accessed June 3, 2009).

Key, V. O., Jr. 1949. *Southern Politics in State and Nation.* New York: Knopf.

———. 1961. *Public Opinion and American Democracy.* New York: Knopf.

———. 1964. *Politics, Parties, and Pressure Groups.* 5th ed. New York: Thomas Y. Crowell.

———. 1968. *The Responsible Electorate: Rationality in Presidential Voting, 1936–1960.* New York: Vintage.

Key, V. O., Jr., and Frank Munger. 1970. "Social Determinism and Electoral Decision: The Case of Indiana." In *Public Opinion and Politics: A Reader*, ed. William J. Crotty. New York: Holt, Rinehart and Winston, 250–67.

Kinder, Donald R. 1998a. "Communication and Opinion." *Annual Review of Political Science* 1: 167–97.

———. 1998b. "Opinion and Action in the Realm of Politics." In *The Handbook of Social Psychology*, ed. Daniel Todd Gilbert, Susan T. Fiske, and Gardner Lindzey. New York: McGraw-Hill, 778–866.

———. 2003. "Communication and Politics in the Age of Information." In *Oxford Handbook of Political Psychology*, ed. David O. Sears, Leonie Huddy, and Robert Jervis. New York: Oxford University Press, 357–93.

Kinder, Donald R., and D. Roderick Kiewiet. 1979. "Sociotropic Politics: The American Case." *British Journal of Political Science* 11 (2): 129–61.

Kiousis, Spiro. 2001. "Public Trust or Mistrust? Perceptions of Media Credibility in the Information Age." *Mass Communication and Society* 4 (4): 251–71.

Klapper, Joseph. 1960. *The Effects of Mass Communication*. Glencoe, IL: Free Press.

Kohn, Bob. 2003. *Journalistic Fraud: How the New York Times Distorts the News and Why It Can No Longer Be Trusted*. Nashville, TN: Nelson Current.

Kohring, Matthias, and Jorg Matthes. 2007. "Trust in News Media: Development and Validation of a Multidimensional Scale." *Communication Research* 34 (2): 231–52.

Koppel, Ted. 2010. "The Case against News We Can Choose," *Washington Post*, November 14, B01.

Kovach, Bill, and Tom Rosenstiel. 2001. *The Elements of Journalism: What Newspeople Should Know and the Public Should Expect*. New York: Three Rivers Press.

Kramer, Gerald H. 1973. "On a Class of Equilibrium Conditions for Majority Rule." *Econometrica* 41 (2): 285–97.

———. 1983. "The Ecological Fallacy Revisited: Aggregate versus Individual-Level Findings on Economics and Elections, and Sociotropic Voting." *American Political Science Review* 77 (1): 92–111.

Krosnick, Jon A., and Laura Brannon. 1993. "The Impact of the Gulf War on Ingredients of Presidential Evaluations: Multidimensional Effects of Political Involvement." *American Political Science Review* 87 (4): 963–75.

Krosnick, Jon A., and Donald R. Kinder. 1990. "Altering the Foundations of Support for the President through Priming." *American Political Science Review* 84 (2): 497–512.

Krugman, Paul. 2002a. "For Richer: How the Permissive Capitalism of the Boom Destroyed American Equality." *New York Times Magazine*, October 20, 62–142.

———. 2002b. "In Media Res," *New York Times*, November 29, A39.

———. 2005. "Losing Our Country," *New York Times*, June 10, A21.

———. 2007. *The Conscience of a Liberal*. New York: W. W. Norton.

Kuklinski, James H., and Norman L. Hurley. 1994. "On Hearing and Interpreting Political Messages: A Cautionary Tale of Citizen Cue-Taking." *Journal of Politics* 56 (3): 729–51.

Kuklinski, James H., and Lee Sigelman. 1992. "When Objectivity Is Not Objective: Network Television News Coverage of U.S. Senators and the 'Paradox of Objectivity.'" *Journal of Politics* 54 (3): 810–33.

Kull, Steven. 2006. "Iraq: The Separate Realities of Republicans and Democrats." March 28. http://www.worldpublicopinion.org/pipa/articles/brunitedstates canadara/186.php (Accessed September 2, 2009).

Kull, Steven, Clay Ramsay, and Evan Lewis. 2003–4. "Misperceptions, the Media, and the Iraq War." *Political Science Quarterly* 118 (4): 569–98.

Kurland, Philip B., and Ralph Lerner, eds. 2000. "Thomas Jefferson to Edward Carrington." In *The Founders' Constitution*. Vol. 5, Amendment I (Speech and Press), Doc. 8. Chicago: University of Chicago Press. http://press-pubs.uchicago .edu/founders/documents/amendI_speechs8.html (Accessed August 8, 2008).

Kurtz, Howard. 2009. "Liberal Radio Talker Schultz Signs On with MSNBC," *Washington Post*, April 2, C05.

Ladd, Jonathan. 2004. "Attitudes toward the News Media and the Acquisition of Political Information." Paper presented at the Annual Meeting of the Midwest Political Science Association, Chicago, IL.

———. 2005. "Attitudes toward the News Media and Voting Behavior." Paper presented at the Annual Meeting of the Midwest Political Science Association, Chicago, IL.

———. 2006. "Attitudes toward the News Media and Political Competition in America." PhD diss. Department of Politics, Princeton University.

———. 2007. "Predispositions and Public Support for the President during the War on Terrorism." *Public Opinion Quarterly* 71 (4): 511–38.

———. 2010a. "The Neglected Power of Elite Opinion Leadership to Produce Antipathy toward the News Media: Evidence from a Survey Experiment." *Political Behavior* 32 (1): 29–50.

———. 2010b. "The Role of Media Distrust in Partisan Voting." *Political Behavior* 32 (4): 567–85.

Ladd, Jonathan M., and Gabriel S. Lenz. 2009. "Exploiting a Rare Communication Shift to Document the Persuasive Power of the News Media." *American Journal of Political Science* 53 (2): 394–410.

Larson, Magali Sarfatti. 1977. *The Rise of Professionalism: A Sociological Analysis*. Berkeley: University of California Press.

Lawrence, Eric, John Sides, and Henry Farrell. 2010. "Self-Segregation or Deliberation? Blog Readership, Participation, and Polarization in American Politics." *Perspectives on Politics* 8 (1): 141–57.

Lawson, Chappell, and James A. McCann. 2004. "Television News, Mexico's 2000 Elections and Media Effects in Emerging Democracies." *British Journal of Political Science* 35 (1): 1–30.

Lazarsfeld, Paul F., Bernard Berelson, and Hazel Gaudet. 1948. *The People's Choice: How the Voter Makes Up His Mind in a Presidential Campaign*. New York: Columbia University Press.

Ledbetter, James. 1998. *Made Possible By . . . The Death of Public Broadcasting in the United States*. London: Verso.

Lee, Martin A., and Norman Solomon. 1991. *Unreliable Sources: A Guide to Detecting Bias in News Media*. New York: Carol Publishing.

Lehrer, Jim. 1992. *A Bus of My Own*. New York: Putnam.

Lemann, Nicholas. 2005. "Fear and Favor: Why Is Everyone Mad at the Mainstream Media?" *New Yorker*, February 14 and 21, 168–74.

Lenz, Gabriel S. 2009. "Learning and Opinion Change, Not Priming: Reconsidering the Evidence for the Priming Hypothesis." *American Journal of Political Science* 53 (4): 821–37.

———. 2010a. "Judging Politicians." Department of Political Science, Massachusetts Institute of Technology. Book manuscript.

———. 2010b. "Misremembering Politicians' Performance." Paper presented at the annual meeting of the Midwest Political Science Association, Chicago, IL.

Levendusky, Matthew. 2009. *The Partisan Sort: How Liberals Became Democrats and Conservatives Became Republicans*. Chicago: University of Chicago Press.

Levitt, Steven D. 1994. "Using Repeat Challengers to Estimate the Effect of Campaign Spending on Election Outcomes in the U.S. House." *Journal of Political Economy* 102 (4): 777–98.

Levy, Frank, and Peter Temin. 2007. "Inequality and Institutions in twentieth century America." National Bureau of Economic Research, Working Paper no. 13106.

Lewis, David E. 2003. *Presidents and the Politics of Agency Design: Political Insulation in the United States Government Bureaucracy, 1946–1997*. Stanford, CA: Stanford University Press.

———. 2008. *The Politics of Presidential Appointments: Political Control and Bureaucratic Performance*. Princeton, NJ: Princeton University Press.

Lewis-Beck, Michael S. 1990. *Economics and Elections: The Major Western Democracies*. Ann Arbor: University of Michigan Press.

Lewis-Beck, Michael S., Helmut Norpoth, William G. Jacoby, and Herbert F. Weisberg. 2008. *The American Voter Revisited*. Ann Arbor: University of Michigan Press.

Lewis-Beck, Michael S., and Tom W. Rice. 1984. "Forecasting Presidential Elections: A Comparison of Naive Models." *Political Behavior* 6 (1): 9–21.

———. 1992. *Forecasting Elections*. Washington, DC: CQ Press.

Lewis-Beck, Michael S., and Mary Stegmaier. 2000. "Economic Determinants of Electoral Outcomes." *Annual Review of Political Science* 3: 183–219.

Lichter, S. Robert, and Richard E. Noyes. 1996. *Good Intentions Make Bad News: Why Americans Hate Campaign Journalism*. 2nd ed. Lanham, MD: Rowman and Littlefield.

Lichter, S. Robert, Stanley Rothman, and Linda S. Lichter. 1986. *The Media Elite: America's New Powerbrokers*. Bethesda, MD: Adler and Adler.

Liebovich, Louis. 1998. *The Press and the Modern Presidency: Myths and Mindsets from Kennedy to Clinton*. Westport, CT: Praeger.

Lippmann, Walter. 1927. *The Phantom Public*. New York: Macmillan.

———. 1931. "Two Revolutions in the American Press." *Yale Review* 20 (March): 433–41.

———. 1995 [1920]. *Liberty and the News*. New Brunswick, NJ: Transaction.

———. 1997 [1922]. *Public Opinion*. New York: Simon and Schuster.

Lodge, Milton, and Charles Taber. 2000. "Three Steps toward a Theory of Motivated Political Reasoning." In *Elements of Reason: Cognition, Choice, and the Bounds of Rationality*, ed. Arthur Lupia, Mathew D. McCubbins, and Samuel L. Popkin. New York: Cambridge University Press, 183–213.

Lord, Charles G., Lee Ross, and Mark R. Lepper. 1979. "Biased Assimilation and Attitude Polarization: The Effects of Prior Theories on Subsequently Considered Evidence." *Journal of Personality and Social Psychology* 37 (11): 2089–109.

Loven, Jennifer. 2009. "Bush's Last Press Conference Monday." HuffingtonPost .com January 12. http://www.huffingtonpost.com/2009/01/12/bushs-last-press -conferen_n_157042.html (Accessed May 4, 2009).

Lupia, Arthur. 1994. "Shortcuts versus Encyclopedias: Information and Voting Behavior in California Insurance Reform Elections." *American Political Science Review* 88 (1): 63–76.

———. 2002. "Who Can Persuade Whom?: Implications from the Nexus of Psychology and Rational Choice Theory." In *Thinking about Political Psychology*, ed. James H. Kuklinski. New York: Cambridge University Press, 51–88.

Lupia, Arthur, Adam Seth Levine, Jesse O. Menning, and Gisela Sin. 2007. "Were Bush Tax Cut Supporters 'Simply Ignorant'?: A Second Look at Conservatives and Liberals in 'Homer Gets a Tax Cut.'" *Perspectives on Politics* 5 (4): 773–84.

Lupia, Arthur, and Mathew D. McCubbins. 1998. *The Democratic Dilemma: Can Citizens Learn What They Need to Know?* New York: Cambridge University Press.

Luskin, Robert C. 2002. "From Denial to Extenuation (and Finally Beyond): Political Sophistication and Citizen Performance." In *Thinking about Political Psychology*, ed. James H. Kuklinski. New York: Cambridge University Press, 281–301.

MacKuen, Michael B., Robert S. Erikson, and James A. Stimson. 1989. "Macropartisanship." *American Political Science Review* 83 (4): 1125–42.

Madison, James, Alexander Hamilton, and John Jay. 1987 [1788]. *The Federalist Papers*. London: Penguin.

Mansbridge, Jane J. 1986. *Why We Lost the E.R.A.* Chicago: University of Chicago Press.

Markus, Gregory B. 1988. "The Impact of Personal and National Economic Conditions on the Presidential Vote: A Pooled Cross-Sectional Analysis." *American Journal of Political Science* 32 (1): 137–54.

———. 1992. "The Impact of Personal and National Economic Conditions on Presidential Voting, 1956–1988." *American Journal of Political Science* 36 (3): 829–34.

Markus, Gregory B., and Philip E. Converse. 1979. "A Dynamic Simultaneous Equation Model of Electoral Choice." *American Political Science Review* 73 (4): 1055–70.

Mayhew, David R. 1974. "Congressional Elections: The Case of the Vanishing Marginals." *Polity* 6 (3): 295–317.

McCarty, Nolan, Keith T. Poole, and Howard Rosenthal. 1997. *Income Redistribution and the Realignment of American Politics*. Washington, DC: American Enterprise Institute.

———. 2006. *Polarized America: The Dance of Ideology and Unequal Riches.* Cambridge, MA: MIT Press.

———. 2009. "Party Polarization: 1879–2008." Voteview.com. January 2. http://polarizedamerica.com/#POLITICALPOLARIZATION (Accessed May 19, 2009).

McCombs, Maxwell E., and Donald L. Shaw. 1972. "The Agenda-Setting Function of Mass Media." *Public Opinion Quarterly* 36 (2): 176–87.

———. 2006. "The Evolution of Agenda-Setting Research: Twenty-Five Years in the Marketplace of Ideas." *Journal of Communication* 43 (2): 58–67.

McCubbins, Mathew D., Roger G. Noll, and Barry R. Weingast. 1987. "Administrative Procedures as Instruments of Political Control." *Journal of Law, Economics, and Organization* 3 (2): 243–77.

McDermott, Rose. 2002. "Experimental Methods in Political Science." *Annual Review of Political Science* 5: 31–61.

McGerr, Michael E. 1986. *The Decline of Popular Politics: The American North, 1865–1928.* New York: Oxford University Press.

McGowan, William. 2003. *Coloring the News: How Political Correctness Has Corrupted American Journalism.* San Francisco: Encounter.

McGuire, William J. 1969. "The Nature of Attitudes and Attitude Change." In *Handbook of Social Psychology*, ed. G. Lindzey and E. Aronson. Reading, MA: Addison-Wesley, 136–314.

McKelvey, Richard D. 1976. "Intransitivities in Multidimensional Voting Models and Some Implications for Agenda Control." *Journal of Economic Theory* 12 (2): 472–82.

———. 1979. "General Conditions for Global Intransitivities in Formal Voting Models." *Econometrica* 47 (5): 1085–112.

McKelvey, Richard D., and Peter C. Ordeshook. 1985. "Elections with Limited Information: A Fulfilled Expectations Model Using Contemporaneous Poll and Endorsement Data as Information Sources." *Journal of Economic Theory* 36 (1): 55–85.

———. 1986. "Information, Electoral Equilibria, and the Democratic Ideal." *Journal of Politics* 48 (4): 909–37.

Media Dynamics. 2001. *T.V. Dimensions.* New York: Media Dynamics.

Mifflin, Lawrie. 1995. "Simpson Case Gives Cable an Edge on the Networks," *New York Times*, February 20.

Miller, Joanne M., and Jon A. Krosnick. 2000. "News Media Impact on the Ingredients of Presidential Evaluations: Politically Knowledgeable Citizens Are Guided by a Trusted Source." *American Journal of Political Science* 44 (2): 301–15.

Miller, Warren E. 1991. "Party Identification, Realignment, and Party Voting: Back to the Basics." *American Political Science Review* 85 (2): 557–68.

———. 1999. "Temporal Order and Causal Inference." *Political Analysis* 8 (2): 119–40.

Miller, Warren E., and J. Merrill Shanks. 1996. *The New American Voter.* Cambridge, MA: Harvard University Press.

Mindich, David T. Z. 1996. "Building the Pyramid: A Cultural History of 'Objectivity' in American Journalism." PhD diss. American Studies Program, New York University.

Moe, Terry M. 1982. "Regulatory Performance and Presidential Administration." *American Journal of Political Science* 26 (2): 197–224.

———. 1985. "Control and Feedback in Economic Regulation: The Case of the N.L.R.B." *American Political Science Review* 79 (4): 1094–116.

———. 1989. "The Politics of Bureaucratic Structure." In *Can the Government Govern?*, ed. John E. Chubb and Paul E. Peterson. Washington, DC: Brookings Institution, 267–329.

Moehler, Devra, and Naunihal Singh. Forthcoming. "Whose News Do You Trust? Explaining Trust in Private versus Public Media in Africa." *Political Research Quarterly*.

Mondak, Jeffery J. 1993. "Source Cues and Policy Approval: The Cognitive Dynamics of Public Support for the Reagan Agenda." *American Journal of Political Science* 37 (1): 186–212.

———. 1995. *Nothing to Read: Newspapers and Elections in a Social Experiment*. Ann Arbor: University of Michigan Press.

Morton, Rebecca B. 2006. *Analyzing Elections*. New York: W. W. Norton.

Mott, Frank Luther. 1950. *American Journalism: A History of Newspapers in the United States through 260 Years: 1690 to 1950*. Rev. ed. New York: MacMillan.

Mueller, John E. 1973. *War, Presidents, and Public Opinion*. New York: Wiley.

Mullainathan, Sendhil, and Andrei Shleifer. 2005. "The Market for News." *American Economic Review* 95 (4): 1031–53.

Mutz, Diana C. 1998. *Impersonal Influence: How Perceptions of Mass Collectives Affect Political Attitudes*. New York: Cambridge University Press.

Mutz, Diana C., and Byron Reeves. 2005. "The New Videomalaise: Effects of Televised Incivility on Political Trust." *American Political Science Review* 99 (1): 1–15.

Near v. Minnesota. 1931. 283 U.S. 697.

Nelson, Harold L. 1959. "Seditious Libel in Colonial America." *American Journal of Legal History* 3 (2): 160–72.

Nelson, Richard, and Michael Krashinsky. 1973. "Two Major Issues of Public Policy: Public Subsidy and Organization of Supply." In *Public Policy for Day Care of Young Children*, ed. Dennis R. Young and Richard R. Nelson. Lexington, MA: D.C. Heath, 9–21.

Nelson, Thomas E., Rosalee A. Clausen, and Zoe M. Oxley. 1997. "Media Framing of a Civil Liberties Conflict and Its Effect on Tolerance." *American Political Science Review* 91 (3): 567–83.

Nelson, Thomas E., and Donald R. Kinder. 1996. "Issue Frames and Group-Centrism in American Public Opinion." *Journal of Politics* 58 (4): 1055–78.

Nielson Media Research. 1972. *Nielson Station Index*. Chicago: A. C. Nielson.

Nisbett, Richard E., and Timothy Decamp Wilson. 1977. "Telling More than We Can Know: Verbal Reports on Mental Processes." *Psychological Review* 84 (3): 231–59.

Niven, David. 2002. *Tilt? The Search for Media Bias*. Westport, CT: Praeger.

Nivola, Pietro S., and William A. Galston. 2008. "Toward Depolarization." In *Red and Blue Nation? Vol. 2. Consequences and Correction of America's Polarized Politics*, ed. David W. Brady and Pietro S. Nivola. Washington, DC: Brookings Institution Press; Stanford, CA: Hoover Institution, 235–84.

Noel, Hans. 2006. "The Coalition Merchants: How Ideologues Shape Parties in American Politics." PhD diss. Department of Political Science, University of California, Los Angeles.

O'Callaghan, Kate, and Patrick Farrelly. 2005. *Left of the Dial.* HBO Video.

O'Reilly, Bill. 2004. "Transcript: Bush Talks to O'Reilly." FoxNews.com. September 24. http://www.foxnews.com/story/0,2933,133712,00.html (Accessed May 3, 2009).

Olasky, Marvin. 1988. *Prodigal Press: The Anti-Christian Bias of the American News Media.* Wheaton, IL: Crossway Books.

Olson, Mancur. 1965. *The Logic of Collective Action: Public Goods and the Theory of Groups.* Cambridge, MA: Harvard University Press.

On the Media from NPR. 2004. "Transcript: Media in a Blue State." Onthemedia.org. November 19. http://www.onthemedia.org/transcripts/transcripts_111904_blue.html (Accessed November 28, 2004).

Ostrom, Elinor. 1999. "Coping with Tragedies of the Commons." *Annual Review of Political Science* 2: 493–535.

Oudes, Bruce, eds. 1989. *From the President: Richard Nixon's Secret Files.* New York: Harper and Row.

Page, Benjamin I., and Richard A. Brody. 1972. "Policy Voting and the Electoral Process: The Vietnam War Issue." *American Political Science Review* 66 (3): 979–95.

Page, Benjamin I., and Calvin C. Jones. 1979. "Reciprocal Effects of Policy Preferences, Party Loyalties and the Vote." *American Political Science Review* 73 (4): 1071–89.

Page, Benjamin I., Robert Y. Shapiro, and Glenn R. Dempsey. 1987. "What Moves Public Opinion?" *American Political Science Review* 81 (1): 23–43.

Pasley, Jeffrey L. 2001. *"The Tyranny of Printers": Newspaper Politics in the Early American Republic.* Charlottesville: University of Virginia Press.

Patterson, Thomas E. 1980. *The Mass Media Election.* New York: Praeger.

———. 1993. *Out of Order.* New York: Knopf.

Patterson, Thomas E., and Robert D. McClure. 1976. *The Unseeing Eye: The Myth of Television Power in National Politics.* New York: Putnam.

Patty, John. 2009. "The Politics of Biased Information." *Journal of Politics* 71 (2): 385–97.

PBS News. 2009. "P.B.S. #1 in Public Trust for the Sixth Consecutive Year, According to National Roper Survey." About PBS News: Press Releases. February 13. http://www.pbs.org/aboutpbs/news/20090213_pbsropersurvey.html (Accessed July 6, 2009).

PBS NewsHour. 2009. "Another Chapter Begins for *NewsHour*." PBS.org. December 4. http://www.pbs.org/newshour/bb/media/july-dec09/pbsnewshour_12-04.html (Accessed February 12, 2010).

Perloff, Richard M. 1989. "Ego-Involvement and the Third Person Effect of Televised News Coverage." *Communication Research* 16 (2): 236–62.

Perlstein, Rick. 2001. *Before the Storm: Barry Goldwater and the Unmaking of the American Consensus.* New York: Hill and Wang.

———. 2008. *Nixonland: The Rise of a President and the Fracturing of America.* New York: Scribner.

Petrocik, John R. 1995. "Reporting Campaigns: Reforming the Press." In *Campaigns and Elections American Style*, ed. James A. Thurber and Candice J. Nelson. Boulder, CO: Westview Press, 126–37.

Petty, Richard E., and John. T. Cacioppo. 1981. *Attitudes and Persuasion: Classic and Contemporary Approaches*. Boulder, CO: Westview Press.

Pew Research Center for the People and the Press. 2004. "Survey Report: Iraq Support Stable, Bush Not Seen as Unilateralist." Washington, DC: Pew Center for the People and the Press.

Pew Research Center for the People and the Press. 2007. "Internet News Audience Highly Critical of News Organizations: Views of Press Values and Performance: 1985–2007." Washington, DC: Pew Center for the People and the Press.

Piazza, Thomas, Paul M. Sniderman, and Philip E. Tetlock. 1989. "Analysis of the Dynamics of Political Reasoning: A General-Purpose Computer-Assisted Methodology." *Political Analysis* 1 (1): 91–121.

Plott, Charles R. 1967. "A Notion of Equilibrium and Its Possibility under Majority Rule." *American Economic Review* 57 (4): 787–806.

Pollard, James E. 1947. *The Presidents and the Press*. New York: MacMillan.

Poole, Keith T., and Howard Rosenthal. 1991. "Patterns of Congressional Voting." *American Journal of Political Science* 35 (1): 228–78.

———. 1997. *Congress: A Political-Economic History of Roll Call Voting*. Oxford, UK: Oxford University Press.

———. 2007. *Ideology and Congress*. New Brunswick, NJ: Transaction.

Popkin, Samuel L. 1991. *The Reasoning Voter: Communication and Persuasion in Presidential Campaigns*. Chicago: University of Chicago Press.

———. 2006. "Changing Media, Changing Politics." *Perspectives on Politics* 4 (2): 327–41.

Pöttker, Horst. 2005. "The News Pyramid and Its Origin from the American Journalism in the 19th Century: A Professional Approach and an Empirical Inquiry." In *Diffusion of the News Paradigm 1850–2000*, ed. Svennik Høyer and Horst Pöttker. Göteborg, Sweden: Nordic Information Center for Media and Communication Research, 51–64.

Price, Vincent, and John Zaller. 1993. "Who Gets the News? Alternative Measures of News Reception and Their Implications for Research." *Public Opinion Quarterly* 57 (2): 133–64.

Prior, Markus. 2003. "Any Good News in Soft News? The Impact of Soft News Preference on Political Knowledge." *Political Communication* 20 (2): 149–71.

———. 2005. "News vs. Entertainment: How Increasing Media Choice Widens Gaps in Political Knowledge and Turnout." *American Journal of Political Science* 49 (3): 577–92.

———. 2006. "The Incumbent in the Living Room: The Rise of Television and the Incumbency Advantage in U.S. House Elections." *Journal of Politics* 68 (3): 657–73.

———. 2007. *Post-Broadcast Democracy: How Media Choice Increases Inequality in Political Involvement and Polarizes Elections*. New York: Cambridge University Press.

Project for Excellence in Journalism. 2007a. "P.E.J. Special Index Report: Anna Nicole Smith, Anatomy of a Feeding Frenzy." Washington, DC.

———. 2007b. "The State of the News Media: An Annual Report on American Journalism." http://www.stateofthemedia.org/2007/ (Accessed April 22, 2009).

———. 2008. "The State of the News Media: An Annual Report on American Journalism." http://www.stateofthemedia.org/2008/ (Accessed April 22, 2009).

———. 2009. "The State of the News Media: An Annual Report on American Journalism." http://www.stateofthemedia.org/2009/ (Accessed April 22, 2009).

———. 2010. "The State of the News Media: An Annual Report on American Journalism." http://www.stateofthemedia.org/2010/ (Accessed September 7, 2010).

Putnam, Robert D. 2000. *Bowling Alone: The Collapse and Revival of American Community*. New York: Simon and Schuster.

Quinn, Sally. 1998. "In Washington, That Letdown Feeling," *Washington Post*, November 2, E01.

Rahn, Wendy M. 1993. "The Role of Partisan Stereotypes in Information Processing about Political Candidates." *American Journal of Political Science* 37 (2): 472–96.

Rahn, Wendy M., Jon A. Krosnick, and Marijke Breuning. 1994. "Rationalization and Derivation Processes in Survey Studies of Political Candidate Evaluation." *American Journal of Political Science* 38 (3): 582–600.

Ranney, Austin. 1975. *Curing the Mischiefs of Faction: Party Reform in America*. Berkeley: University of California Press.

Rasinski, Kenneth A. 1989. "The Effect of Question Wording on Public Support for Government Spending." *Public Opinion Quarterly* 53 (3): 388–94.

Rich, Frank. 2005. "Gonzo Gone, Rather Going, Watergate Still Here," *New York Times*, March 6, sec. 2, p. 1.

Richardson, James D., ed. 1908. *A Compilation of the Messages and Papers of the Presidents, 1798–1907*. Vol. 6. New York: Bureau of National Literature and Art.

Riker, William H. 1980. "Implications of the Disequilibrium of Majority Rule for the Study of Institutions." *American Political Science Review* 74: 432–47.

———. 1982. *Liberalism against Populism: A Confrontation between the Theory of Democracy and the Theory of Social Choice*. Prospect Heights, IL: Waveland Press.

Rivers, William L. 1962. "The Correspondents after Twenty-Five Years." *Columbia Journalism Review* 1 (1): 4–10.

Robert, Christian P. 1994. *The Bayesian Choice: A Decision-Theoretic Motivation*. New York: Springer-Verlag.

Rosenblum, Nancy L. 2010. *On the Side of the Angels: An Appreciation of Parties and Partisanship*. Princeton, NJ: Princeton University Press.

Rosenstiel, Tom, Carl Gottlieb, Lee Ann Brady, and Dan Rosenheim. 2000. "Time of Peril for T.V. News." *Columbia Journalism Review* 38 (4): 84–92.

Rosenstiel, Tom, Marion Just, Todd L. Belt, Atiba Pertilla, Walter Dean, and Dante Chinni. 2007. *We Interrupt This Newscast: How to Improve Local News and Win Ratings, Too*. New York: Cambridge University Press.

Rosenstone, Steven J. 1983. *Forecasting Presidential Elections*. New Haven, CT: Yale University Press.

Rosenstone, Steven J., and John Mark Hansen. 1993. *Mobilization, Participation, and Democracy in America*. New York: Macmillan.

Ross, Charles G. 1911. *The Writing of News: A Handbook with Chapters on Newspaper Correspondence and Copy Reading*. New York: Henry Holt.

Rubin, Donald B. 1974. "Estimating Causal Effects of Treatments in Randomized and Nonrandomized Studies." *Journal of Educational Psychology* 66 (5): 688–701.

Rubin, Richard L. 1981. *Press, Party, and Presidency*. New York: Norton.

Sabato, Larry J. 1991. *Feeding Frenzy: How Attack Journalism Has Transformed American Politics*. New York: Free Press.

———. 2000. *Feeding Frenzy: Attack Journalism and American Politics*. Baltimore, MD: Lanahan.

Sanford, Bruce. 1999. *Don't Shoot the Messenger: How Our Growing Hatred of the Media Threatens Free Speech for All of Us*. Lanham, MD: Rowman and Littlefield.

Schattschneider, E. E. 1942. *Party Government*. New York: Holt Rinehart and Winston.

———. 1975 [1960]. *The Semisovereign People: A Realist's View of Democracy in America*. Fort Worth, TX: Harcourt Brace Jovanovich.

Scherer, Michael. 2009. "Calling 'Em Out: The White House Takes on the Press." Time.com. October 8. http://www.time.com/time/politics/article/0,8599,1929058,00.html (Accessed April 14, 2010).

Schickler, Eric. 2001. *Disjointed Pluralism: Institutional Innovation and the Development of the U.S. Congress*. Princeton, NJ: Princeton University Press.

Schmitt-Beck, Rudige. 2003. "Mass Communication, Personal Communication and Vote Choice: The Filter Hypothesis of Media Influence in Comparative Perspective." *British Journal of Political Science* 33 (2): 233–59.

Schofield, Norman. 1978. "Instability of Simple Dynamic Games." *Review of Economic Studies* 45 (3): 575–94.

———. 1983. "Generic Instability of Majority Rule." *Review of Economic Studies* 50 (4): 695–705.

Scholz, John T., and B. Dan Wood. 1998. "Controlling the I.R.S.: Principals, Principles, and Public Administration." *American Journal of Political Science* 42 (1): 141–62.

———. 1999. "Efficiency, Equity, and Politics: Democratic Controls over the Tax Collector." *American Journal of Political Science* 43 (4): 1166–88.

Schudson, Michael. 1978. *Discovering the News: A Social History of American Newspapers*. New York: Basic Books.

———. 1990. *Origins of the Ideal of Objectivity in the Professions: Studies in the History of American Journalism and American Law*. New York: Garland.

———. 1995. *The Power of News*. Cambridge, MA: Harvard University Press.

———. 2005. "The Emergence of the Objectivity Norm in American Journalism." In *Diffusion of the News Paradigm 1850–2000*, ed. Svennik Høyer and Horst Pöttker. Göteborg, Sweden: Nordic Information Center for Media and Communication Research, 19–35.

———. 2008. *Why Democracies Need an Unlovable Press*. Cambridge, UK: Polity.

Schulman, Howard, and Stanley Presser. 1996 [1981]. *Questions and Answers in Attitude Surveys: Experiments on Question Form, Wording, and Context*. Thousand Oaks, CA: Sage.

Sears, David O., and Jonathan L. Freedman. 1967. "Selective Exposure to Information: A Critical Review." *Public Opinion Quarterly* 31 (2): 194–213.

Shadish, William R., Thomas D. Cook, and Donald T. Campbell. 2002. *Experimental and Quasi-Experimental Designs for Generalized Causal Inference.* Boston, MA: Houghton Mifflin.

Shafer, Jack. 2007. "In Defense of the Anna Nicole Feeding Frenzy: And Other Pulp Journalism Run Amok." Slate.com. April 4. http://www.slate.com/id/2163504 (Accessed April 6, 2007).

———. 2009a. "Alms for the Press? The Case against Foundation Ownership of the *New York Times*." Slate.com. February 3. http://www.slate.com/id/2210333/ (Accessed March 2, 2010).

———. 2009b. "Nonprofit Journalism Comes at a Cost: The Downside of Nonprofit News Organizations Like MinnPost, Voice of San Diego, and the Washington Independent." Slate.com. September 30. http://www.slate.com/id/2231009 (Accessed March 2, 2010).

Shaw, David. 1996. "Beyond Skepticism," *Los Angeles Times*, April 17, 1.

Shea, Danny. 2010. "N.P.R. Bans Employees from Jon Stewart's and Stephen Colbert's Rallies." HuffingtonPost.com. October 13. (Accessed October 14, 2010).

Sheffrin, Steven M. 1989. "Evaluating Rational Partisan Business Cycle Theory." *Economics and Politics* 1 (3): 239–59.

Sheppard, Si. 2008. *The Partisan Press: A History of Media Bias in the United States.* Jefferson, NC: McFarland.

Shepsle, Kenneth A. 1979. "Institutional Arrangements and Equilibrium in Multidimensional Voting Models." *American Journal of Political Science* 23 (1): 27–59.

Shepsle, Kenneth A., and Barry R. Weingast. 1981. "Structure-Induced Equilibrium and Legislative Choice." *Public Choice* 37 (3): 503–17.

Shull, Bernard. 2005. *The Fourth Branch: The Federal Reserve's Unlikely Rise to Power and Influence.* Westport, CT: Praeger.

Sinclair, Upton. 1920. *The Brass Check: A Study of American Journalism.* Pasadena, CA: Self-published.

Sloan, Wm. David, and Julie Hedgepeth Williams. 1994. *The Early American Press, 1690–1783.* Westport, CT: Greenwood Press.

Slovic, Paul. 1995. "The Construction of Preference." *American Psychologist* 50 (5): 364–71.

Smythe, Ted Curtis. 2003. *The Gilded Age Press, 1865–1900.* Westport, CT: Praeger.

Sniderman, Paul M., Richard A. Brody, and Philip Tetlock. 1991. *Reasoning and Choice: Explorations in Political Psychology.* New York: Cambridge University Press.

Sniderman, Paul M., and Douglas B. Grob. 1996. "Innovations in Experimental Design in Attitude Surveys." *Annual Review of Sociology* 22: 377–99.

Sniderman, Paul M., and Sean M. Theriault. 2004. "The Structure of Political Argument and the Logic of Issue Framing." In *Studies in Public Opinion: Gauging Attitudes, Nonattitudes, Measurement Error and Change*, ed. Willem E. Saris and Paul M. Sniderman. Princeton, NJ: Princeton University Press, 133–65.

Sniderman, Paul M., and Robert P. Van Houweling. 2005. "The Political Logic of Downsian Space." Department of Political Science, University of California, Berkeley.

Snijders, Tom A. B., and Roel Bosker. 1999. *Multilevel Analysis: An Introduction to Basic and Advanced Multilevel Modeling*. London, UK: Sage.

Snyder, James M., Jr., and Michael M. Ting. 2002. "An Informational Rationale for Political Parties." *American Journal of Political Science* 46 (1): 90–110.

Sobel, Joel. 1985. "A Theory of Credibility." *Review of Economic Studies* 52 (4): 557–73.

Solomon, Norman. 2005. *War Made Easy: How Presidents and Pundits Keep Spinning Us to Death*. Hoboken, NJ: Wiley.

Sparrow, Bartholomew H. 1999. *Uncertain Guardians: The News Media as a Political Institution*. Baltimore, MD: Johns Hopkins University Press.

Stanley, Harold W., and Richard G. Niemi. 2010. *Vital Statistics on American Politics 2009–2010*. Washington, DC: CQ Press.

Starr, Paul. 1984. *The Social Transformation of American Medicine*. New York: Basic Books.

———. 2004. *The Creation of the Media: Political Origins of Modern Communications*. New York: Basic Books.

Steenbergen, Marco R., and Bradford S. Jones. 2002. "Modeling Multilevel Data Structures." *American Journal of Political Science* 26 (1): 218–37.

Stensaas, Harlan. 1986. "The Objective News Report: A Content Analysis of Selected U.S. Daily Newspapers for 1865 to 1954." PhD diss. School of Mass Communication and Journalism, University of Southern Mississippi.

———. 2005. "The Rise of the News Paradigm: A Review of the Scientific Literature." In *Diffusion of the News Paradigm 1850–2000*, ed. Svennik Høyer and Horst Pöttker. Goteborg, Sweden: Nordic Information Center for Media and Communication Research, 37–49.

Stewart, Potter. 1974–75. "Or of the Press." *Hastings Law Review* 26 (3): 631–37.

Stockmann, Daniela C. 2007. "Propaganda for Sale: The Impact of Newspaper Commercialization on News Content and Public Opinion in China." PhD diss. Department of Political Science, University of Michigan.

Stokes, Donald E. 1966a. "Party Loyalty and the Likelihood of Deviating Elections." In *Elections and the Political Order*, ed. Angus Campbell, Philip E. Converse, Warren E. Miller, and Donald E. Stokes. New York: Wiley, 125–35.

———. 1966b. "Spatial Models of Party Competition." In *Elections and the Political Order*, ed. Angus Campbell, Philip E. Converse, Warren E. Miller, and Donald E. Stokes. New York: Wiley, 161–79.

Stratmann, Thomas. 2005. "Some Talk: Money in Politics. A (Partial) Review of the Literature." *Public Choice* 124 (1–2): 135–56.

Streckfuss, Richard. 1990. "Objectivity in Journalism: A Search and a Reassessment." *Journalism Quarterly* 67 (Winter): 973–83.

Streissguth, Thomas. 2006. *Media Bias*. New York: Benchmark Books.

Stroud, Natalie Jomini. 2008. "Media Use and Political Predispositions: Revisiting the Concept of Selective Exposure." *Political Behavior* 30 (3): 341–66.

Sudman, Seymour, and Norman M. Bradburn. 1987. "The Organizational Growth of Public Opinion Research in the United States." *Public Opinion Quarterly* 51 (2): S67–S78.

Sweeney, Paul D., and Kathy L. Gruber. 1984. "Selective Exposure: Voter Information Preferences and the Watergate Affair." *Journal of Personality and Social Psychology* 46 (6): 1208–21.

Swensen, David, and Michael Schmidt. 2009. "News You Can Endow." *New York Times*, January 27, A31.

Taber, Charles S., and Milton Lodge. 2006. "Motivated Skepticism in the Evaluation of Political Beliefs." *American Journal of Political Science* 50 (3): 755–69.

Taylor, Shelley E., and Susan Fiske. 1978. "Salience, Attention, and Attribution: Top of the Head Phenomena." In *Advances in Experimental Social Psychology*, ed. Leonard Berkowitz. New York: Academic Press, 249–88.

Tebbel, John, and Sarah Miles Watts. 1985. *The Press and the Presidency: From George Washington to Ronald Reagan*. New York: Oxford University Press.

Tempelman, Jerry H. 2007. "A Commentary on 'Does the Fed Contribute to a Political Business Cycle?'" *Public Choice* 132 (3–4): 433–36.

Tesler, Michael. 2010. "The Growing Cable News Divide in Midterm Vote Preference." YouGov.com. November 1. http://today.yougov.com/news/2010/11/01/growing-cable-news-divide-midterm-vote-preference/ (Accessed November 5, 2010).

Thomas, Isaiah 1810. *The History of Printing*. Worcester, MA: Self-published.

Thompson, Krissah. 2009. "White House Officials to Appear on Fox News." *Washington Post*, October 19, A3.

Tourangeau, Roger. 1987. "Attitude Measurement: A Cognitive Perspective." In *Social Information Processing and Survey Methodology*, ed. Hans-J. Hippler, Norbert Schwarz, and Seymour Sudman. New York: Springer, 147–62.

Tourangeau, Roger, and Kenneth A. Rasinski. 1988. "Cognitive Processes Underlying Context Effects in Attitude Measurement." *Psychological Bulletin* 103 (3): 299–314.

Tourangeau, Roger, Lance J. Rips, and Kenneth Rasinski. 2000. *The Psychology of Survey Response*. New York: Cambridge University Press.

Tsfati, Yariv. 2002. "The Consequences of Mistrust in the News Media: Media Skepticism as a Moderator in Media Effects and as a Factor Influencing News Media Exposure." PhD diss. Annenberg School for Communication, University of Pennsylvania.

———. 2003. "Media Skepticism and Climate of Opinion Perception." *International Journal of Public Opinion Research* 15 (1): 65–82.

Tsfati, Yariv, and Joseph N. Cappella. 2003. "Do People Watch What They Do Not Trust? Exploring the Association between News Media Skepticism and Exposure." *Communication Research* 30 (5): 504–29.

———. 2005. "Why Do People Watch News They Do Not Trust? The Need for Cognition as a Moderator in the Association between News Media Skepticism and Exposure." *Harvard International Journal of Press/Politics* 7 (3): 251–71.

Tuchman, Gaye. 1972. "Objectivity as Strategic Ritual: An Examination of Newsmen's Notions of Objectivity." *American Journal of Sociology* 77 (4): 660–79.

Tufte, Edward R. 1978. *Political Control of the Economy*. Princeton, NJ: Princeton University Press.

Turner, Joel. 2007. "The Messenger Overwhelming the Message: Ideological Cues and Perceptions of Bias in Television News." *Political Behavior* 29 (4): 441–64.

U.S. Census Bureau. 2002. *Statistical Abstract of the United States*. Washington, DC: U.S. Government Printing Office.

Valentino, Nicholas A. 1999. "Crime News and the Priming of Racial Attitudes during Evaluations of the President." *Public Opinion Quarterly* 63 (3): 293–320.

Vallone, Robert P., Lee Ross, and Mark R. Lepper. 1985. "The Hostile Media Phenomenon: Biased Perception and Perceptions of Media Bias in Coverage of the Beirut Massacre." *Journal of Personality and Social Psychology* 49 (3): 577–85.

Veblen, Eric P. 1975. *The Manchester Union Leader in New Hampshire Elections*. Hanover, NH: University Press of New England.

Villard, Oswald Garrison. 1923. *Some Newspapers and Newspaper-Men*. New York: Knopf.

Wald, Abraham. 1950. *Statistical Decision Functions*. New York: Wiley.

Waldfogel, Joel. 2007. "T.V. Is Good for You: If You Are a Woman in Rural India at Least." Slate.com. August 20. http://www.slate.com/id/2172474/ (Accessed August 21, 2007).

Watson, Roland, and Gerard Baker. 2005. "The *Times* Interview with President Bush: Transcript." TimesOnline. http://www.timesonline.co.uk/tol/news/uk/article538900.ece (Accessed May 3, 2009).

Watts, Mark D., David Domke, Dhavan V. Shah, and David P. Fan. 1999. "Elite Cues and Media Bias in Presidential Campaigns: Explaining Public Perceptions of a Liberal Bias." *Communication Research* 26 (2): 144–75.

Weber, Max. 2002 [1905]. *The Protestant Ethic and the Spirit of Capitalism: And Other Writings*. New York: Penguin.

Webster, James G. 2005. "Beneath the Veneer of Fragmentation: Television Audience Polarization in a Multichannel World." *Journal of Communication* 55 (2): 366–82.

Weingast, Barry R., and Mark J. Moran. 1983. "Bureaucratic Discretion or Congressional Control? Regulatory Policymaking by the Federal Trade Commission." *Journal of Political Economy* 91 (5): 765–800.

West, Darrell M. 1999. "The Rise and Fall of the Media." *Inside Politics: Your Guide to State and National Politics*. October 10. http://www.insidepolitics.org/heard/heard101099.html (Accessed May 4, 2009).

———. 2001. *The Rise and Fall of the Media Establishment*. Boston: Bedford / St. Martin's.

———. 2009. "The New Digital Press: How to Create a Brighter Future for the News Industry." Issues in Governance Studies, Brookings Institution.

White, Graham J. 1979. *F.D.R. and the Press*. Chicago: University of Chicago Press.

Whitman, Willson, ed. 1945. *Jefferson's Letters: Selections from the Private and Political Correspondence of Thomas Jefferson, Telling the Story of American Independence and the Founding of the American Government*. Eau Claire, WI: E. M. Hale.

Wilcox, Nathaniel, and Christopher Wlezien. 1993. "The Contamination of Responses to Survey Items: Economic Perceptions and Political Judgments." *Political Analysis* 5: 181–213.

Wiley, David E., and James A. Wiley. 1970. "The Estimation of Measurement Error in Panel Data." *American Sociological Review* 35 (1): 112–17.

Wilmer, Lambert A. 1859. *Our Press Gang; or, A Complete Exposition of the Corruptions and Crimes of the American Newspapers.* Philadelphia: J. T. Lloyd.

Wilson, Woodrow. 1885. *Congressional Government: A Study in American Politics.* Boston: Houghton, Mifflin.

Winfield, Betty Houchin. 1994. *F.D.R. and the News Media.* New York: Columbia University Press.

Winkler, Robert L. 2003. *An Introduction to Bayesian Inference and Decision.* 2nd ed. Sugar Land, TX: Probabilistic Publishing.

Wlezien, Christopher, and Robert S. Erikson. 1996. "Temporal Horizons and Presidential Election Forecasts." *American Politics Quarterly* 24 (4): 492–505.

———. 2002. "The Timeline of Presidential Election Campaigns." *Journal of Politics* 64 (4): 969–93.

Wlezien, Christopher, Mark Franklin, and Daniel Twiggs. 1997. "Economic Perceptions and Vote Choice: Disentangling the Endogeneity." *Political Behavior* 19 (1): 7–17.

Wood, B. Dan. 1990. "Does Politics Make a Difference at the E.E.O.C.?" *American Journal of Political Science* 34 (2): 503–30.

Wood, B. Dan, and Richard W. Waterman. 1991. "The Dynamics of Political Control of the Bureaucracy." *American Political Science Review* 85 (3): 801–28.

———. 1993. "The Dynamics of Political-Bureaucratic Adaptation." *American Journal of Political Science* 37 (2): 497–528.

Wood, Gordon S. 1993. *The Radicalism of the American Revolution.* New York: Vintage.

Wooldridge, Jeffrey M. 2003. *Introductory Econometrics: A Modern Approach.* 2nd ed. Cincinnati, OH: South-Western College Publishing.

Woolley, John T. 1984. *Monetary Politics: The Federal Reserve and the Politics of Monetary Policy.* New York: Cambridge University Press.

———. 1993. "Conflict among Regulators and the Hypothesis of Congressional Dominance." *Journal of Politics* 55 (1): 92–114.

Wooster, Martin Morse. 2007. *The Great Philanthropists and the Problem of "Donor Intent."* 3rd ed. Washington, DC: Capital Research Center.

Wuthnow, Robert. 1989. *Communities of Discourse: Ideology and Social Structure in the Reformation, the Enlightenment, and European Socialism.* Cambridge, MA: Harvard University Press.

Zaller, John R. 1985. "Pre-Testing Information Items on the 1986 N.E.S. Pilot Survey." Report to the National Election Studies Board of Overseers.

———. 1991. "Information, Values, and Opinion." *American Political Science Review* 85 (4): 1215–37.

———. 1992. *The Nature and Origins of Mass Opinion.* New York: Cambridge University Press.

———. 1994. "Elite Leadership of Mass Opinion: New Evidence from the Gulf War." In *Taken by Storm: The Media, Public Opinion, and U.S. Foreign Policy in the Gulf War*, ed. W. Lance Bennett and David L. Paletz. Chicago: University of Chicago Press, 186–209.

———. 1996. "The Myth of Massive Media Impact Revived." In *Political Persuasion and Attitude Change*, ed. Diana C. Mutz, Paul M. Sniderman, and Richard A. Brody. Ann Arbor: University of Michigan Press, 17–78.

———. 1998. "Politicians as Prize Fighters: Electoral Selection and Incumbency Advantage." In *Politicians and Party Politics*, ed. John G. Geer. Baltimore: Johns Hopkins University Press, 125–85.

———. 1999a. "Market Competition and News Quality." Paper presented at the Annual Meeting of the American Political Science Association, Atlanta, GA.

———. 1999b. "A Theory of Media Politics: How the Interests of Politicians, Journalists, and Citizens Shape the News." Department of Political Science, University of California, Los Angeles. Book manuscript.

———. 2003. "A New Standard of News Quality: Burglar Alarms for the Monitorial Citizen." *Political Communication* 20 (2): 109–30.

———. 2004. "Floating Voters in U.S. Presidential Elections, 1948–2000." In *Studies in Public Opinion: Attitudes, Nonattitudes, Measurement Error, and Change*, ed. Willem Saris and Paul M. Sniderman. Princeton, NJ: Princeton University Press, 166–212.

———. 2007. "Madison's Error: Political Communication and Presidential Selection." Paper presented at the Changing Media and Political Accountability conference, November 30, Center for the Study of Democratic Politics, Princeton University.

Zaller, John R., and Dennis Chiu. 2000. "Government's Little Helper: U.S. Press Coverage of Foreign Policy Crises, 1945–1999." In *Decisionmaking in a Glass House: Mass Media, Public Opinion, and American and European Foreign Policy in the 21st Century*, ed. Brigitte L. Nacos, Robert Y. Shapiro, and Pierangelo Isernia. Lanham, MD: Rowman and Littlefield, 61–84.

Zaller, John R., and Stanley Feldman. 1992. "A Simple Theory of Survey Response: Answering Questions versus Revealing Preferences." *American Journal of Political Science* 36 (3): 579–616.

Zechman, Martin J. 1979. "Dynamic Models of the Voter's Decision Calculus: Incorporating Retrospective Considerations into Rational-Choice Models of Individual Voting Behavior." *Public Choice* 34 (3–4): 297–315.

Index

The letters *t* or *f* following a page number denote a table or figure on that page.